DEATH CONFOUNDED!

TRUE STORIES

CATHOLIC ✠ ARCHIVES

DEATH CONFOUNDED!

TRUE STORIES

Diary of a London Priest, 1840's

by

Father E. Price

Caritas Publishing

Printed with
Ecclesiastical Approval
2024

This is a compilation. The stories were taken from *Life Stories of Dying Penitents,* or *Sick-Calls, from the Diary of a Missionary Priest,* 1902.

🄫 Free of copyright. With the Evangelists and Saints throughout history, you are *encouraged* to copy and freely share this material for the glory of God and the salvation of souls!

Paperback ISBN: 1945275650
Hardback ISBN: 1945275642

By you we were created, in you we were re-created in the Blood of your Son. Your mercy preserves us, your mercy caused your Son to do battle for us, hanging by His arms on the wood of the Cross—life and death battling together. Then *life confounded the death* of our sin, and the death of our sin destroyed the bodily life of the Immaculate Lamb. But which was finally conquered? *Death!* And how? *By your mercy!*

~ St. Catherine of Sienna, *Dialogues*

ST. JOSEPH, PATRON OF THE DYING

Contents

The Infidel 1
A Priest's Sunday Work 26
The Dying Burglar. 31
The Dying Banker 49
The Miser's Death 66
The Hospital 87
The Wanderer's Death. 94
The Dying Shirt-Maker 112
The Broken Heart 129
The Destitute Poor 138
The Cholera Patient. 143
The Drunkard's Death. 147
The Merchant's Clerk. 173
Death-Beds of the Poor. 201
The Magdalen 217
The Famished Needle Woman. 239
Appendix. 261
   How to Help the Dying 261
   The Divine Mercy Chaplet 268
   Recommendation for a Departing Soul 270

The Infidel

IT WAS early in the spring of 1845 that I first conceived the idea of penning these reminiscences of a missionary life. I had just escaped, through the mercy of God, from the horrors of a long and dangerous fever, from weeks of delirium, and the languid helplessness of convalescence. I was then residing in a quiet nook on the Sussex coast, enjoying the hospitality of the same kind and venerable friend who, three-and-twenty years ago, received me into the Church. The sea air soon restored my shattered health. It was my favorite occupation to wander alone at sunset on the smooth sands; to watch the tiny white sail of the fisher's boat till it faded,—was lost on the far distant horizon; to gaze with musing eye on the graceful flight of the seagull, dipping its delicate white wing in the crested billow; and then following with eager look the flitting purple shadows, as they scudded rapidly over the darkening bosom of the sea. Then, to seat my wearied limbs on the jutting fragments of a rock, listening with rapt attention to the booming surf, as it slowly, but surely won its way. And then, lulled by the dreamy music of that surf, to think on bygone days, and the many strange and mournful events I had encountered. And then the fair and beautiful moon would arise from that far-distant line, where sea and sky seem to meet and mingle; throwing, in one long and silvery track, her brightness over the dark, blue waters. And then the twinkling stars would appear and shine in the firmament; and they all proclaimed, in their own silent eloquence, the glory, the majesty of their Omnipotent Creator.

It was on such an evening, that the following narrative occurred to my recollection. One by one, the events shaped themselves in my memory, until the whole stood clear and as well defined as if those events had been of recent occurrence.

In these days of unbelief, it may be that someone of that unhappy class, who, with reckless folly, with pitiable hardihood, deny the efficacy, the truth of revealed religion; who coolly scoff at its salutary power, and resign themselves with apathy to the gloomy thought and conviction of their soul's annihilation; who say there is no hereafter; and that the soul, or thinking principle of man, perishes like the brute beast of the field—it may be, someone, perchance, of this unhappily numerous class, may glance his eye over this narrative; let him not despise the warning it conveys; let him see infidelity stripped of its boasted shield and panoply of philosophy, in its last solemn conflict with death. Let him come, and stand by the death-bed of him who, in his folly, said there is no God,—there is no hereafter—and witness, if he can, with an unblanched cheek, the reaction of fears too agonizing for utterance; the overwhelming conviction of an hereafter, alas! utterly unprovided for. Let him see, in fine, whether infidelity, the panacea of a diseased mind, can impart peace or consolation in the closing scene of human existence.

"Remember next Thursday," said my old friend, Mrs. B—. "Mind and be punctual at six; and don't forget it is our wedding day. By the by," she continued, "you will meet a cousin of ours at dinner. I wish sincerely you would make his acquaintance. He is, I am sorry to say, an unbeliever: you may have some influence over him; try and do what you can for him."

I promised acquiescence, but had strong doubts of succeeding.

Thursday evening came. The husband of Mrs. B— was an old friend of mine,—in fact, we were at the same school together in early youth, and a warm friendship had been ever maintained between us. He and his wife had both become converts a few years previously, and I had the happiness of receiving them into the Church. They had no family, but enjoyed, in the highest degree, domestic harmony and felicity.

On my entering the drawing-room, I received, as I always did, the warmest welcome from my host and hostess. Two more guests arrived, and then the expected cousin. He was a tall, gentlemanly man, about five-and-thirty years of age; slightly, but well made; of a pale and thoughtful cast of feature, and a magnificently expansive brow. He was evidently a man of high intellect, and his voice had a most winning and persuasive intonation. His smile, too, had a melancholy sweetness; and I thought I rarely beheld a more dangerous or captivating advocate of unbelief. On my introduction to him, the usual courteous salutations ensued, and the ordinary topics of the day were discussed, until dinner was announced.

We were seated opposite, and I had a good opportunity of making a quiet study of that incomprehensible being,—a sceptic. Dinner passed as dinners usually do. After the cloth was removed, and the dessert and wines placed in all their tempting array, the conversation took a widely discursive and cheerful strain. Every topic, save that of religion, was well and lightly touched on. Politics; the merits of the premier; the chance of a dissolution; the last crack speech in the House; O'Connell and his rent; Ireland, her long sufferings,—her faults, and many virtues; steam,—and its stupendous advancement; America; France; and many other subjects of interest, came successively on *the tapis*; and on all and each of these Mr. H—, the sceptic cousin, spoke well and fluently. He had the rare merit of never speaking for effect; but what he said was well said and just, and no more than was sufficient to make you perfectly cognizant of the fact.

After coffee, we had a little—just enough—of most excellent music. One of Beethoven's lovely trios was charmingly played. Mrs. B—, our hostess, presided at the piano; her husband played the violoncello, and their cousin, the violin. Then followed a

duet for the violin and piano—one of Pasiello's finest. Mr. H—
was the best amateur player I ever heard. His tone was pure and
exquisitely vocal. In an *adagio* he poured forth a strain of such
plaintive melody, so thrilling and mournful, that every listener
was moved almost to tears. His playing showed that he had a
heart which had been deeply tried by sorrow.

The conversation took a musical turn. Mrs. B— mentioned
to me that her cousin had a fine collection of old violins; upon
which I expressed the great pleasure it would give me to see
them. He laughingly acceded, and said:

"I have heard, sir, that you are as great an enthusiast as myself
about a Cremona. I shall be most happy to see you to-morrow,
and you can judge for yourself."

The hour was arranged, and I departed with a strong feeling of
compassion for this highly- gifted man, deprived of the only solace—religion—which can mitigate the evils and sorrows of life.

On the morrow, I paid my promised visit. He lived in the
neighborhood of Bedford-square. I was shown into his library,
which contained several thousand volumes, all well bound, and
in fine condition. In a few minutes he came in, and, at once, I
found myself at home with him. Our conversation took a liter-
ary turn, and he showed me the treasures of his library. I almost
envied him his collection. But in one of the bookcases, which
was protected by a brass wire screen, and under lock and key, I
beheld, to my sorrow a fearful array of French and English infidelity. Every work of those demon intellects who strove to sap
and mine Christianity was there. Alas! how many thousands,
perhaps, are now suffering in hell from those very works; and
what a fearful account will those unhappy writers have to render
at the judgment-seat of God, for the poison they have strewn in
the path of their fellow-men! The very atmosphere of the room
became hateful to me, tenanted as it was by such an infidel host.

"I perceive, sir," said Mr. H—, with a grave and courteous
smile, "that these works are not at all to your taste. But I am unwilling to shock the prejudices of anyone. These books, you see,
I keep under lock and key, and no one has access to them but

myself. But come, I have metal much more attractive for you. We will adjourn to my music-room, and try the violins."

I willingly acceded. The room in which he kept his instruments was large and wainscoted. No curtains, no carpet, no sofa or stuffed chairs to deaden the sound; but it looked, as it really was, a music-room, in which every tone could be heard in all its purity, and to the best advantage.

A grand piano, three or four music desks, some shelves, on which reposed several violin cases, formed the contents. His violins were all of the first class. Two, a Guarnerius and a Stradiverius, were of unrivalled beauty of tone. I looked on them with reverence. Through how many generations have these delicate and fragile Cremonas survived! How many kingdoms have been lost and won; how many dynasties have been changed, since that frail and perishable wood was put together at Cremona; how many countless thousands have listened with rapt attention to their melting strains, and who are now dead, and perhaps forgotten! Mysterious instruments of melody! the art of producing you has perished with your makers. Science and skill have been tried in vain, to imitate—to reproduce you. You stand, O Cremonas, alone in your glory!

He tried one of the finest of his violins. Chords the most pure, sweet, melodious, and brilliant, streamed from beneath his bow; then he achieved, with incredible lightness and precision, the widest intervals,—ascended and descended, with marvelous facility, the chromatic and diatonic scales, and exhausted, within the space of a few bars, the whole range of chorus and sounds possible upon the instrument. Then his spirit seemed changed; a mournful, fleeting, intangible vision,—a sort of shuddering fury, as if of recollected wrongs, seemed to seize him, and tones the most appalling, strains the most agonizing, pealed from the excited strings—until I trembled for the hapless being whom I beheld and heard. Then he played *Nel cor piu,* to which he imparted a tone so plaintive and desolate, that the heart was torn by it. Intermingled were tones that seemed to be wrung from the deepest anguish of a broken heart: and then he finished with a light and graceful *rondo.*

The loosened notes fell in a silver shower and left me breathless with admiration and delight. His violin appeared a part of himself by which he could best portray the workings of his mind. He would, if he had been a professional player, have rivalled Paganini.

He finished, exhausted with his efforts.

"It is seldom," said he, "that I meet with one who can appreciate the resources of the violin. Marvellous, indeed, they are, and who can tell the extent of its limits? To the common, unobservant eye, it is only a fiddle; but who ever heard Paganini, and did not at times almost imagine that his fiddle contained a soul? And thou," said he, apostrophizing his Cremona, "my fine old fellow, thou wilt, perhaps, long survive me; thy melodious tones will be heard,—will quicken the pulses of others, when I shall be no more,—when this mysterious, sentient, thinking principle by which I exist, will be annihilated—will rest in the eternal sleep of death."

"My dear sir," I rejoined, "are you *quite* sure,—are you *quite* satisfied, that such will be the termination of your earthly career?"

"Perfectly so," he replied. "Long ago, by intense study, by deep and mature reflection, I arrived at a calm and deep conviction, that there is no hereafter."

Here I pondered, for a few moments, on the best method of dealing with so fearful a spiritual disease; and reflecting on the great force of what is called the pride of intellect, I determined to avoid, in the commencement, any and all collision with the metaphysical objections, which, indeed, I felt I could overthrow, but to which, I perceived, he was so wedded, that to do that would only estrange him still farther from the truth. These thoughts flashed rapidly through my mind, and I determined on a very opposite, and, as my experience in this and in other cases has invariably shown me, a much more happy and effective plan.

"Allow me to ask," I said, "has this conviction tended to promote your happiness?"

"Happiness!" he exclaimed, with a ghastly smile, "happiness has long fled from this lacerated heart of mine. I seek no longer for happiness. It is a bubble,—a dream; and oh, how miserable is the awakening! But come, sir, I must apologize for my hasty expression. It escaped from me I know not how. I am ever most careful not to shock, what I conceive the prejudices of others. I have chosen my path, sir; it may not be the best, perhaps, but such as is, it has given me content."

"But you would not like to die, sir, professing those opinions of unbelief? I have seen many hundreds of death-beds, and I have often witnessed extraordinary changes in the mind and heart of man in the solemn hour of dissolution. I have never witnessed one, however thoughtlessly he had lived, who was not then deeply impressed that there *is* a hereafter, and that he has a strict account to render to the God that made him. Happy indeed are those who are prepared for that last hour!"

"It is bootless," said he, "to argue those points. I am proof against conviction; and, as to death,—oh, gladly would I lay me down and die! I have tried all the boasted resources of life, and have found their hollowness,—their deception. I have plunged madly into what is called pleasure,—it soon palled on my jaded senses. I have tried literature, science, travel; thinking, by a change of scene, to alleviate the insupportable burden of existence; but all, alas! failed. I have tried friendship,—was deceived, betrayed. No matter. I suppose I must still live on,—still drag on this hated life. My pride forbids; it would be cowardice to resign it by my own act and deed."

As my time was limited, my first visit soon came to an end. He requested me earnestly to see him again soon, adding, that though we differed on religious grounds, he would have great pleasure in cultivating my acquaintance.

I left him, saddened at heart to perceive so many fine talents, so many noble qualities, buried in the grave of infidelity. For in the heart of the infidel there are no joys, but such as are like scentless flowers, that one plucks to pieces for sport; no passion, save that which is akin to delirium or debauchery; no medicine of the soul that is healing, but the damning dose of madness, apathy, or despair. Ay, though calm and impassible may be the exterior of the infidel, a wounded and withered heart exists within.

But I did not despair of his conversion. I commended him fervently to the infinite mercy of God.

One day, in paying my round of visits to the sick, I unexpectedly encountered him in the garret of a poor Irish tailor, who was slowly recovering from a long illness. The poor fellow had a large family,—all too young to aid him. His wife was near her confinement. He was in arrears for rent, and to increase his troubles, his club, from some slight infringement of their rules, withheld their small weekly contribution.

Mr. H— had accidentally heard of his distress, and, like the good Samaritan, hastened to relieve it. He had paid the rent; given handsomely for their present support; and, what was better than all, promised the man employment when his health was restored. Both husband and wife were thanking him with a grateful burst of feeling, as I entered and prevented his escape. This, however, he soon effected, I then learned from the poor tailor that it was incredible the good he did; that a great part of his large income must be given away in deeds of unobtrusive charity; and that numbers of aged widows, and other poor persons, whom, by his benevolence, he preserved from the cold charity of the workhouse, were praying for him day and night. I had heard obscurely of the "good gentleman who did not wish his name to be known." He was the man.

Several other instances of great generosity, of extreme kindness of heart, came shortly afterwards under my notice, and made me more anxious than ever to attempt his conversion. But every plan, however ingeniously laid, failed most signally. He always maintained a chilling and stern reserve whenever religion was mentioned, and immediately forced the conversation into some other channel. Still, I did not despair.

One morning I paid my visit at the usual hour. The servant informed me that his master was very ill, and could see nobody. I expressed my concern, and asked how long he had been unwell, as it was more than a week since I had seen him.

"Why, sir," said the man, "master went out last night quite well, and returned home very bad indeed. He could hardly get out of the cab. And what is worse, sir, he has been walking up and down the library all night, and hasn't been to bed. The housekeeper went to him, crying, this morning, and begged him to have advice. But he won't, sir."

A tear was in the poor fellow's eye, which showed that he had a grateful heart, and had a kind master.

I left my card.

About an hour after I reached home, I received the following note:

"Dear Sir,—By all that *you* hold sacred, come to me immediately. Yours, F. H."

I went immediately, and found him on the sofa in the greatest distress and anguish of mind. His cousin, Mrs. B---, was with him, endeavoring in vain to soothe him. He wrung my hand in silence; gave me one piercing glance with his blood-shot eyes, and burst into tears. I was little less agitated myself to see that powerful mind so prostrated.

"Do not," he gasped, "do not speak to me yet, or I shall die of suffocation. Where is now my boasted philosophy! it is humbled in the dust."

He was silent for some minutes, and then rallied.

"I am ashamed, sir, for you to witness such emotion, which you may deem unmanly; but when you know the cause, you will hardly blame me. Be seated, sir, and listen as patiently as you can to the tale of a heart-broken man. I also need your service in a work of charity, which must plead my apology for your hasty summons. It is necessary to give you a sketch of my previous life, that you may understand my present position.

"It is now twenty years since I entered Eton and to my entrance there do I owe much of my after unhappiness. I soon contracted a warm friendship with young C—, who was the pride of the school. He was three forms above me, and I was four years his junior, He was very athletic, finely formed; was our best cricketer, pulled the stroke oar in all our matches, and was the terror of all the bargemen in the neighborhood. We were inseparable until he went to Oxford; I, also, in the course of time, joined him at Christ Church. He was there also a universal favorite; and we recommenced a warm, and what to me proved a fatal friendship.

Young as he was, he was already a confirmed free-thinker, and spared neither pains nor time in inoculating his associates with his opinions. I long held out firm against every attack; and argued, as I thought, successfully, against every withering sarcasm which he freely quoted from Hobbes and Voltaire. I had been bred a strict Protestant, and member of the Church of England, and I well knew the pain it would give my mother to hear that her son had become an infidel.

"Finding mere argument inoperative, he tried the seductive arts of pleasure. Here, alas! he fatally succeeded. I look back now with bitter regret, to the calm and innocent days of my youth, when I was obedient to a mother's kind and affectionate warning. Then, religion though I now know it to be a fallacy,—a delusion,—gave me unspeakable happiness. But regret is idle. At first, I stood, like a timid bather, on the brink of corruption, but soon plunged madly in. Drink and debauchery consumed my nights; my days passed in languid feverish exhaustion, only to be alleviated by the same infernal round of nightly excess. At length, after a long career of suicidal excess, I was laid up; human nature could stand no more. *Delirium tremens* laid its gaunt and spectral hand on my fevered brain. A powerful constitution pulled me through, but for weeks I was helpless as a child. Never shall I forget the mental horrors I endured in my slow recovery. The fear of future punishments haunted me day and night. I felt a miserable, anguished regret at my past consummate folly, and I made many vows of amendment.

"I was laid up during the long vacation; no one came near me but my scout and the doctor, and I had time for reflection. Term time came and with it the fast men, my former associates in guilt. Among these, the first that visited me was C—. I was glad enough to see him, as I felt so lonely and miserable. I told him the horrors I endured, and that nothing could tempt me to retrace my former steps. He laughed gayly at my fears, derided with the keenest irony what he called the bugbears of a weakened brain, and told me, when I got on my legs, I would laugh at them as he did.

"'By-the-by, old fellow,' said he, 'seriously—would advise you to pull in a little for the present: no constitution could stand the wear and tear you have given yours. I am reckoned a tolerable fast man myself, but you beat me hollow.'

"Well, sir, I recovered, and though I lived freely, was tolerably careful of my health. But my good resolutions had long since gone to the winds. As I fell deeper into systematic vice, every early religious impression, so tenderly fostered by my kind mother, gradually faded from my mind. The idea of an hereafter became so hateful to me, that I sought with frantic eagerness to dispel every lingering faith on the subject. My mentor in evil was soon perfectly successful in making me one like himself. He was the president of a free-thinking club, and I was enrolled as an associate. We met at each other's rooms every week, and little did the orthodox dons dream of the nest of hornets they were fostering in the bosom of old Oxford.

"I felt more tranquil now. I had neither fear nor hope to disturb or agitate my mind. The present was my only life, and I resolved to enjoy it to the utmost. I soon got disgusted with my former coarse and revolting debaucheries, and became an Epicurean in my tastes and enjoyments. It was then that I devoted myself with passionate enthusiasm to music, for which I had always a great fondness. On leaving Oxford, I travelled for three years, with C— for my companion. We did not confine ourselves to the usual route of travelers, but ransacked the treasures of the East.

"On my return to England I shortly after married. For a while I was intoxicated with happiness. My wife was exquisitely beautiful and we were devotedly fond of each other. Our tastes, too, harmonized. I must now tell you sir, that I then made what I consider the greatest, foulest mistake, of my life. My wife was a Catholic; I allowed her at first the free exercise of her religion, and was careful never to express a doubt, never to utter a word against Christianity in her presence. But when we had been married about a year, an irrepressible desire tempted me to shake her trust in religion and in her God. In this, what I now think an infernal scheme, I was zealously aided by C—. Our plan of operations was laid—was followed out with exquisite tact. Like the constant dropping of water on stone, an impression was slowly but surely made. She began to be indifferent, and then to neglect her religion altogether. So far, we succeeded, but no farther. We found a woman's heart, a woman's imagination, and peculiar susceptibility to religion, a more difficult thing to manage than we expected. We could not make her a free-thinker, but we soon made her restless and unhappy. I began even to think that her affections to myself were changed. The thought was insupportable—was madness. C— was our constant visitor. Under a fatal delusion, I firmly believed him to be a true friend. One day I received a letter from Devonshire, announcing the sudden illness and expected death of my uncle, Sir J— D—. He was an old officer, knighted for his bravery, and tenderly attached to me. The letter was written by his medical man, and urged me to start immediately, if I wished to find my uncle alive. I was reading the letter to my wife, when C— entered the room. I told him its contents.

"'Go, my dear fellow,' said he, 'you have no time to lose; and I hope, before you return, Mrs. H— will have recovered her good looks.'

"She had been suffering slightly from indisposition.

"I rang the bell, told my valet to pack up, and order post-horses to be ready in an hour.

"I had a short interview with C— in my dressing-room. His heart seemed full of the deepest friendship to me and mine.

"'I am afraid,' said he, "Mrs. H— has been moped too much lately; she seems to have lost all her buoyant spirits. Pray write to her often and write kindly. If I can be of any service to her during your absence, which I hope will not be long, you know you may command me. I am an idle man.'

"I thanked him warmly, begged him to look in as often as he could, and to use an old friend's privilege during my absence. My parting with my wife was painful. We had never yet been separated. She clung to me, embraced me again and again, and burst into tears when I bade her farewell. I never loved her so fervently as I did at that moment, and could have died willingly to have done her the slightest service. I travelled all night as fast as four fleet horses could whirl me along. On my arrival at my uncle's seat the next afternoon, I found to my great joy that he had unexpectedly rallied, and, though extremely weak, no immediate danger was apprehended. My interview with him, after he had been prepared for my reception, was full of tenderness and affection. The fine old man was propped up with pillows; his white hair floated on his shoulders; his face was pale and emaciated from severe illness, but lit up with a feeling of happiness and reverent submission; his dark intellectual eye gleamed with delight, when, pressing both my hands in his thin wasted ones, he told me how glad—how exceeding glad—he was to see me.

"'I thought, Fred, it was all over with me, that I never should see you again. But thanks be to God and his infinite mercies, I am spared a little longer to make a better preparation for heaven. And can you stay with me, my dear boy, till I am gone? It will soon, very soon happen—for though so much better than yesterday, I feel that sinking at the heart, that certain intelligence within, which tells me I must indeed die soon.'

"I promised, as well as my grief would allow me, that no other hands than mine should close his eyes.

"He lived, sir, seven weeks longer, in almost daily expectation of his death. During that period, I wrote very frequently to my wife, and received the most affectionate replies. Mv uncle's last hour approached. I envied him his death; it was that of a truly good man; and I felt that religion, all delusive as I then believed and now think it, must have wondrous power in soothing the agony of a dying pillow. I had written to Emily to announce my uncle's death, and my succession to the estates. In a few of her last letters I thought I perceived something of coldness of tone; but the hurry and anxiety I was plunged in, gave me no time for thought. This time, however, I received no answer; I wrote again, still no answer came. I was in an agony of fear—imagining she was ill, and fancied a thousand horrors, which kept me from sleeping at night. I could endure my suspense no longer. On the evening of the funeral—when all was over, the guests dismissed, and the last instructions given to the steward—I threw myself into the carriage, and posted at headlong speed to London.

"It was midnight when I arrived—there were no lights visible in the house. 'Emily's retired to rest,' I thought,—'poor darling! I hope she is not ill—how surprised she'll be to see me:—I am sure my letters miscarried.'

"My valet thundered at the door again and again, I began to feel a suffocating throbbing at the heart. At length the door was opened—I rushed in, and found Mrs. Jones, the housekeeper, and two more of the servants, in the hall; they were pale, trembling, and only half dressed, as if they had hastily risen from their beds.

"'Mrs. Jones,' I exclaimed, my agitation nearly choking my utterance, 'how is my wife?—she is ill!—she is dead!' I almost screamed, grasping her by the arm as she hesitated to return me an answer; 'Tell me, woman, this instant, or I shall go mad!'

"'Oh, sir,' said she, sobbing violently 'do not ask me here, I would almost die rather than tell you.'

A strange unnatural horror crept with benumbing influence through my veins. I stood for some seconds in a dreamy state of torpor, with my eyes fixed, dilated, on the woman.

"At length my tongue, which cleaved to the roof of my mouth, found utterance: 'Come with me to the library.' We entered.

"I turned to question her: she had fallen on her knees, the tears streaming down her aged cheeks, and her hands clasped together in passionate sorrow.

"'Woman,' I again asked, 'where is my wife?' 'Oh, my dear sir,' said she, bear with fortitude what I am going to tell you—bear it like a man—I dared not tell you my suspicions before you left town. Now they are confirmed. Your unhappy wife eloped last night with your pretended friend, Mr. C—.'

"'Eloped!' I exclaimed, or rather screamed, with a pang of unutterable agony; a sudden blaze of light seemed to flash before my distended eyeballs—a roar like thunder pealed in my ears—I fell stricken to the ground.

"What followed, I know not; a long and fearful dream ensued, filled with unmitigated horror; visions unearthly, despairing, held for months my senses captive. At length I awoke to a dim consciousness of existence—I was in the cell of a madhouse! my hands and feet manacled; and my dull and leaden eye gazed with apathy at the whitewashed wall, and the narrow light of a window about ten feet from the ground.

"I remained, I suppose, about an hour speculating on my strange situation, and wondering what it all meant—my confused brain puzzling itself to prove my identity, and that it was not all a dream; when the door of my cell slowly opened, and two men entered. One was evidently a gentleman—the other I supposed was an attendant, or perhaps my jailer. What crime had I committed that I should be thus immured?

"The gentleman, who had a kind and benevolent look, advanced to the side of my rude pallet, to which I was bound, felt my pulse, laid his hand on my forehead as if to examine its temperature, and gave a look of surprise and pleasure to the attendant.

"'Where am I, sir?' I asked.

"'Hush, my dear sir,' said he, 'don't talk now, you have been very ill, but will soon be quite well—you are in the hands of friends. James, undo the bandages.'

"They were instantly removed with great care and tenderness. A composing draught was given me, and I soon sank into a profound slumber. I was told afterwards, that I slept more than twenty hours. I awoke much refreshed, and my mind somewhat clearer than before.

"Day after day, as my strength returned, did the horrible story of my wrongs make itself clearer, more distinct to my memory, until the whole burst upon me with the force of an overwhelming avalanche. I wrestled against my returning madness—I fought against despair and suicide, I nursed my every faculty for revenge—I brooded over those mighty wrongs of mine, until every fibre of my frame was restrung by an insatiable desire of revenge. My happiness was crushed and blasted—I lived only for revenge—I would pursue the villain to the uttermost bounds of the earth, and devote all that I had for his destruction. Strange to say, my bodily health throve under this burning desire of vengeance. In a month's time I was conveyed home; was pronounced sane and perfectly cured.

"I instantly made inquiries in every direction. For some time I was baffled—they, the guilty pair, had been traced to Paris and were then lost sight of. I flew to Paris, determining to ransack the whole city till I found them. I bribed the police, and had several keen agents in pay, but, for a month, there was no intelligence. I visited every place of public resort, but with no success.

"And now, how I cursed my folly—how I cursed the very name of friendship, since I had been so betrayed. How bitterly I deplored the insidious arts I had used in perverting my wife from her religion! it would have been her best safeguard, if, like a venomous reptile, I had not poisoned her peace. I felt that I was the author of her ruin—but woe be to him who has blasted my honor, and trampled under foot my happiness and peace! And he was my friend! the friend whom I thought the soul of honor; and who, I thought in my folly, was bound to me by every tie of gratitude! for when his resources had been crippled by his gambling losses, I supplied him with several thousands, and threw his note of hand into the fire. My purse, my home, my heart were his—and yet, how foully he betrayed me.

"One morning the porter of the lodge came to my bedside at daybreak, and said an agent of police wished to see me immediately. He brought me golden news, and was well rewarded. The last night he received certain information from a courier, that they were residing in Florence, under a feigned name.

"My passport was ready, signed, before eleven—and at twelve that morning I was speeding on the wings of vengeance to Florence.

"I will spare you the detail, sir, of nearly twelvemonth's hunt after this wretched couple, through almost every state in Europe. I rarely lost my clew, which I followed with all the tenacity of a sleuth-hound—but the chances were against me. Once, at Baden-Baden, I almost caught him—he had started in the morning, after losing a very considerable sum at the gaming table. I arrived in the evening—got scent of him, and should have run my quarry to the death, had not my carriage, from the headlong speed at which I was driven, overturned; and I was compelled, from several severe contusions, to remain a week at a miserable German inn, cursing my fate, and frantic with delay.

"The scent was lost, and never recovered. Two years I wandered about in hopeless misery but to no avail—*they* were not to be found. I then, wearied in body and mind, miserably broken down, returned to England. My cousin here, Mrs. B—, at whose house we first met, has been very kind to me: if it had not been for her, I think I should have long since died of a broken heart."

Here he paused, as if from exhaustion, drank some laudanum and water, and continued.

"I now come, sir, to what I have so long, perhaps intentionally, delayed. My agent, who manages my country property, is in town. I went to him last night to give directions about the renewal of a lease, and as I had had no exercise during the day, I preferred walking home. I left him about eleven. It was a bitter cold night. A thin, chilling sleet was falling; scarcely a passenger was in the deserted streets, and I muffled my cloak over the lower part of my face to keep out the night-air.

"In threading my way through the devious intricacies of the Seven Dials, I beheld a woman meanly clad advancing slowly and feebly towards me. I got ready a half-crown to give her, as she seemed from her feebleness to be in want of food, perhaps was ill. Before I could give her the money, she had, however, in the humblest, gentlest tone of entreaty, solicited charity. The tones of that voice, though scarcely raised above a whisper, struck with an icy chill upon my heart. I thought I remembered them. Horrible thought! it could not be—but, as I placed the money in her cold, trembling hand, I gazed earnestly in her face; her eyes were downcast, they did not meet mine. The lineaments of that face were the same: but, in expression, in beauty, how changed! She was my *wife!*

"I was stunned—paralyzed for some seconds. She had hastily left me, happily without recognizing me. But the miscreant must be at hand, it is for *him* she has then begged for charity in the public streets. I followed her with noiseless steps, like those of the tiger dogging his victim before he makes the final spring. With feeble steps she crept towards a neighboring public house, and I peered though the half-open door. She purchased with the money some wine and biscuits, placed them carefully under her thin shawl, and hurried off. I followed her through several streets: she stopped at the door of a miserable house, and entered. She had not once looked round, nor closed the door. I heard her ascend with panting and labored breath two flights of stairs. I marked with vigilant ear the room she entered. In an instant I had sprung up the stairs, and was at the door. I heard the same sweet plaintive voice, which a few minutes before had struck like a death knell upon my ear. I heard also the hoarse and muttered tones of that incarnate fiend, C. I could bear no more; I burst the door open and was upon them: now should my hoarded vengeance be satiated. It was, sir! My revenge was satisfied, but by another hand than mine.

"I beheld on the bed the miserably squalid form of C—, death stamped on his hideously wasted face, his clothes in rags, foul and loathsome. *She* was kneeling by the bedside, and helping him to a biscuit soaked in a cup of wine, which he feebly but ravenously devoured. They gazed on me as I entered the room. His eyes dilated, glared fearfully for an instant, then closed, as if he would shut out for ever an appalling vision, the whole visage became convulsed, distorted, the jaw fell, and he sunk back a corpse.

"She, too, had fallen, had fainted, the moment her eyes met mine. I called loudly for assistance. I could not touch her, nor raise her from the ground; but I felt an excessive trembling of the heart, that told me my love for her was not quite extinguished.

"The landlady ran up; I hastily explained that the man died as I entered the room, and the unhappy woman had fainted; I forced my purse upon her, told her to do what was necessary, and reached home as if ten thousand furies were lacerating my heart."

He drank some more of the laudanum, wiped the clammy dew from his forehead, and continued:

"I have had, sir, last night and this morning, a sore and hard struggle; but happily, I have conquered. Revenge, I think of, I desire, no more. He, the miscreant, is dead. But, sir, she must not starve. You will lay me under an infinite obligation if you will see to her wants. Take this pocket-book, it will amply provide for her present necessities. I will direct my solicitor to settle on her a sufficient annuity. But, sir, I cannot—will never see her again."

He gave me her direction hastily written in pencil on a card. I then departed on my mission of mercy.

I found the unhappy woman in bed, carefully tended by the humane landlady, who had removed her to her own room. She had suffered much from hysteria, but was more composed, though greatly exhausted. She had all the remains of exceeding great beauty, but was pale and thin, and evidently not long for this world. I explained the motives of my coming as briefly and as tenderly as I could, for I was unwilling to add a pang to a heart that seemed well-nigh broken.

"And it is my husband, my Frederick, who has done all this for his poor guilty wife! Oh. sir! I have sinned deeply, almost beyond repentance, but not so much as he thinks I have done. Tell him, sir, I was betrayed, that I did not meditate guilt, and that the rest was frenzy, madness, and despair! Tell him that on the very night of my elopement, I left the partner of my guilt—left him I thought for ever*—that I have remained ever since in these poor lodgings, earning my daily bread by the most menial offices; and by bitter tears of repentance endeavoring to make my peace with Heaven. Tell him, sir, that coming home last night, penniless, and unsuccessful in obtaining work, I met the miserable partner and author of my crime in a dying state. He knew me at once, and piteously implored me to give him food and shelter; he had eaten nothing for two days, and for weeks had slept in the open air. I could not, sir, though I had suffered such bitter wrong from him, refuse his request. I took him to my lodgings, and hurried

---

* This was found afterwards to be true. Mrs. H— left C— at Dover, and returned from London. C— proceeded alone to Paris, where he induced by his arts a thoughtless young creature to accompany him on his travels. He soon discarded her; returned to England; lost every shilling of a fine property by gambling; became the bonnet of one of the minor hells; was kicked out for his frauds and insolence; sank from one degree of degradation to another, until he was thus found, starving and dying in the streets, by her whom he had betrayed and ruined.

out to obtain some sustenance for him. It may be wrong for me to have done so, but I could not see him perish for want, and not endeavor to relieve him. Sir, I have suffered unutterable agony during these seven years since I left my husband; but I owe my unhappy fall entirely to my neglecting religious duties. It is when we forget—we neglect—our God, that the tempter is busiest with us. But God has been exceedingly merciful to me. He gave me grace immediately to return to Him, and to expiate by a life of penance my exceeding great sin. I have no wish now but to obtain my husband's forgiveness, and, if it be God's holy will, to die. Often, sir, when the nights have been coldest, have I walked the street for hours where my husband lives—where, alas, I have spent so many innocent, happy days—and watered the pavement with my tears. Often have I knelt at midnight on the stone steps of his door, and prayed to Heaven to pardon me, and to bless him. Tell him this, sir, and that, if my guilt was great, my sorrow and repentance have been also great and enduring."

Every reader, I am certain, will sympathize with this afflicted, repentant heart. That day she was removed to a comfortable, respectable lodging, where she had every attention her precarious situation required. I sent for her director by her request, to whom she had gone to confession for the last seven years. He attended her daily. I also saw her as frequently as I could, but at each visit I perceived that death was nearer at hand.

In a fortnight's time I received a note from her landlady, to say that she was dying and wished to see me. I hastened to her immediately. I found her rapidly sinking—the pulse scarcely perceptible, the breath short and quick, the face of an ashy hue, but calm and tranquil in expression. She had that morning received with edifying piety the last rites of the Church.

"I have sent for you, sir," said she, with a sweet and dying smile,—"I have sent for you to give you my last grateful thanks for all your kindness. Tell my husband, that with my last breath I bless him and pray for him."

"Would you not like to see him," said I, "before you die?"

"Oh, sir," she replied, a flush mantling on her pallid brow, "it would be too great a happiness; I am utterly unworthy to see him again; and yet I should die so happy to see him once more, to hear from his own loved lips that he forgave me."

I threw myself into a cab, telling the man to exert his utmost speed. Happily, I found Mr. H— at home.

"My dear friend," I hurriedly said, "your poor wife is dying."

"Well, sir," said he, sternly, "and what then?"

I had before given him his poor wife's exculpatory message, at which he appeared much moved.

"My dear sir," I replied, "you will not, I am sure, refuse her last earnest and dying request. She wishes to see you before she dies, and to have your forgiveness."

He sank on a chair, and for some minutes was plunged in an agony of grief.

"Come, sir," said he, taking me by the arm, "the struggle is over. Poor Emily—I do indeed forgive thee, and I myself have much to be forgiven."

We entered the cab, which returned at the same rapid pace.

We met the landlady at the door, who was in tears and anxiously awaiting us. He pressed me to accompany him, as he thought the trial would be too much for him alone.

We entered the room together. The injured husband, the repentant wife, were locked in each other's arms in a long and fond embrace. It was a sight that angels might rejoice at in heaven.

"Frederick," she faintly whispered, "do you forgive me?"

"The fault was mine, love," he replied. "As we first met, so let us part now: all is forgotten."

She looked on him in an ecstasy of love and gratitude; and, in that look of happiness expired.

She was buried plainly and unostentatiously. Her husband and myself were the only mourners.

On the morning after the funeral, his valet came to me in a great hurry, requesting to see me. On his admittance, he told me that his master had gone out late last night, and was brought home that morning in a hackney-coach, wet through, and almost insensible. He was put to bed; a doctor sent for, who had somewhat relieved him; and that, if possible, I was to go to him immediately.

I hastened to him, under the impression that he had attempted self-destruction. Such, however, was happily not the case. I found him in bed, sadly altered, and showing strong signs of approaching fever.

"My dear friend," he said, "I have been very foolish; but I could not help it. I felt so miserable last night, so broken-hearted about poor Emily, that the very air of the room was stifling to me. I rushed out of doors, going I know not where, my brain throbbing as if it would burst, when I found myself, how I know not, by Emily's grave. I threw myself upon it, and thought long and bitterly on all her matchless excellence and love, and on all her after sorrows. You may think it a weakness, but I thought then there must be a hereafter, and that her disembodied spirit was then looking down upon me from a place of rest and happiness. I felt an emotion within me too strong to be resisted; it was perfectly independent of my reasoning powers; it was the deep, overwhelming conviction of my heart, that there is a God, a hereafter, and a religion by which we are to be saved. I wept abundantly, and prayed—the first time for many years—on her grave, to that same Divine Eternal Spirit, that He would aid me, would direct me what to do. I suppose I must then have fallen into a sleep or a trance, for I was found the next morning by the sexton in a state of insensibility, and wet through with the rain, which fell heavily during the night. I rely, sir, on your friendship. You, I am sure, will assist me."

I replied it would give me the greatest joy to do so; and that, if he persevered, his past sorrows might yet be exchanged for peace and happiness.

"Alas, sir, I fear not. I am every moment getting more seriously ill. It may be my last. My constitution is shattered—broken up; and I fear there is little time or opportunity for the close employment of clear intellect it requires."

"Do not depend, sir, too much on your own strength,—on the resources of your own reasoning powers; but pray fervently to God, whom you now acknowledge your Creator, to aid you with his mercy and grace."

"Farewell, sir, for the present," said he, wringing my hand. "I must now tell you, though it is a humiliating confession, that my infidelity has long made me truly wretched, has poisoned every enjoyment of my life; and, in my heavy sorrows, it was a poor and miserable support, and has now failed me in my utmost need. Pray for me, sir, and see me again soon."

I did pray for him; and the many poor he had relieved by his discriminating charities, prayed for him too. Their prayers are all-powerful with God.

For three weeks he lay under a severe attack of brain-fever. His sufferings were horrible. For days together he heaped appalling maledictions on the departed C—, cursing himself as an infatuated fool for having been made his tool, his victim; then, blasphemies too fearful to think on. Then he would scream with pitiable terror, that the spectre of C— was standing by the foot of the bed, and grinning and mocking him with insulting scorn. Night after night, he would address this spectral creation of his own distempered brain, and urge against him the whole catalogue of his many wrongs; that it was he who had destroyed his faith in God, poisoned his peace, and blasted his happiness. Then would he shudder and wring his hands, and cry sorrowfully that he would not, could not die; that he was now sure there was a hell, and that he had damned himself by his own folly.

But the prayers of the poor prevailed. He had shown mercy and forgiveness to his wife, and mercy was shown to him. He recovered, but was a helpless cripple: he had lost the use of his limbs, from exposure that night on his wife's grave. He was, however, very patient and resigned; and expressed his great thankfulness that his intellect was restored. He set himself earnestly to read, to inquire, to think and to pray. He read through, with deep attention, the whole of the Bible.

"I am satisfied, sir," said he, "this is the word of God. I am satisfied the Christian religion is the emanation of the Divine will—the immediate work of the Son of God. No other religion tends so much to purify the mind, to subdue the passions, and to make men happy. Its austere, sublime, and self-denying principles, prove to me that it must come from God; and the greatest proof of its Divine authority to me is, that so large and intellectual a part of mankind have embraced it. Sir, I now sincerely profess myself a Christian, though a most unworthy one, I must now study to choose my creed among the many phases of Christianity."

In his library was an extensive collection of controversial works. These he perused with eagerness. In a few weeks, he avowed his intention of becoming a Catholic. I asked him his reasons.

"They are few," said he with a smile, "but fundamental. For a Church, such as I conceive to be the work of its Divine Architect, must, in the first place, be *One;* no varieties of belief: yours has never changed. Secondly, it must have *infinite sanctity,*—yours is the fruitful mother of all the saints; and I cannot sufficiently deplore my blindness, in having so late discovered the immaculate purity of her doctrine. Thirdly, she must be *Catholic,* or the Church of all nations,—yours is essentially so, and no other can lay claim to that venerable name. Fourthly, she must be *apostolic,* coming down from the apostles in an unbroken chain of episcopal and priestly descent. Now, sir, every other Church has come into the world too late to claim this title; some several, some many hundred, years too late to make me wish to join their communion. Besides, sir, in my thinking, no other Church but yours provides so well for the wants and happiness of man. She is ever the same kind and watchful mother to man in life; and, when he dies, she has her departed child in prayerful, sacrificial remembrance. Sir, I am a Catholic in heart: I pray you, make me one in reality."

I did so. I received him into the Church. He became one of the humblest, the most contrite, and fervent of her members. He had bent the whole power of his acute mind and great intellect to the task. He had prayed to that God who never refuses the humble, trustful suppliant, and his last days were full of Christian peace, and serenity, and joy. Never shall I forget his last hour: it was the Christian's triumph; it was the departure of a soul purified by repentance, strengthened by faith, animated by hope, and glowing with charity. In his last reverent reception of the sacraments, he was sustained against the fear and the agony of death. He prayed that his life, his sufferings, the retributive justice which had so severely tried him, might be a warning to those who, like him, had imbibed the poison of infidelity. He prayed that the same mercy which had been extended to him, might be vouchsafed to them; and that they might never experience that most awful of God's judgments, that of dying in their infidelity, and awakening to their belief in God in the eternal fire of hell.

Such was his end. Let the freethinker pause, and meditate what his end is like to be.

A Priest's Sunday Work

WEIGHED down, and frequently exhausted, by his heavy and laborious duties, a London priest is but ill-prepared to meet the increased exertions of the Sunday, and especially the duties of the pulpit. I will exemplify this by briefly narrating one Sunday's work, which I went through in the month of May, three ago.

I must first premise, that I heard the confessions of nearly a hundred penitents the evening before, and that it was past midnight before I retired to rest, completely fatigued, and longing for a good night's sleep, to set me up for the labors of the ensuing day. I was not, however, thus to be gratified. I had been asleep little more than an hour, when my dreamless slumbers were rudely disturbed by a sick call of an urgent nature. It was one of my penitents, who was dying. Go I must; so hurrying on my clothes, I got ready my ritual, the holy oil, and the pix, containing the blessed Sacrament. It was a miserable stormy night, and about two o'clock when I started. The poor dying man resided in a little street near the New road, that was nearly two miles distant. There was no cab to be found in any of the neighboring stands, so, buttoning my great coat tight, I trudged on as fast as the gusty wind allowed me.

At length, after a long and weary walk, I reached my poor penitent. I had attended him a few days previous, and heard his confession. Happy it was I did so. His malady had gained rapidly and fearfully upon him. He was now speechless: he wished to say something more in confession, but could not. A low, inarticulate moaning was all I heard. His countenance, pale, anxious, and bedewed with the agony of approaching dissolution, was at times fearfully convulsed. He clasped and wrung his emaciated hands together, raised himself partially in his bed, and when he could not make himself understood, fell back on his pillow, with anguish stamped on every fading lineament. His hearing, however, was perfect, and to each question I propounded he answered by signs. I remained long with this poor dying brother. By degrees his agitation lessened; his features lost their haggard restlessness,—a look of calm and holy resignation succeeded his former troubled state of mind; and as I read in a low and distinct tone the beautiful and consolatory prayers of the Church, previous to administering the last sacraments for the dying, large, and to me, blessed tears flowed plentifully down his wasted cheeks. That heart, so soon to be stilled by the mighty hand of death, was now reconciled to its Father and its God. A look of meek and unrepining resignation, of an entire trust in the merits of his only Redeemer, stole over his face, like a dying sunset on a wasted land, when he received for the last time Him who died for his sins on the cross.

He was much spent when I applied the holy anointing, but his lips moved ceaselessly in prayer. The last blessing, and solemn Plenary Indulgence for the dying, completed my ministerial duties; and, with a few earnest exhortations to resign himself with an humble, yet pious confidence, to the mercy of his God, I returned to my home and my bed.

It was long before I got to sleep. I thought again and again on the dying scene I had witnessed. I thought again and again on the folly of those who delay their repentance to the last hour. Happy it was for that poor dying man, that he had repented, and confessed in time; for, in his death-hour, speech was denied him. I thought over, in sadness of heart, of the many whom I had attended in their last hour who were like him thus similarly afflicted; who had lost the power of confessing their sins, but who, for many years, had lived strangers to their religious duties. They had lived the usual lives of sinners, reckless, unrepenting, confident that all would be well with them at their last hour, but when that last hour came, they sank overwhelmed with that stern and holy truth; "As a man lives, so shall he die."

A shuddering came over me, as I thus reflected an the miserably unprepared state in which a soul, so stained with crime, so unpurified by repentance, is thus hurried suddenly before its God. Four o'clock struck,—then five, and I fell asleep. At seven I was called to hear confessions. I arose, tired and unrefreshed; my head throbbing, and very much inclined to sleep the whole day: but it might not be. Duty, imperative duty, was before me, and the day's toil began again.

I heard confessions till nine: I then said Mass. Now, I thought, I should have a quiet hour to prepare and recollect my thoughts for my approaching sermon at eleven. No such thing. In the middle of my breakfast there came another sick call. It was a sore trial for my patience; for through a press of business, through being very unwell, I had thought little of my approaching sermon. But the sick call must be attended to, and I went.

It was a melancholy, though too frequent case; one of delirium tremens. Drink, miserable drink, had reduced an unhappy man to the last stage of premature decay. He possessed the wreck of once noble features: had been once in affluence, but drink, insatiate drink, had thus prematurely destroyed him. He, too, was on his death-bed, but he knew it not: his consciousness had deserted him. He was in bed, and his wasted form exhibited, in all its hideousness, the staring wildness and restless unappeasable anxiety that characterize his malady, as well as the universal trembling whence it derives its name. The tendons of his hands and arms were spasmodically convulsed. His knees were sometimes, for a few minutes, drawn up to his chin, and then his feet would be thrown forward with extraordinary force, and, at times, like the fatal disorder tetanus, or lock-jaw, the body would form an arch, resting on the head and the heels. The most mournful and appalling groans would then issue from his dark and crusted lips,—more like the expiring howl of a wild beast, than the voice of agony from a human being. Alas! that an immortal being should thus live, should thus die.

It was a quarter to eleven when I reached home, with my nerves completely unstrung by the terrible scene I had just witnessed. But, nerves or no nerves, I must preach my sermon, and in twenty minutes I had a glimmering of what I intended to say. I entered the pulpit; the chapel was intensely hot—thermometer at ninety-two. A severe headache, great languor, and mental depression, gave me indifferent grounds of hope that I should make even a tolerable discourse. However, God, in his infinite mercy, strengthened me for the contest. As I proceeded, and warmed with my subject, my languor left me, my ideas shaped themselves clearer in my mind, and I preached a few home truths on the evils of a death-bed repentance. But if any strangers had been present, they would have little thought on what I had gone through before preaching that sermon.

Human nature, however, is seldom outraged with impunity. My powers of mind and body had been taxed beyond their strength: for an hour I felt thoroughly prostrate, but fresh duties were to be performed; I had to christen at a quarter-past one. I descended to the hot and reeking chapel, scarcely able to stand, and baptized about ten children. This long ceremony over, I played with a bit of dinner, for I was too faint to eat. At three, vespers. After vespers, I heard several confessions. Scarcely had my last penitent departed, when a violent ring at the door-bell told me plainly enough there was a sick call. I was right. Away I had to go, post haste, to a dying woman. She, poor thing, died before I reached her. I found her on her humble bed, the room full of weeping relatives, and a still-born infant by the side of its dead mother. This was another trying scene to go through: and it is in scenes like these that the consolatory power of religion is so admirably shown. I made them all kneel down, while I read the prayers for a departed soul; and while they prayed the mercy of Heaven for that departed soul, though they wept much, they were comforted.

It was now six o'clock, and I had the evening service to perform, and to preach at seven. There was no time to be lost, so I took a cup of tea, and buckled myself to my task. But it is severe mental labor to summon your languid thoughts to their post of duty, when sinking under long-continued and excessive fatigue. But mind triumphed over matter. I got through the long evening service, preached as usual, without showing any signs of distress, though I was nearly fainting several times. The evening service over, I had again several confessions to hear,—those of poor servant girls, who are only allowed to attend their chapel on a sabbath night.

The reader may now imagine my hard day's work was over. No such thing. I had all my office to recite; for until then I had not a minute of the day to myself. It was eleven when I finished. Then came *another* sick call; and at twelve I retired to rest, as tired and exhausted as any individual in her majesty's dominions.

Now, in penning this sketch I entreat the reader to believe that I am uninfluenced by any miserable feeling of vanity in thus publishing the details of a Sunday's missionary toil. I have selected this Sunday, because the events from several causes, are better fixed in my memory than others; but I have passed many such Sundays, and some of them of even much greater severity. I do not even publish it to the world as any thing uncommon or out of the way. Many of my respected brethren in London do usually as much, and some even more, as their average routine of Sunday work. They might, as a body, justly challenge a safe competition for pious, well-regulated, and persevering priestly exertion, with any ecclesiastics in Christendom. But in humility and silence they have done their appointed work, and they have done it well. They have won, by their own personal piety,—by their unwearied zeal and exertions, the respect, the gratitude and unshaken affections, of their flocks. But they look not for their reward on earth; they humbly expect it in heaven.

The Dying Burglar

"PLEASE, sir, there's a Sick call," said my ancient housekeeper one dull, winter's afternoon, and, placing a clumsily-folded note in my hands, she waited till I had perused it. It ran as follows:

"Reverend sir,—Your spiritual attendance is most earnestly requested at No. 17— Court Field-lane. The sick man's name is Alick Leary.

"From your obedient servant,
"Mary Donovan."

"Is any one waiting?" I asked.

"Yes, sir; a woman is below. Shall I tell her to step up?"

"Yes," I replied "send her up immediately."

A few minutes after, I heard a slow, and apparently a wearied footstep climbing the stair: and then, a timid knock at my room door. Upon my saying "Come in," a young and decently dressed young women entered, and stood with downcast eyes before me. She was apparently about five-and-twenty years of age, with good features, and of a pleasing and modest appearance. She trembled at first slightly; and then a blush—it seemed to be of shame—dyed her pale countenance to a crimson tint. Her hands were clasped together, as if in entreaty for me to go to the sick man; but there was no ring on the third finger of the left hand. I did not wish unnecessarily to wound her feelings; but I felt it necessary to know the truth beforehand, in order to see how I should act.

"Is it your husband that is ill?" I asked.

The poor thing was silent a few seconds; her chest heaved; the tears sprang to her eyes; but, by a strong effort, she repressed all external emotions of grief.

"No sir," she sadly replied; "he is not my husband—I am not his wife; would to God I were. Then I should have a right to attend upon him in his illness, for I fear it will be his last."

She spoke with such a touching tone of earnestness, with so much apparent sorrow and regret, that my heart fairly melted within me. We are told in the sacred books of Holy Writ, "The bruised reed thou shalt not break; the smoking flax thou shalt not extinguish." Why should I heap additional coals of fire upon this unfortunate creature's head? why add additional pangs to those which, of too plainly evidenced, she had already endured? why probe with stern and unrelenting severity, the wound which sin had made in that poor lacerated heart? I could do none of this, but spoke kindly and soothingly to this poor child of sin and sorrow—for such she evidently was.

"What is the matter with him?" I asked.

"Oh, sir, he has met with such a bad accident!'

"Why didn't you send him to the hospital, where he could be so much better attended than in the poor place he is in now?"

"I was not with him then, sir," she replied, and for the first time fairly raising her eyes to mine. "I left my situation as soon as I found out how ill he was, and have nursed him ever since. But, oh! sir, I'm afraid he will die tonight, he is so very bad. But, father—I must tell you the truth, it is no use to deceive you— poor Alick was a good boy once; but he was led astray by bad companions; first drink, then loss of work, then thieving; and so on, from bad to worse, till he became a confirmed housebreaker. It was on Sunday night fortnight, that he, and three other men, broke into a house to rob it; they were disturbed by the police, and nearly caught; and Alick, jumping from a window, got a bad fall and was almost killed. The men that were with him carried him to the place where he lodged; and, the next morning, one of them came to me, and told me all about it. I was so miserable, that I could not stop in my place. There were only a few shillings due to me; and with that, and pawning my things, I have managed to pay the doctor, and to get what Alick wanted. He would not go to the hospital for fear of being discovered. I have begged and prayed him to let me go for the priest; but he would not. He said it was no use for him to repent; that he could not remember the tenth part of his sins; and if he got over it, he should most likely do the same things again. But last night a change for the worse came sadly over him. He then began to pray; and I, sir, prayed with him, and for him. I had still by me my little Prayer Book, which was given me when I made my first communion, and which, in all my troubles, I have never parted with; and out of that blessed book I read the prayers for confession, and other good prayers, to move his poor heart to repentance, and to turn him towards God, who, I am sure, will forgive him, if he makes a good confession before he dies. Oh, sir, he was the good boy when we were childen together, and when we were in our own poor country. Little did I think then that he would take to the evil courses, and go to the bad entirely; and to be dying now, and him so young.

"But he left me, sir, to seek his fortune in England; and the light left my eyes, as I gazed, and gazed, upon the ship that took him from Cork. I stood upon the quay, half-blinded with the tears; and when I could no longer see the vessel, or her purty white sails, I felt quite broken hearted—I thought I should have dropped. The world, sir, had gone against us, and we were afraid to marry; but we were pledged to each other. We met the night before he sailed; and upon my mother's grave, we both knelt down, and he drew the ring over my finger and promised that when times would mend he would send for me, and marry me afore the priest. In the sight of God, I considered myself then as his wife. Maybe I was mistaken, maybe I was wrong; but I had no one then to look to but to him. He had won my heart; and I lived but for him. Oh, sir, if I had thought then more of God, more of my duties, more of heaven, and less of this world, I should not be now here before you; I should not regret so bitterly what I have done, and which I would give the world not to have done. And a year after he was gone, he wrote me word that he had got a fine situation, and was earning a mint of money; and that he wanted nothing more than to make me his good little wife. He sent me money to pay my passage; and I left my own native place and came to London. Oh, sir, black was the day that I entered London. I had been a giddy, laughing girl, but there had been no harm in me. I had been thoughtless, but I had never the heart-scald of bitter, bitter grief till I entered this terrible place. I had my own little savings, in addition to what Alick sent me; and I lodged at a good widow's, who came from my own town-land. Alick used to see me often, and was very kind; but I wondered why he did not speak of marrying me. He took me to plays and dances. I did not like them at first; but I got too fond of them at last. As I got fonder of them, I neglected more and more my prayers; I went seldomer to confession and my duty, and at length stayed away entirely. It is like a terrible dream to me, sir, what I then did, but I shall never forget it: it is burnt like fire into my memory. I was delicate in urging him to marry me, and he kept putting off, and putting it off; and at times I got very uneasy. Still I hoped for the best: I never dreamed that he would deceive me. But the day of marriage never came, sir. I loved him more than my God, and—and—"

Here she paused, and burst into tears. In a minute or two she recovered her utterance, and proceeded:

"Father, you may guess the rest. From that moment I lost my peace of mind for ever. It was perhaps more my fault than his, for I should have checked him; but I did not, or, if I did, I was weak and wavering. But I did not, father, remain long in the sin. I could then have died of shame and sorrow for my fall; but I was afraid to die. The heavens seemed to look black upon my guilty face, whenever my eyes were turned upwards. I used to wake in the night, full of fear and trembling, as I thought that, if I was to die that night, my soul might be in hell. It was in vain that he tried to keep me with him: I should have gone mad, or destroyed myself. I left him, father; and the same evening, I saw a chapel-door open, and lights within. For a long time I stood trembling at the door, and was afraid to enter. I thought the roof of the holy chapel would fall down and crush me, if such a wretch as I should enter. But something urged and persuaded me, or rather compelled me, to enter. It was the good thought, sent from the good God, which whispered to me—I could almost hear it speak—that, however much I had sinned, if I truly repented and confessed, the Almighty would surely pardon me. I remembered then the sermon I had heard in my own parish-chapel in Ireland, years ago, upon the blessed Mary Magdalen; and I thought that, if God pardoned her, He would also pardon me. And then came the fear, and the bitter shame, of confessing my sins, and what would the priest think of me! That almost drove me away; but thanks be to God, and blessed for ever be His holy name, the courage came to me and drove out all fear. I entered, and threw myself upon my knees in the confessional; and told all that I had done, to the good priest, and promised him faithfully never to sin again. Oh! what a weight was taken off my heart when I had finished my confession! I could then hope; before, I had despaired. My confessor spoke so kindly and fatherly to me,—he gave me such good advice how I should avoid sin for the future, and what sort of life I should live in order to get to heaven. I cried all night afterwards; but those tears I shed were not the bitter, scalding tears that used so frequently to run down my face, when I thought of the shame and disgrace I had been to my parents' memory. Thank God, they were dead before my fall—they were spared the dying of broken hearts for their child's disgrace and sin. The good priest to whom I confessed,—he, too, is now dead. God rest his soul,—recommended me to a situation. I have since remained in service; and have endeavored to get my bread honestly, and to do my duty as well as I could, to God. I often used to hear of Alick and of the bad courses he took to; but I never went near him. I was determined to keep myself out or the way of temptation, though my heart at times felt very sore for him. But, father, when I heard that he was so ill, and might die; that he was in distress, and there was no one to tend him—for all his evil companions abandoned him when most he wanted their help, and even robbed him of all that he had—when I heard this, I could not refrain from going to see him; and when I saw him—- so faint, so ill and miserable, and his poor soul in such a sad, sad state—sir, I could not leave him to die alone. I went back to my place, packed up my things, and have remained with him ever since. The landlady kindly allowed me to sleep with her children; but it is little sleep I have had for this fortnight I could not rest for thinking of him, and whether he could make his peace with God. Oh, sir, tell me, is it too late? is there any chance of his being saved? is there yet time? is there any hope?" The poor girl's countenance was now flushed with hope, now paled with fear. I told her that God would reward her for her pious endeavors to bring this unhappy man to a sense of his miserable condition; that, while there was life, there were yet hopes, provided the repentance was sincere; and that I would lose no time in seeing the sick man.

I was much and deeply affected at the simple, yet touching narrative of this good girl, who was so forgetful of the cruel wrong done to her by one who should have guarded her innocence but who ruthlessly destroyed it; who made a market of her affections, to gratify his own licentious desires; and who, as I learned afterwards, had well-nigh broken her heart by his savage and inhuman treatment. But thus it ever is; the flower is plucked, and then thrown aside to wither and to die, and its fading leaves are trampled underfoot by the cool and indifferent destroyer. It was another—yet now a new—chapter of woman's meek endurance of a most cruel wrong, and of perfect forgiveness to him who had blighted all her youthful hopes, and poisoned the current of her after life. For, though she had sinned, she had erred perhaps more from frailty then from malice—more from the inability to deny any thing to the object of her affections, than from any motive self-gratification. She had trusted, and she was betrayed. And she did more than forgive: she imperilled even her own recovered good name, by thus attending the last moments of the now repentant burglar. She stripped herself of all her slender stock of wordly goods that she might feed and nourish the betrayer of her innocence; she deprived herself of her rest, to soothe and comfort that moaning heart, to allay the throbbings of that fevered head, and to whisper holy words of faith and hope and repentance to that distracted mind, and to cleanse the perilous stuff from that polluted soul, by leading it, even in its agony, to Him who pardoned the dying thief on the cross. I hoped for him even against hope. But, alas! I fear that very, very few are saved in their last moments of contrition, if their repentance has been deferred till then. It is a most miserable, and a most broken reed to trust to in man's sternest and most perilous extremity, that deathbed repentance. The tempter lures them on through life; glides, serpent-like, into their hearts and inmost desires; preaches unctuously, rapturously, to them the joys of present carnal gratification, the realization of present sensualities, and the self-flattering prospect of making their peace with an all-merciful, all-forgiving God, when age has chilled their passions, when the recuperative powers of nature no longer lend their aid for a prolongation of mere animal enjoyment. And the devil laughs, as well he may, when he thus gulls besotted fools to sin, and to wallow in iniquity, in the insane hope of repenting in their old age, and of seizing to themselves that delusive perspective of a deathbed repentance. Worn out by debaucheries, stricken down by fever, or cut off by accident, they commonly expire in the very prime of manhood; and then the wailing, agonizing cry for mercy is more than met by confirmed and rooted despair—a despair that plunges their departing souls into the most profound of all human griefs—a despair that unrolls to their dying eyes the joys, the felicity of heaven, and contrasts them most horribly with the tortures of the damned—a despair that reveals to them the infinite goodness, the mercy, the long-suffering patience of God, with their own base and black ingratitude, and the infinite enormity of their sins—a despair which rivals that of Cain, who proclaimed, conscience-stricken, that his sin was too great to be forgiven.

And then comes the last and most terrible struggle with the prince of darkness, and the often-unavailing efforts of angel guardians with that proud, subtle, and powerful fiend. And the sinner has then to bid adieu—a farewell for ever—to this beautiful world; to the blue sky above and its starry hosts, and to all on earth that he holds nearest and dearest to his dying heart. Yes, it is a beautiful world; for the Spirit of God is upon it. At the separation of chaos it came over the waters, and has since remained with us, everywhere, but invisible. We see His hand in the variety and beauty of creation, but His Spirit we see not. Yet do we feel it in our soul; and, by the eye of faith we inly see it; and in the voice of revelation we hear it; and in the solemn hour of prayer, and in the holy temple, we also see it, and hear it, and feel it; it is around us, and in us. And in the hour of sin we forget it; and in the hour of after-recollection we fear it, if, conscience-stricken, we haply awake from the sleep, the dream of sin.

The dying sinner is summoned to the land of spirits. What does he know—what do we know—of these incorporeal beings? What do we know of the world of spirits! Little or nothing, beyond what faith and revelation afford. Still, we know that they surround us; that they hover over us; that they accompany us whithersoever we go; and that, even in the inmost tabernacle of the soul, they penetrate and have their being. Good spirits and bad are around us. Good spirits to aid us, to waft our lame and imperfect prayers to heaven, and to protect us in the hour of temptation or peril: "He shall give His angels a charge over thee, lest thou dash thy foot against a stone." Bad angels, too, are around us, and against us; percolating through every avenue of the soul, inflaming the imagination, warping the judgment, tainting the will, and too often, alas! perverting it to perdition. Bad angels are around us, even in the protecting sanctuary of God's Church, when summoned, permitted there by the subdued and corrupted will of man. Bad angels are around us in every walk, and rank, and condition, and event of life; we see them not, but they hover over us and around us, and they penetrate within the mysterious precincts of the soul, by many a foul and unholy thought, by many an evil suggestion to sin. And they triumph, and they gibber in their unholy glee whenever they tempt and prevail. They triumph, and they laugh the insulting laugh, whenever they steep to the lips in sin an unhappy mortal, and fasten upon him the mocking thought and determination of a deathbed repentance. That is their battle-ground—the battle-ground of victory. The standard of deceit is then triumphant: the captive is delivered bound into their hands, to do with as they wish—to be tormented according to the refinement of their infernal pleasure: "He shall be delivered unto the torturers."

What do we know of the fallen angels? Much does the priest of God's Church know of their power in the hour of death, in the last consuming agony of the dying and unrepenting sinner. Unrepentant! Why, he had for years and years hoped for repentance, promised himself repentance, and, in the languid intervals of sin, when the powers of nature collapsed from excess of animal enjoyment, had featly rehearsed his part, and played the play of dying in the grace of God. The hour comes. The grace of God is not found. It is sought for in the last delirious effort of expiring mortality; but it descends not into the foul abyss of that dying sinner's heart. He prays, he shrieks for mercy and forgiveness; but his prayers and his shrieks are whistled to the winds by the accusing spirit, who hovers around his bed, impatient to seize his prey. That infernal spirit is then, and too often, all-powerful. He has been a suppliant in the hour of temptation—a fawning wheedling slave, he is now the imperious master, the annihilator of good, the impenetrable veil which conceals the mercy of the Omnipotent. He is then rampant and despotic. It is his last conflict with a departing soul, and he improves his past advantage to the uttermost. He even quotes Scripture, the words of Holy Writ, in the very teeth of the dying wretch's petition for mercy. "As a man lives, so shall he die," is whispered with hellish malice by this foul tormentor to the departing soul. "God will render to every one according to his works," is again and again reiterated, and with paralyzing effect. In vain does the minister of the altar present to his filmy gaze the crucifix, the badge of hope, the Christian's helm in the stormy conflict with death. Satan whispers, "Thou hast trampled upon Christ, thou hast spurned His blood by thy repeated transgressions." The dying sinner is urged by his director, urged by those tears of paternal agony and concern for his departing soul, to confess his sins while yet there is time to repent—while yet there is time to move the illimitable mercy of God. But the dullness and the apathy of despair are again and again thrown into his soul by the accusing spirit; and the memory of the past is to him but the vague and shadowy outlines of a far-gone dream. And if the good angel should prevail in this terrible conflict; and if the expiring sinner's recollection should brighten up like an almost extinguished torch, and he should remember some of the most prominent and appalling of his past transgressions, their remembrance plunges him further into despair. Again and again is that condemnatory text quoted by the tormentor: "As a man lives, so shall he die."

Is it thus with all who lead a life of sin, and are suddenly stricken with death? God forbid that I should say so; but I fear and tremble. True, the mercy of God is infinite. Early impressions of piety then sometimes return with most beneficial effect. That prayer, which the most abandoned, the most reckless of sinners has often repeated, "Holy Mary, Mother, of God, pray for us sinners now and at the hour of our death," may, and doubtless does, move the mercy of God wonderfully in behalf of many of those who are suspended over the precipice of death. But still there is much, and terribly much, to fear in a death-bed repentance. God grant that none of my readers may cling to that frail and shifting plank in the last shipwreck of life.

I was about to test this mighty problem in my approaching visit to the dying burglar.

Most of my readers are aware of the bad repute in which Field-lane and its immediate vicinity was held some six years since. Indeed, for a century or two it was the prime resort of burglars, cut-purses, and vagabonds of either sex. In squalid misery, in the outward and visible signs of vice and ruffianism, and intense debauchery, it far excelled the rookery of Westminster, the Borough Mint, or the worst localities of Loke's Fields. It was the chief stronghold, the principal fortress of London crime, where decency was expelled, where law was laughed at, and where burglars might find a secure haven, and most safe sanctuary. Its numerous narrow and winding streets, and lanes, and courts, and alleys, seemed originally erected to defy pursuit. They spread like a foul net-work all around the northwest angle of old Smithfield. The new Farringdon-street has cut this impure artery in two. It has levelled to the ground one-half of Field-lane, and other notorious haunts of vice, and dispersed a whole colony of receivers of stolen goods. The other improvements have destroyed a vast number of the most atrocious nests of crime in this unhappy locality. But six years ago the pollution was untouched, and to this miserable quarter of the metropolis I bent my way in search of the dying Alick Leary. I was pretty well acquainted with the court in which he resided, as my spiritual duties had led me sometimes there.

I will not detain the reader by describing its filth, its disgusting odor, nor the ruffian-like blackguardism that distinguished this misshappen alley and its inhabitants. Three drunken rows, with much swearing and unmitigated blasphemy, were going on at one and the same time. As my person was well known, I was immediately recognized, and the fighting stopped as I reached No. 17. Coarse, brutal, men, and haggard women, with blood flowing down their bruised and hideous faces, sullenly retreated to their several doorways, and the whisper ran, that the priest was going to the cracksman Leary. I stayed not to listen to their ribald jeers, nor the torrent of blasphemies which were showered upon his supposed repentance. I hastened up stairs. As in many of my sick calls, I had to feel my way cautiously up the broken and dilapidated staircase, for light there was none. I climbed as far as the back garret. This I was thankful for, as the roar and turmoil from the crowded court were here almost inaudible.

As I stopped at the top landing to get my breath, which was somewhat impeded from the steep and long ascent, and the noxious fumes of sulphury coke that filled every portion of the house, the door of the back-room opened, and poor Mary Donovan stood before me. A little sky-light, about a foot square in the roof, enabled me to recognize the good girl. She looked at me so gratefully, so humbly, and so imploringly, and that mute and expressive look seemed to request my kind pity and forbearance for the miserable man within. Not a word passed, for she was too much agitated to speak. I entered.

The sick man lay on a poor bed on the floor, but it was clean and neatly arranged. He lay on his bed, stretched out more like a corpse than a living being. One arm was stretched down by his side, while the other lay outside the clothes, apparently helpless from exhaustion: he looked terribly emaciated. His beard had evidently not been shaven for weeks, so that there was little of his face visible from amidst the black fell of hair that surrounded it. His shrunken forehead was white and sallow, upon which the blue veins could be easily traced; his nose was sharp, and wasted away nearly to a point; his cheek-bones were frightfully prominent, so completely had the flesh fallen in and wasted away; his lips, which were a little open, could scarcely be seen from the thick beard that surrounded them, but the front teeth were visible, and from their ghastly whiteness, gave to the whole countenance the look of an unwashed corpse. The clammy dew of approaching death trickled slowly down that poor squalid face, and he lay in a sleep still as the grave, and, but for slight heaving of the bed-clothes, I should have thought that the spirit had already fled. Though terribly wasted away, the huge congeries of bones and tendons that marked the outlines of his chest and arm, showed that when in health he must have been a man of immense strength, and enormous muscular power.

Mary whispered to me that he had slept the last two hours, She had left him sleeping when she came for me, and he was now in the same dull and death-like state of repose. I gazed upon this poor burglar for some minutes, and in profound silence, and prayed fervently to God in his behalf. At length the bandaged arm that was extended without the bed-clothes, moved with a slight convulsive start; the fingers were unclenched, passed slowly through his matted hair, the eyes opened, gazed vacantly around, then closed, and in the feeblest tone he faintly whispered, "Mary."

"I am here, Alick dear," she gently whispered in return. "Do you feel any better after your long sleep?"

"No, my poor girl, I don't; I am going, going fast. My day of life will soon be spent, and then the night comes; the night of death, in which there is no waking."

"But you have prayed, Alick dear, have you not, that God Almighty would have mercy on you, and that you might be prepared for death?"

"I have, Mary; but what chance is there for a sinful wretch like me? No, no, no," he bitterly exclaimed, "there is no hope for mercy. I have lived in sin, and I shall die in my sins. My sins are more numerous than the hairs of my head, or the sands of the sea-shore. I tell you, girl, I have no hope. I shall be damned everlastingly as sure as you stand there beside me. Oh! cursed, cursed fool that I have been! But no matter, Mary, don't cry so," he continued, as his ear caught the sound of her violent weeping; "don't cry so, Mary; it will soon be over, and God bless you, for you have been the good and true girl to me. Would that I had treated you better."

"Oh, Alick," said she, "don't think about that, it is all, all forgiven; but turn your heart to God, for His forgiveness. Alick, dear," she said, kneeling down by his side, so that every syllable she uttered might be distinctly heard, "I have brought a priest to hear your confession,"

The sick man, with an incredible effort, started up in bed, and gazed wildly around him. I had stood in deep shadow at some distance from the bed; I now came forward, and as his excited eye met mine he looked upon me long and earnestly; his lips quivered, every muscle of his countenance was strongly agitated, and oh! blessed sign of repentance, the large tears coursed their way rapidly down his cheeks, and he fairly sobbed aloud.

"And you will repent, my poor fellow," I said; "you will try and make your peace with God?"

"Too late, too late!" he mournfully exclaimed as he sank back exhausted upon the pillow.

As I was going again to urge upon him the infinite mercy of God, and the all-atoning merits of his Redeemer, I heard footsteps rapidly ascending the staircase; they stopped at the door, it opened, and an old and venerable-looking man, with white hair, and decent garb, advanced hurriedly into the room.

"I beg your reverence's pardon," said he, "I see you are a priest; but tell me, is Alick Leary here?"

"He is; and there," said I, pointing to the bed, "is the poor fellow."

The old man looked at the bed, and as he looked, a gasping, choking sob seemed almost to strangle him. He bent eagerly over the bed, as if uncertain of what he saw. At length the terrible recognition was made. He tossed his hands on high, and piteously exclaimed:—

"Alick mavourneen, my poor darling boy, it's your old father come to see you. Sure you won't die yet, Alick, when I've come all the way from could Ireland to try and make you honest and good. And your poor mother, Alick, who died last winter, with her last breath prayed for you, and only wished that she might set eyes again upon her bouchal before she went to God. Alick dear, I am alone now in the world; you'll come back with me, darling; sure, we'll go home to the old place; you'll be an honest man yet, and we'll be so happy together."

The sick man turned his face to the wall and wept.

"My mother, my mother," he hoarsely muttered, "my good kind mother. Another crime to answer for; I killed her; I broke her heart."

"No, Alick, my son, you didn't. She died happy, with all the rites of the Church, and her love to you was wonderful when she was going. The last word on her lips was a blessing for you, and that God might spare you to repent. And you will repent, and you do repent; do you not, my son?"

"Father, I do, and from my inmost heart; but oh! how black and terrible have been my crimes." He then suddenly joined his hands, as if in prayer, and he vehemently exclaimed: "Oh, blessed God, my God, my God! God of infinite mercy, pardon me; forgive me my sins."

"He will, he will, my darling boy. An' why should you despair? Sure the mercy of God, Alick dear, is a thousan' and a million times greater than your sins. But, Alick avillish, here is the priest of God's Church; wouldn't it aise your mind, and lighten your troubled heart, to lay aside the heavy load that's upon it, and to feel, ahagur, that the black burden of your whole life is taken off it?"

"I will, father; I will confess, for I feel now that the mercy of God is indeed infinite."

Sacred influence of paternal love! How beautifully, how convincingly the pure charities of the heart gushed forth from the lips of this old but eloquent man!

He turned round to me with the tear and the smile upon his aged cheek. When he saw Mary for the first time, his look grew troubled, and somewhat stern.

"I hope, young woman, that you do not keep company with my son?"

In a few whispered words I more than satisfied the old father. He pressed warmly the hand of the weeping girl, and in a tone of great tenderness said to her:—

"Mary asthore, I ax your pardon for not remembering you. God bless you, and reward you kindly, for all you have done for my poor boy. Come, darling, let us leave Alick alone with the clargy."

The room was cleared; it was now the time of trial; it was now the time whether the good or the bad angel would prevail; whether sin was to be pardoned, and an immortal soul to be saved. I carefully fastened the door by its rude wooden latch, and seating myself by the bedside of the now repentant and dying man, I applied myself earnestly and prayerfully to my sacred functions… An hour or more had elapsed… The good angel prevailed. That dying man was, I fervently hope and trust entirely reconciled to his God. His confession was made. The full gushing tide of contrition accompanied him throughout. On its purifying waters he was borne along. If he had sinned much, he repented much, and truly and deeply. He laid hold, in these his last moments, on the saving Cross of Christ; he remained in that last and most contrite embrace until the merits, and the healing, and the atoning blood of his Saviour had been applied to his poor sinful soul. Full of faith, full of hope, and I may say, full of charity and contrition, he received the sacramental absolution and remission of all his sins. Full of the same divinely inspired sentiments he received the last anointing, and the last solemn blessing and plenary indulgence of the Church. And then in words, few but deeply eloquent, he murmured forth his grateful thanks to God, his entire submission to His holy will, his reverent, cheerful acceptance of his approaching death; offering most humbly, most contritely, his present and future sufferings as some small atonement for his many and repeated crimes.

"It only grieves me now, father," said he, "that I cannot make restitution to those whom I have wronged." Something I whispered in his ear; the result will be seen.

His confession, and the holy anointing, had a wonderful effect upon him for the better. I saw there was no danger that night, and told him to prepare himself to receive the blessed Sacrament the following morning. His look was gratitude itself.

I then called in his father and poor Mary. I also whispered something to her, at which she blushed, and looked so happy and thankful. The result will be seen.

The following morning I took him the adorable Sacrament. God seemed to have touched the hearts of the miserable indwellers of this wretched court; for I now met with naught but respectful looks and anxious inquiries after poor Alick. These I answered, and with brief admonition to amend the error of their ways. That, too, was kindly taken. I found the worthy old Leary with the right hand of his son affectionately clasped in his, and poor Mary kneeling by his humble bed, and reading, in a singularly sweet and gentle tone, the prayers before communion. She was just finishing as I entered. But how changed was the countenance of my penitent! He had been shaved, clean linen had been brought him by his father, and he sat propped up in bed by several pillows. Though death was making rapid and unmistakable advances upon him, yet his look was singularly calm and happy. He was fully prepared. I gave him the bread of angels, even the body of our Lord in the most holy viaticum. At every time that I pronounced those words of faith and humility, "Lord, I am not worthy that Thou shouldst enter under my roof; say but the word only, and my soul shall be healed," he struck his breast with the same humble sentiments of compunction as the good publican is said to have done by our Saviour in the parable. Surely his good angel had joy in that blessed moment of communion with his God, and surely the dark angel of sin fled away from that bed of peacefully approaching death.

He remained for about ten minutes in silent prayer. His thin wasted hands were closed together over his eyes, but through his fingers the quiet tears flowed long and plentifully. I then read aloud the commendation of a departing soul, for the gray shadow of death was stealing fast over his countenance, and rendering his features sharper each instant. I soon concluded.

"Reverend sir," he said, "you yesterday spoke to me about making restitution. To those whom I have robbed and plundered it is unhappily out of my power. God knows I would do so, and most gladly, were it possible. This is even now a sore grief to me. But, sir, there is one whom I have most cruelly and shamefully wronged, and, thank God, it is not too late to make, even at the last moment, some small compensation. Father," said he, turning to his aged parent, who was eagerly listening to every word that his child spoke: "Father, I have ruined this good dear girl who now stands beside you. I foully, wickedly ruined her under the promise of marriage and that promise I never was honorable enough to redeem. But if you, reverend sir, will join our hands together, I will marry her now, in some respects, her good name may be restored, and that God may be more merciful to me when I am gone."

"Alick acushla!" said the weeping old man, "you have said the thing that is right: you will die happy after you have done this good deed. But do you consent, my darling child?" he asked of the also weeping Mary.

"Oh, yes," she meekly said; "I shall then look you in the face, Mr. Leary, without shame, when dear Alick puts the ring upon my finger, as he promised me he would years and years ago."

She had been the previous evening to me to confession, so she was fully prepared. I then repeated the marriage service, and as I went on, faster and faster the gray shadow of death stole over the face of the dying bridegroom. Mary knelt upon the bed for him to put the ring upon her finger. It was done; the prayer, the blessing was given. "My wife!" he fondly, tenderly exclaimed. "My dear, dear husband!" was her heartfelt reply. One long and most loving embrace followed this sacred rite of marriage, when the old father said:—

"Let me to him, Mary, my child: let me to him, alanna; let me too kiss my darling boy before he is taken from me."

And so saying he cast himself upon the bed, entwined his arms around the neck of his son, and pillowing his head upon his loving, aged breast, he laid that fading cheek to his, and poured forth a multitude of the fondest endearments, and of the most devotional kind. Among the rest he effectionately whispered:—

"Alick, mavourneen, you are going to your blessed God, and his ever virgin Mother. You are going to your own mother who bore you and loved you so tenderly, and who with her last breath, prayed that she might see you happy with her in heaven. Her prayers have been heard for you, my darling boy, and God, glory be to His heavenly name, has been wonderfully good to you in your last moments. And shall I never see you more in this cold world, pulse of my heart? Ah, but Alick dear, I will lead the good life, that we may be all happy and united hereafter, with Christ and his blessed saints in glory! Amen."

"Father," said the dying man, "my sight is gone; I cannot see you now, but I hear your voice; I die happy now. Father dear, bless your Alick, and let me lean my head once more on the heart of my dear Mary; I shall die happier so."

The blessing of the aged parent was solemnly, fervently given. His young wife stept noiselessly to the other side of the bed, and supported the head of her departing husband upon her bosom, and watered his face with her gushing tears. She could not repress them. Again I prayed for him, and on repeating the holy name of Jesus, he pressed a little crucifix gently to his lips, and in that mute action of repentant love he calmly expired.

The Dying Banker

DRURY-LANE AT NIGHT

IT HAS very frequently happened to me to have an urgent sick call on a Saturday night—the most inconvenient night in the week, when the duties of the confessional are generally extended to a late hour. It is of no use to scold the messenger, and ask why you were not sent for at an earlier period of the day; go you must, and that very speedily, when the sick person is reported to be in danger. You leave the confessional, around which is a crowd of kneeling penitents absorbed in prayer, the examination of their conscience, and imploring the mercy of God for their past sins. You leave that edifying train of penitents, silent and prayerful; the atmosphere of the loved old chapel breathing naught but mercy and reconciliation, the strengthening of humble hope, and the putting away the works of the most wicked one. It is the very sanctuary of peace. You leave it with regret, for much good remains to be done there that night; and having got ready the holy oil, the stole, and ritual, you then start on your errand of mercy, and exchange the quiet of your chapel for the noise, and turbulence, and sinful doings of the street.

I was thus summoned on a busy Saturday night some three years ago. The beadle knocked smartly at my confessional door, and informed me that a young lady wished to see me immediately. I went to the bottom of the chapel, and found her near the entrance-door. She was crying bitterly. She told me that her father was suddenly very much affected in his head, that she was afraid he was losing his senses. She begged earnestly that, if possible, I would see him that night; for she trembled to think of what his state might be on the morrow. I, of course, consented, and prepared immediately for my sick call.

The direction given me was in a small street near Drury-lane. My nearest way lay through Clare market, which was densely thronged with purchasers and venders of fish and vegetables, and perambulating stalls of nondescript refreshment.

It was about eleven o'clock as I turned into Drury-lane; and here let me give a slight sketch of this celebrated locality, which is never seen to such picturesque effect as on this hour of a Saturday night.

The palaces of old Drury-lane are long since departed; it is no longer a favorite site for residences of the English nobility, or the foreign ambassadors, as it was in the reigns of James II and of William III. Pawnbrokers, gin-palaces, and provision-shops have long since usurped their place and state; and its immediate purlieus—once laid out in fair and stately gardens and shady walks, where fountains glistened in the noonday sun, where birds warbled heir thrilling melodies, and the ambient air was redolent of choice and richly-scented flowers,—these once beautiful environs now fester in rank squalor and filth, the abodes of crime and pollution, and peopled with the vilest of the vile. As you turn into Drury-lane, there are several pawnbrokers right and left. Each banker of the poor generally contrives to get a location at the corner of a court or alley, or some quiet passage, where his customers may step in and out unperceived by the passers-by. Let us take as a specimen yon densely stored establishment which has relieved the necessities, or administered to the vices of the poor for some generations past. From basement to attics it is piled with pledges; each in its pigeon-hole, ticketed and numbered, and ready for delivery at a moment's notice. To save time, there is a speaking-trumpet in the shop, which communicates by a zinc pipe to the various store-rooms; and when a pledge is about to be redeemed, the word is passed up the pipe, and the article is slipped down a mahogany well, which goes through every floor. How often have I gazed at that curious shop, and stared at the motley contents which are hung about its door,—pendant groups of shawls, and sheets, and blankets, and every description of wearing apparel, gaudy silk handkerchiefs of the real bird's-eye spot, and faded gowns of every variety of shape, and color, and material. Suspicious old violins, too, are there, which arrest the hurried step of many a fiddling genius, and cause him to inspect their shape and varnish, in the delusive hope that one may turn out a veritable Cremona. Husky old flutes are there in abundance; and children's corals, and warming-pans, and fashionable stocks with a cataract of satin enriched with crimson stripes; and mosaic gold chains and studs, and shirt-pins with little chains and arrow-like devices; and a tempting old oil painting is sure to be there, with "George Morland" freshly painted in the corner, or some other celebrated and taking name, by which a stray collector is often taken in and done for; and a magnificent collection of plate is there also—plated of course—but which, in the gaslight, looks as bright and as costly as silver soup-tureens and dish-covers of an antiquated pattern, bottle-holders, tea-services, and candle sticks in rich profusion, strike the eye of the pool passenger with an inexhaustible idea of boundless wealth; and real silver spoons are there too, glistening in a row, and making the hearts of housewives pine with envy when they array at tea-time their scanty stock of Britannia metal.

But look at that stream of laden women, who, shunning the street-entrance, are groping their way round the corner of the alley! Whither are they bound? What do they carry with so much furtive care and circumspection? Glance your eye round the corner, and you will see. A dozen paces down that alley there is another, and a secret entrance, dimly lit by a slender thread of gas inside the open doorway. This is the real business inlet, and through which these women so stealthily enter. A long passage leads at right-angles from the door, and facet two-thirds of the extensive shop. This long passage is divided into little dens, each with its wicket, and about three feet wide. The unhappy suppliants for the pawnbroker's assistance are thus screened from observation, and enabled to make their pitiful bargains in desired privacy. This nicety of feeling, however, only applies to the uninitiated in pawnbroking; the *habitues* of the locale lounge with their elbows on the counter, thrust their moppy heads forward, and laugh and chat with the shopmen as with old and long-tried acquaintances.

But it is at the window you are gazing, resplendently lit up with external tin sconces, from which the light is reflected, and, joined with numerous bright jets within, they shed the light of day on all around. And what an extraordinary museum does the window of that pawnbroker present, from the flat-iron of the drunken laundress, the ragged jacket of the starved mechanic, to the diamond ear-rings or necklace of the spendthrift lady of fashion! Each and every article has its ticketed price; and if each article could tell its painful tale, what a series of romantic facts, stranger and sterner than ever fiction imagined, could be gleaned! A row of wedding-rings hangs on one of the small brass rods. How many domestic tragedies do these worn and battered rings denote! Heart-broken widows, famished wives, profligate mothers, who would sell or pawn their souls for gin, bring here the first sacred pledge of wedded love—that love which is either buried in the grave, or crushed out of life by crime or debauchery. A little tray contains articles of jewelry, marked from three-and-sixpence upwards; lockets containing hair—the hair of a dead lover, a dead parent—-garnered and cherished so many years, until grim poverty and starvation compelled the heart-broken survivor to pawn the sacred relic.

How many mournful kisses, how many sad and unavailing tears have fallen upon that locket! But there was no resisting the grinding, pinching famine. We may guess the feelings of shame and timidity of that poor creature, as she neared the pawnbroker's shop, the lingering, hesitating step that trembled at the threshold, the feeling that she was about to commit a crime;

but the Rubicon is passed, and from henceforth that threshold is worn with her frequent footsteps. See that small Breguet gold watch: it belonged to a gambler and ruined spendthrift. He pawned it to have a last chance at hazard: all was lost, and in an hour afterwards his corpse was floating down the Thames. Look at that diamond pin. It was plucked from the bosom of a drunken reveller by a street-walker: and she, too, soon after committed suicide—leapt, in a fit of frenzy, from the fatal bridge, which, more than that of Venice, has been the bridge of sighs. A terrible history stares you in the face from each trinket in the group: the prison and the hulks, the madhouse and the midnight grave of the self-destroyer hold possession of their late owners; and they stand and glisten through the begrimed windows, mementos of past sorrows and follies, and unatoned-for crimes.

But pass we on to a very different scene. A butcher's shop stands invitingly open; there are no plate-glass windows, nor meretricious ornaments about this humble establishment. Its front is tenantless of windows, its usual decorating joints are sold, and the sturdy butcher sits in still complacency within, thinking over, and counting mentally, the gains of the past week. The rows of iron hooks that garnish his shop boast not of their usual load of ruddy sirloins, of savory, juicy legs, and prime fillets of veal. They are sold and the butcher is chinking the welcome cash in his capacious breeches-pockets. The huge block is fresh scraped for the ensuing week, clean sawdust is thickly spread on the floor, the gas flares out in a lengthened stream from the open neck of the pipe—now almost extinguished, it shows a ghastly blue stream of flickering light, now a flaming sword of fire, as the wind plays upon it, hustles it, and strives to extinguish its sturdy blaze, which alternately plunges the shop into intense light and deep shadow. The knight of the cleaver sits grim and silent and thoughtful; his favorite bulldog sleeps soundly at his feet: his stock, all but the refuse, is sold, but he keeps a wary eye on the large board at the open front, which is covered with little heaps of miserable scraps and cuttings of meat—it is the usual diet, or feast of the poor. A dozen or more of wretchedly clad women hang wistfully before that board, and turn the scraps over, one by one, bringing their noses as closely as they dare, to test the sweetness, while the fat butcher looks sullenly on. The bargain is concluded; three pennyworth of offal is cheerily carried off for the Sunday's festal dinner.

And in the classic region of Drury-lane gin-shops reign pre-eminent. They have not the flaring, rampant way of displaying their magnificence, that the more western emporiums exult in exhibiting to the squalid and miserable drunkard, though several are smart enough in external stucco, plate-glass, mahogany counters, and a battalion of immense casks or vats, labelled with gigantic letters, "Old Tom," "Cream of the Valley," "Splendid Gin," "The Nonpareil," and other tempting varieties of this villanous and poisonous compound—for villanous and poisonous it is to the stomach and brains of its unhappy and besotted recipients—being doled out in countless drams, at a much lower rate than if issued from the distiller. But the gin-palaces of Drury-lane have their peculiar type of debauchery, perhaps unmatchable in any other quarter of this overgrown metropolis, and their flaunting glories shine forth with redoubled splendor as the eleventh hour approaches on a Saturday night

Reader, take your stand at that corner slaughterhouse, so celebrated for its cheap and burning gin: the poor folk love what warms and stimulates them. They are reckless of the vitriol, so that they are oblivious for a brief hour of the icy and depressing calamities of life. Fix your eyes for ten minutes consecutively on that mahogany swing-door, through whose ceaseless opening a hot and stifling stream of spirituous compounds of bad beer and worse tobacco, and the breaths, foul and tainted, of a serried rank of drinkers, clamorous, pugnacious in their bestial draughts, issues, reeking and overpowering, into the cold midnight air. The ear is almost stunned with the noisy uproar inside those gates of death, the eye is pained with its quickly-recurring glimpse of the doings within, and the pitying heart is saddened with the consciousness of the near vicinity of a pandemonium, little less frightful and abhorrent than hell itself. About two score of men, women, and children, are congregated about that gaudily-decorated bar,—hard-working, ragged mechanics, with their wives, madly spending a great part of the earnings of the previous week; drunken trulls, whose flushed and swollen visages proclaim habitual intoxication, and whose every second word is one of obscenity or blasphemy; young, daring, and insolent-looking costermongers, with their girls scarcely past the innocent age of juvenility; ancient fish-women, squatting upon their empty baskets, with the short and blackened pipe in their toothless mouths, crooning together over the day's market and scanty gains; cadgers in every variety of costume—the pretended sailor, the broken-down tradesman, the starving agriculturist; the hoarse ballad-singer, who has wound his remaining and unsold stock of sentimental ditties (three yards long for one halfpenny) round his greasy and dilapidated hat; poor famished needle-women, who have no food to eat, who have but three halfpence in the world, and who strike the balance in favor of a glass of gin that sends them to bed in a dreamy reminiscent state of better and happier days. Young boys and girls, too, are there, whose discerning palates are well acquainted with gin, and who stand on tiptoe at the capacious bar to imbibe their small glass,— their pennyworth of poison. Mothers, too, are there, with babies in their arms, pouring down the throats of their offspring, with maudlin tenderness, the draining of the scarce-emptied glass. It is a scene of horrors. And on a sudden the fierce uproar succeeds that hoarse murmur of sound within. Screams, quick and agonizing, are heard; oaths deadly and blasphemous, and most appalling; and then the quick and repeated blow, the struggle, the smash of glass, the sob of agony, the terrible imprecation, the blasphemous appeals to that God whose name they profane, the cries for the police, the rush, pell-mell, through the doors, of a hideously blent crowd of fighting combatants, of shrieking wives and fiend-like husbands and terrified children, the renewed battle with the police, the capture of the most violent, their drooping, repentant walk to the police station at Bow-street, the gradual clearance of the crowd:—and then all is quiet in Drury-lane for the next quarter of an hour.

The Sick Room

"How do you find yourself, sir?" said I to an elderly gentleman of prepossessing appearance, who was seated at a table covered with numerous manuscripts. His daughter, the young lady who had summoned me, was standing by his side, pale and tearful, and anxiously watching her parent's looks.

The old man had gazed on me, as I entered the room, with a troubled look as if he were puzzled at my intrusion.

"Papa," whispered his daughter, "this is the clergyman whom I requested to see you for spiritual consolation. You know, dear father, how much we talked about it the other day. You then promised me that you would be good, and go to confession."

Her father turned his eyes alternately from his daughter to me, without replying. His mind seemed lost in vacancy. It was then that something extraordinary struck me about his eyes. They were very glassy and tremulous; the muscles about the orbit of the eye were working with a twitching motion. His look was wandering, inquiring, anxious, and a tinge of imbecility had overspread his entire features. His mouth, though beautifully cut in nature's happiest mood, was slightly twisted aside, and a deep and internal distress give it an appearance of anxiety most painful to contemplate. His forehead was magnificently developed. Gall would have been in ecstasies to have handled it. Slight as my knowledge of phrenology was, yet I could perceive the more noble organs of humanity beautifully and prominently developed. Its external formation showed high intellect, deep sagacity, and a happily balanced brain. What then could have so disturbed its functions? It was *paralysis*—stealthily, but surely approaching—laying its gaunt hand on every faculty of the brain, and eye, and speech.

"Father, dear father, will you not speak to the clergyman,—-your own clergyman,—a Catholic priest from the Sardinian chapel?"

No answer, but a wild and incoherent look.

The poor girl wrung her hands, suppressed with difficulty a hysterical sob, and looked piteously at me with a heart-broken despondency.

I was much and deeply moved. They seemed alone together in the world, or some friend or relative would have been summoned on this afflicting occasion. There was, too, an air of shabby gentility in the room, that betokened poverty, though every precaution was taken to conceal it. In the rapid side-glance that I took of its appointments on entering, I saw that everything was much worn, and of ancient workmanship. Everything, though in respectable order, looked faded and past its date, and valueless, save to its possessors. There were two exceptions. A beautiful miniature over the mantelpiece—a lady of exquisite beauty—painted in enamel, which I afterwards found out was the portraiture of the mother of the sobbing girl before me; and also a double-actioned harp, with a covering of green baize.

What could be done? I drew a chair beside the aged man, and laid my hand gently on his shoulder. He turned his poor demented countenance, and looked at me long and piteously. At length he spoke. "I am an old man, sir; take care of my daughter when I am gone." His words were slowly, very slowly, articulated. There was a thickness in their utterance, and a hesitation, that showed that both tongue and brain were affected.

"You love your daughter," I replied.

"Love her! dearly, dearly, sir. But what are you come for? Come, Ellen," he said, turning sharply round; "I have no time to waste I must go on with my work."

So saying, he drew before him several folio sheets of paper, which were nearly covered with figures and memoranda.

His daughter sank at his feet, resting her clasped hands on his knees, and burst into a violent fit of weeping.

"Ellen," said he, "why do you cry? Why does this gentleman stop here? He is hindering me from retrieving my embarrassed fortunes. Aye," he muttered, "they say that I am poor and bankrupt; but they will soon see me win back more than my former wealth."

That this afflicting case may be intelligible to my readers, I must make them acquainted with what the weeping, trembling girl told me an hour before. Her father had been a country banker. The firm was one of considerable standing and importance in a distant county, and bore a high character for stability and prudential dealings. When Mr. Danby (for so I must call him) began to feel the infirmities of old age, he resigned the active management of the bank to his head clerk, whom he had taken into partnership, and retired with his daughter to a beautiful country residence, which he had lately purchased. A few years passed happily away in calm retirement, when the old man's happiness was suddenly blasted, and his fortunes shipwrecked, by the insolvency of his bank. His new partner had plunged recklessly into every wild and specious speculation, in the delusive hope of realizing speedily a colossal fortune. As fast as one scheme failed, another was eagerly taken up. A heavy drain was continually going on upon the available resources of the bank; the most disgraceful, dishonorable expedients were resorted to, from time to time, to raise money; stock, standing in his name, but belonging to minors and married women, was sold out; charitable, and even religious trust property was misappropriated; but a curse from Heaven seemed to blight every plan or expedient this dishonest banker took in hand. His American securities, in which he had embarked such enormous sums, became waste-paper in the market—his patented inventions all failed—and the crash of several other banks and influential firms, suddenly completed his ruin.

And curses, loud and deep from the ruined widow and orphan—from the decayed gentlewoman—from the broken tradesman, followed this miserable man wherever he went. No one pitied him. But every one lamented over the entire ruin of the excellent Mr. Danby, whose only fault had been that he had no suspicion that his partner was a scoundrel, and that he had not kept a watchful eye on his proceedings. Everything that Mr. Danby possessed in the world—funded property, house and land—was sold to provide the miserable fraction of a dividend for the creditors. An old and faithful clerk purchased at the sale the harp and miniature for his beloved master and child, and devoted the whole of his savings to getting them comfortably settled in the metropolis, where Mr. Danby thought he might have a better chance of employment, and might be at a greater distance from the scene of his late disgrace and misfortune.

For the five preceding years he had struggled to gain a scanty livelihood by keeping the books of tradesmen, and making up their Christmas bills. His daughter also did her best by exerting her accomplishments as a daily governess. But her employment was scanty, and her remuneration trifling. Her meek and quiet temper was often sorely tried by the cold insolence and unfeeling conduct of her employers. Still, they struggled on, with God for their support, and to Him they looked for consolation in all their trials.

In the year preceding the opening of my narrative, Mr. Danby's mind seemed strangely affected. He became peevish, querulous, and fretful. His natural good temper deserted him entirely. He brooded more and more over his past misfortunes, and the poor old man complained at times bitterly about his shattered fortunes. He uttered terrible threats against his late partner; declared repeatedly that he was an infamous villain, who richly deserved hanging, for bringing him and his child into so much and undeserved calamity, and so many poor tradesmen to ruin who had trusted to his honor. It was in vain that this sweet child endeavored to soothe and pacify him. He said he was sure she hated him for his folly in not looking sharper after the concerns of the bank. It was in vain that she pleaded her constant love and veneration for her poor old and irritated parent; in the exacerbations of his mental misery he would shun all society with her—lock himself in his bedroom, and remain the whole day without food. And then his hitherto firm and ardent trust in Divine Providence began to fail him; he looked with a gloomy and jaundiced eye at the dispensations of Heaven, and muttered threats, that if it were not for his child, he would put an end to his life and his sorrows together.

Then it was that he began to absent himself from confession, which he before said was his great comfort and support. He thought himself an outcast from Heaven, and gradually withdrew from attendance at chapel. This caused his daughter, as she told me, many bitter tears. They had hitherto prayed together, knelt together, and received together the bread of life, and it was with an aching heart that she now performed alone these sacred duties.

His next aberration was a fancied discovery how to pay off the national debt. He neglected his slender appointments in bookkeeping, and spent days and nights in the working out his scheme. He expected a magnificent reward from government for his discovery; wrote repeated and incoherent letters to the Chancellor of the Exchequer, which, of course, were unanswered. Suspense and disappointment deprived him of sleep, took away his appetite and, finally, brought on partial paralysis of the brain. It was in this state that I found him.

"My dear young lady," said I, "your poor father requires medical aid, and that immediately. I can be of no service here in his present sad state—allow me to send a doctor."

She hesitated for a moment, requested to speak with me in the small anteroom, and then told me, with downcast eyes and blushing cheeks, that she would have sent for one before, but they were too poor to incur much expense for medical advice, and she could not bear the idea of applying for the parish doctor.

"Do not, my dear child," I replied, "make yourself uneasy about it. I will see to it, and a friend of mine, if disengaged, will see your father to-night."

The poor girl put her trembling hand in mine, pressed it warmly, and looked at me with eyes full of grateful tears. Promising to see her father on the following Monday, I then departed in search of a physician.

He came, bled him copiously, and partially restored him to consciousness.

On Monday afternoon I visited him again. He then knew me, welcomed me kindly, and spoke with resignation as to his present state, and past troubles. He embraced the opportunity to make his confession, and the tears rained down the poor old man's cheeks when he received that priceless boon, the sacramental absolution of his sins.

"Sir," said he, "I can never sufficiently thank you for having imparted peace to an almost broken heart. God give me grace to bear my cross patiently. In the days of prosperity I was never sufficiently thankful to my heavenly Father for all his blessings; but, now that He has withdrawn them, pray for me, sir, that my hope in him may remain to the end unshaken."

On the morrow I gave him the holy communion. He then began slowly to recover.

But God had prepared for him still further trials.

A month afterwards, his daughter sent a lodger in the house, requesting me to come immediately to her father.*

She was waiting for me on the staircase, and appeared much agitated. "Oh, sir!" said she, "I am afraid something serious has happened to my father: pray go to him." I entered his sitting room. He was seated in an old arm-chair at a table, pen in hand;

---

* In proof that my sketches are not exaggerated, when I had finished writing the above paragraph, I had a sick call. I am now returned home, and will faithfully narrate what I have done, and seen, and heard. I have been attending a poor little girl about twelve years of age, who, two months ago, caught the typhus fever. She recovered; but, from going out barefoot in cold wet weather, had a relapse, and is now in a dying state. I have heard the innocent child's little confession, anointed her, and given her the last blessing. I left her with her poor little wasted hands joined together, praying heartily to God. This is such an everyday occurrence, that I should not mention it were it not for attendant circumstances. The father is a carpenter—an honest, hard-working man. He was laid prostrate with typhus fever about six months since. He was dreadfully ill for four weeks, but rallied, and now creeps about, the shadow of his former self. Another priest attended him then; and was good and kind to him, or he must have starved. He has been out of work since his recovery, as his skeleton frame shows little capability for much exertion, and no master-carpenter will employ him. I saw his tools neatly arranged around his little parlor, in No. 48 Parker-street, Drury-lane. The poor man held the candle while I anointed his child; and he trembled from weakness while holding his slight burden. In addition to his troubles, after his recovery, his wife was taken ill of fever; but God brought her round. Then followed the sickness of the poor child of my last hour's ministration. It is a climax of suffering. When the poor mother came to me, crying, and begging me to come to her child, they had been starving all day—had neither fire nor candle. When, on leaving, I put some silver into the poor man's hand, his chest heaved, and he fairly sobbed in striving to utter his grateful thanks. And yet, with all this accumulation of most bitter distress, there was not the least complaint or murmur; but cheerful, heartfelt, unaffected piety, and the utmost resignation to the will of God. Again, do I say, blessed are the virtuous poor, for theirs assuredly is the kingdom of heaven.

but his eyes were fixed, not upon his paper, but upon the ceiling, and he appeared absorbed in thought. A bright sunbeam, with its countless particles, came from the window, and glancing athwart his countenance, lit up every feature; but it gleamed powerless across the old man's open eyes. They shrunk not, nor quivered. No lightning's flash could move their dull tranquility. He was blind.

"Bring the candle, Ellen,'' said the old man, "it is quite dark; how strange that night should have come so soon!"

"Father," said his daughter, "dear father!"

"Hush!" said I, in a low tone; and beckoning her to come near me, I whispered to her startled ear:—

"I fear, my dear child, your poor father is deprived of sight. Be calm, or fatal consequences may ensue."

A deep sob, but instantly repressed with heroic effort, escaped the grief-worn bosom of this hapless daughter. She fell on her knees; bowed herself down in earnest prayer to that adorable Being who alone can comfort the broken heart.

"Ellen," exclaimed the old man, in a sharp and querulous tone, "why don't you bring the candle? Time is money; I must not waste it."

"Dearest father," she answered, the tears coursing their way rapidly down her cheeks, "don't write any more to night—let me lead you to bed. I am sure you are tired."

He was patient and submissive in her hands,—he knew the extent of his calamity,—he wondered why night had come so quickly,—he wished it would go, and leave him to work again.

I went instantly to my friend the physician who was fortunately at home. He came back with me, and carefully, and in silence, examined his patient's eyes. On his return to the little sitting-room, Ellen anxiously asked if her father was really blind?

"It would be cruel in me to deceive you,' was the reply of the benevolent physician; "I am afraid there is little hope of cure."

"Oh, no!" she exclaimed; "do not say that, sir. It is so sudden, it will break my heart. O merciful Father! strengthen me to bear this great trial."

My heart melted within me as I witnessed the grief of this poor afflicted girl. The bruised reed was indeed well-nigh broken.

The Death-Bed

I took particular interest in Mr. Danby's case, and as his residence was near the chapel, managed to see him almost daily. It was indeed a touching and a melancholy sight to witness this aged man so suddenly deprived of one of God's greatest blessings,—a gift rarely sufficiently appreciated while this important organ is in a sound and healthy state; but when endangered—or partially, or, alas! totally, deprived of its magnificent utility,—it is then we value it at a right estimation.

My slender funds, in addition to a liberal donation from my dear kind friend, the physician, enabled me to provide a nurse and all requisite necessaries for the poor blind man. His daughter had the good fortune to get a little needle-work from one of her late employers.

This timely occupation prevented her mind from being corroded by grief, and enabled her to sit constantly by the bedside of her father, and speak to him from time to time those words of affection, which none but a good true-hearted woman can so effectually use in the sick chamber of suffering man. It is then that the helpless lords of the creation pine after the soothing ministry of woman's tenderness and compassion. Their own sex are too apt to regard their sufferings with calm and stolid indifference: not so a wife, or daughter, or sister, whose loving hand smooths the tossed and tumbled pillow,—whose pitying eye is ever kindly directed towards you—and whose voice is ever low and gentle, and full of comforting influence.

My good old penitent was very calm and resigned; much so more than I expected he would be under his terrible privation. He was highly educated, and his mind was enriched with the best stores of ancient and modern literature. I rarely enjoyed an hour's chat more than I did with this good old man. The paralysis had spent its efforts in depriving him of his sight, and his mind seemed clearer and calmer than ever. Our conversation was generally of a varied description. He was deeply read in the Holy

Scriptures, and he would delight in clothing biblical stories of blind men in his own terse and eloquent words. He made out to me, clearer than I ever heard before, the infinite tenderness and compassion of God to blind men. He was never tired of recurring to the old Tobias, who had an angel sent from heaven to cure his blindness.

"I do not, my dear sir," he calmly said, "I do not myself expect, or even hope, for this high privilege. It is God's will I should be blind: Thy will be done, my heavenly Father!" He would then touchingly dilate on the advantages of blindness in our last moments: the more perfect concentration of mind upon God and eternity that necessarily results from the absence of all distractions of sight. He thought it an unhappy thing in a person about to die to have his sight gradually obscured by the film of death, and to have his longings after immortality disturbed by the dimly seen agonies of weeping relatives around his dying bed. He had one sacrifice less to make—the last, longing, lingering look at his child. He spoke firmly upon this trying point. He had no misgivings in God's all-protecting providence. "He who suffereth not a sparrow to fall to the ground without His divine permission, would not assuredly permit his much loved Ellen to suffer overmuch, without grace to support it, when he was taken from her."

He seemed never wearied in talking of the joys of heaven; he had a rapturous, though humbly tempered, wish to be there, and see God face to face, and in the clear vision of His celestial glory for ever to be inebriated with the plenty of His house. And then, at times, he would break out into a murmured and ecstatic thankfulness on the goodness of God, who had thus chastened him before receiving him into His heavenly kingdom. The infinite, all-atoning love of his Saviour was dwelt upon with rapture: and in his frequent communions his soul was more and more purified—more nearly united to the martyred Lamb of God.

His daughter read to him morning and night, and frequently during the day, those beautiful prayers of the *Garden of the Soul,* which have prepared and fitted so many souls for heaven. She never seemed so happy, and tranquil, and resigned, as when she was assisting her father to die the death of the just. There was a fervor and spirituality about every tone of her low and musical voice, that vibrated tenderly through every chord and fibre of the heart. Her father felt it; for his countenance would glow, and his sightless eyes would be raised towards heaven with a reverential appearance that showed that, though corporal sight was wanting, the eye of faith steadily contemplated the ineffable glories of that eternal kingdom to which he was now rapidly hastening.

And his death-bed was most beautiful and consolatory. He was anointed; but it was not expedient for him that God should heal his bodily infirmities. But his heavenly Father wonderfully consoled him in his last moments. They were moments of joy and of overflowing tenderness. A little space before he died, he desired the nurse to raise him up in bed.

"Ellen, my child," he feebly whispered, "my dear, darling child, let me die in your arms. You have ever been the kindest, most dutiful of daughters to me; let me have this last happiness upon earth."

Almost fainting, tear upon tear flowing down her pale and convulsed cheek, her heart throbbing with unutterable anguish, yet keeping down, by a strong effort, every audible expression of grief, the dear child arose quickly from her knees, in which reverent posture she had joined in the prayers for the dying, leaned over the pillow of her father, laid his poor dying head upon her bosom, clasped him tenderly round the neck, kissed again and again his pale brow and lips, and whispered tremulously words of heavenly peace and hope to his dying ear.

In a few minutes he faintly said; "Ellen, my darling child, God eternally bless you; may we meet in heaven. Reverend father, God Almighty bless you, too, for all your kindness to me—look to my poor child when I am gone."

His right hand was slightly agitated. His daughter quickly divined the cause; she reverently raised it, kissed it, and placed it on her own head. The old man's lips were tremulous with unuttered words; a tear rolled down his cheek: a smile, prophetic of his heavenly heritage, lit up his every feature; and with that look of happiness he expired.

The Miser's Death

ONE afternoon I received the following note:

"Rev. and respected Sir:—I hope you will pardon the liberty I take in addressing you, but my poor old master has not long to live; he cannot last many days, and I would be very thankful if you would see him before he dies. He does not know that I have written this, and I am afraid will not receive you kindly; but pray have the charity to come.

"From your most humble servant,
"Martha Wilson"

The direction was to a small street in the suburbs, one of those shabby-genteel localities in which small rickety houses shoot up with mushroom growth; their stuccoed fronts generally displaying in a couple of years several unsightly cracks; the streets ill-paved, and badly drained.

After several fruitless inquiries, I at length found myself at my destination. I knocked and was admitted by Mrs. Wilson. She was the housekeeper to the old gentleman who was sick, and had been long a penitent of mine. She was a woman of rather superior education, as appears from her note, and had been many years in the service of her master. She was about sixty years of age, of a tall, thin figure, a mild intellectual cast of features, and was dressed in faded black silk, that looked as if, like her, it had seen better days.

"Oh, sir," said she, "thank God you are come! but have the goodness to step into the parlor before you see my master, as I wish to speak to you about him."

She showed me into a small dingy room, plainly furnished, but everything clean and in scrupulous order. One side, opposite the window, from the floor to the ceiling, was occupied by large japanned tin boxes, with many an aristocratic name emblazoned in large capital letters. An old worm-eaten bureau stood in a corner, by its side reposed a massive iron safe; and a large office-table with numberless drawers, and thickly strewed with papers tied with faded red tape, occupied the centre of the apartment. The only redeeming features in the room were two exquisite paintings in oil: one, a Murillo, a Holy Family, in which breathed the tenderest piety—the other, a portrait of a Spanish cavalier, by Velasquez, and painted with extraordinary force and breadth. I could have gazed long at these beautiful paintings, which gave an intellectual tint to the griping, penurious air of the room, but my conductress was anxious to obtain my attention. Her information was somewhat prolix,—it was the outpourings of an overcharged heart, and was accompanied with many tears. What I remember is as follows:—

Her employer's name was Hamilton.* He was the youngest son of an ancient but decayed Catholic family. With a younger brother's scanty portion, he devoted his talents, which were of no mean order, to the law. He was articled to a respectable solicitor of large practice in a wealthy town in Yorkshire. After finishing with a London conveyancer, and passing a successful examination, he entered into partnership with his late master. They lived together in apparent harmony for some years, until his partner died. Left unshackled to his own resources, and the full development of his keen but daring mind, he rapidly acquired wealth, chiefly by lending money on mortgage to country

---

* This name, of course, is assumed for certain reasons.

squires who lived too fast for the welfare of their estates, and who stood in need of a temporary supply to meet their forthcoming engagements.

On his forty-fifth anniversary he was still a bachelor, though, from his reputed wealth, it had been easy for him to have selected a willing bride from the neighboring families who had unmarried daughters to dispose of.

"He was then, sir," said the house keeper, "a very different-looking man to what he is now—tall, well-made, and of dignified carriage; he impressed reverence, and, if not love, a certain fear by his presence. His face was pale and very thoughtful; he never entered into any amusement, except an occasional rubber at whist, at which he excelled.

"It was at this time that he had to manage the affairs of an old East India colonel of the name of Graham. The colonel had retired from his profession with a large fortune and an only daughter. His constitution was much shattered by thirty years' campaigning in India, and he lived alternately at Bath and Cheltenham, for the benefit of the waters, varying his enjoyments with an annual visit to London in the season. But his sanguine temperament could not endure the inaction of a quiet life. He engaged keenly in gambling; at first, merely as a stimulus to kill time, but afterwards as the great business of his life. His days and nights were devoted to this fatal and all-absorbing pursuit. His daughter Emily, a beautiful and accomplished girl of eighteen, and in whom he had centred all his cares and happiness, was forgotten, or but dimly remembered in the languid intervals of the maddening excitement of hazard and *rouge et noir*.

"At first he won largely;—crowds of unsuccessful and ruined gamesters would hang behind his chair and envy his luck as he nightly swept his winnings from the board. He was called the lucky colonel; and the *croupier* and the partners of the *hell*, though respectful and lavish in their insidious hospitality, used at length to tremble at his approach. It was a house where heavy and almost unlimited stakes were played. At length fickle fortune made a dead set against the colonel. Night after night he lost, until not only his immense winnings had disappeared but he had dipped considerably into his ample fortune. Stung with disappointment, he redoubled his efforts to retrieve himself; played higher stakes,—but in vain. The result was still the same,—he was pursuing the beaten track—accomplishing the usual end of the gambler—to be sucked down and overwhelmed in the vortex of ruin.

"His disconsolate child had long witnessed with grief this fatal and absorbing passion of her father. In vain had she, with tears and earnest prayers, remonstrated with her parent that he would abandon play for ever, and leave that scene of horror where his ruin was nightly threatened, for the pure and quiet pleasures of a country life. 'No, Emily,' he would say, with a stern and sad smile in which anguish and grief were mingled—'no, my dear child—I must regain from those ruffians what they have robbed me of,—no, my child, your future life must not be impoverished by my past fatal folly. I will yet win back with interest from those knaves all and more than I have lost.'

"One night fortune again smiled on him. Before midnight he had won fifteen hundred pounds. Exulting from success, he joined the supper table, where every luxury, every costly wine provoked the languid appetite, and gave temporary relief to the votaries of hazard. He could eat but little, for his appetite had long failed him, but he quaffed many bumpers of champagne in congratulatory libations to his success. With a heated and excited brain he returned again to the gaming table, and flushed with wine, he seized again the fatal castors. Fatal they were to him. He lost again, and again, and again, until he had given notes of hand for every shilling he possessed, with the exception of his commission, and a small property in Yorkshire. With every rigid feature fearfully convulsed, with an execration too fearful to utter, and which made the callous *habitues* of the *hell* start and stare with wonder, the colonel seized once more the dice-box, which was nearly crushed in his clenched fingers, and rattling the dice with frantic vehemence for some moments, dashed them with maniac force on the board. 'Seven's the main,—I stake my commission on the event.' His bet was taken. He lost. Rising from his seat, he strode into the middle of the *salon*—stopped—raised his eyes to the ceiling, until their bloodshot white was alone visible:—his clenched hands were outstretched and rigid—his lips moved convulsively, but not a sound was audible—his chest heaved and shook—and he fell to the floor in a fit.

"'Call a coach for the colonel,' said the *croupier*, with unmoved apathy and *sang froid*. 'Gentlemen, make your game.' And the game was renewed, as if a fellow-being had not been ruined, the demon of despair at his heart, and his life in deadly peril.

"An acquaintance of the colonel, who had more humanity than the rest, accompanied him. He stopped the coach at a surgeon's by the way; had him bled, which restored him to a dreamy consciousness, and left him not until he had seen him conveyed to bed.

"He soon recovered, but he was an altered man. That night's ruinous loss had made him many, many years older. His hair became thin and of a silvery whiteness. His gait was feeble and the bold and energetic conqueror in many an Eastern fight was now a timid, and querulous, and peevish old man. By the advice of his daughter—for his mental energies seemed paralyzed and incapable of suggestion—a letter was despatched to my master to come and aid them with his counsel. He had been many years the colonel's agent, and had ever professed a high regard for the unfortunate old man.

"He came, and the colonel's affairs were placed in his hands. His commission and the small estate in Yorkshire were sold; and, after all liabilities were discharged, but a few hundreds remained for the support of the colonel and his daughter.

"My master dined with them daily, and he certainly spared neither time nor trouble in making their desolate lot as comfortable as possible. I know not how it was, or how he succeeded, but certain it was, in a few weeks he married Miss Emily, and settled a handsome annuity on her now almost imbecile and broken-hearted father. I suppose, poor child, she did it to save his few remaining years from penury, and surround him again with those comforts to which he had been long accustomed, and which seemed necessary for his very existence.

"And then, sir, my master brought home his young bride. She looked like a drooping flower, so pale, so beautiful; her low and gentle voice, so pitying in its accents for the griefs of others, for she had drank deeply of her own cup of sorrow. I believe my master was as kind to her as his stern, proud, and cold nature allowed him. But, alas! he soon seemed to weary of her presence. The pursuit of wealth soon again absorbed his every faculty. They had no visitors except now and then a client with whom my master wished to drive a hard bargain, and whom he made pay dearly for his calculating hospitality. My poor young mistress rarely went out; she never complained—locked up her sorrows in her own gentle heart, and seemed only to live for a devout preparation for another and a better world.

"In two years' time she was confined with her first child. Oh, sir, never shall I forget that night. It is now six-and-twenty years ago: but it breaks my heart now to think of it. She died an hour after giving birth to an infant daughter, after hearing the first cry of that innocent child—after giving it her first and last embrace. Oh, there was heavy sorrow in our house that night! We all cried bitterly for the loss of so kind, and gentle, and good a mistress. But I am wrong—there was one who shed no tear, and gave no outward sign of grief. My master stood by the bed of death, and gazed with a stern and apparently unmoved countenance upon the cold and insensible clay of her whose innocent soul I do trust was then with God. I brought him his poor motherless babe, thinking that might move him. But he looked upon it with the same cold and stony gaze.

"'Take it away,' said he sternly, 'it has killed its mother.'

"He gave one more long and earnest look at the corpse, and walked slowly out of the chamber of death.

"Yet I think he felt her loss acutely. Night after night, he paced his bed-chamber with heavy and measured strides; but in a month he was again as calm and as stern as usual."

Here the old lady left me for a few moments, to see how her master fared.

"He is still sleeping," said she on her return; but it is not a natural sleep; he is groaning and moaning fearfully. All his sleep is now produced by laudanum.

"Well, sir, his child was named after her mother, and I tried in my poor way to do a mother's part by her. She grew up the image of her departed angel mother. When she was thirteen, my master suddenly relinquished his business for a valuable consideration to his chief clerk, and settled in London. He took a house in a fashionable street at the West-End, furnished it handsomely, and I thought he was going to introduce his daughter into that society which her birth and fortune required. But I was mistaken. He had struck out a new source of wealth, and pursued its acquisition with a calculating mind that never relaxed its efforts. He became a bill-discounter; and though throngs of carriages with coronets on their panels were daily driven to our door, our fare was of the humblest description. True, he did not neglect the education of his child; he had the best of masters to instruct her at home; but even with them he drove a hard bargain.

"Things went on thus for some years; my master daily adding to his now enormous wealth, and daily abridging his own comforts, so that I wonder how he could exist on so little food. His dress became daily more penurious, and he wore his clothes until they were quite threadbare. Almost every night he would hurriedly pace his bedroom.

"I could hear him, for my sleeping apartment was over his. And I would listen shudderingly to the unhappy old man's frantic exclamations, 'I am robbed—I am robbed. And then I could hear his iron safe unlocked, and heavy bags of money dashed hastily on the table, and the clinking sound of the gold as he slowly counted piece after piece,—and then the gasping exclamation, 'Thank God, it is all right; I am not robbed; I am not yet a ruined man!'

"Indeed, sir, it soon appeared clear to me that the extreme and absorbing love for wealth was fast undermining my poor master's powerful intellect. He abruptly stopped the course of his daughter's education, and told her, 'She must now work for her subsistence, for he was a poor man, and could no longer afford to maintain her in idleness. He worked hard, very hard, for the little he got—why should not she do something for the bread she eats?'

"She told me this at night, sobbing with many tears, and asked me what she should do. I advised her not to thwart her father, but to promise compliance to his wishes, and perhaps in a few days his present strange intention would fade from his memory.

"But it did not. Day after day, he reiterated his stern command. He did more,—he repeatedly cursed her, and said with many imprecations, 'if she did not work, she should not feast at his expense.' Poor thing, it was little she eat; the color was leaving her thin cheek, and I was afraid I should soon lose my motherless and now almost fatherless child.

"One day a gentleman came on business. He was a young officer in the army, and I had formerly known him in Yorkshire when his regiment was quartered there. My master was out, and Captain Etherington waited for him in the drawing-room. My young mistress went there to seek for some embroidery, and they then renewed an acquaintance that was commenced in happier times.

"Suffice it to say, in less than a month he offered her his hand. She was too fondly attached to him to refuse, but said she could not marry him without her father's consent. The captain did ask my master's consent, and a pretty storm of abuse he got for his pains.

"'Marry my daughter, you walking piece of animated pipe-clay! Pray what settlement do you intend to make upon her? I believe, sir, your whole estate consists of your beggarly commission and some ninety pounds a year, and which your present extravagance will in a few weeks or months deprive you of.'

"'Mr. Hamilton,' said the other, 'I do not wish to marry your daughter for money.'

"'You would be disappointed if you did,' replied the excited old man. 'I tell you what, sir, if you marry my daughter, she shall be no longer a child of mine. I will never see her again; never give her sixpence; and don't expect anything after my death. I would rather leave what I have to an asylum for stray dogs. There, sir, you have your answer. Good morning, sir.'

"Poor Miss Emily soon became most wretched, and almost heartbroken in the mental strife and misery she endured in her father's house. To upbraiding, bitter and relentless, which pierced the heart of his innocent victim, he one day added blows. He struck to the ground the pale, defenseless girl. One faint, smothered scream, and all was still. I could endure my agony of suspense no longer. I rushed into the room, and beheld the poor child stretched upon the carpet apparently lifeless, and my old master coolly employed in entering into his ledger that day's gains of usury.

"On my upbraiding him for his cruelty, he merely replied: 'Take the girl away; let her marry him if she likes, it is no concern of mine —she is no longer a child of mine.'

"'You do not deserve to have a child, sir, to treat her with such cruelty.'

"'Leave the room, woman,' said he, looking at me with intense bitterness.

"I carried out the pale, inanimate form of my dear child, for so I shall ever call her; and by applying some simple restoratives, she soon recovered. Her grief was pitiable. The last connecting link that bound her to her parent was now rudely severed. That night, sir, the demon again returned to the heart of that unfortunate old man. He expelled her from his house. But she did not go alone. I went with her. I got her a temporary asylum with a respectable widow lady, with whom I had some slight acquaintance, and who felt for her sorrows as if she had been her own daughter.

"In a short time, she married Captain Etherington. I saw them occasionally, and then by stealth; and most thankful I was to find they always seemed truly happy. But misfortunes, sir, soon followed them. They lost two children out of five; and last year, the captain died tto; and poor Miss Emily, or rather Mrs. Etherington, is now a widow, with only a small pension for her support and that of her three children.

"Eight years ago, sir, and shortly after his daughter's marriage, my master gave up his house, which he said was too expensive for him, and came to this poor little abode. All the furniture was sold off, as if he left in distress, with the exception of those two pictures, and a few in his bedroom upstairs; for my master had always a passionate love for pictures, and they were the only luxuries he ever purchased. Some of them, however—and the best—he got cheap from his titled debtors, when their extravagance prevented their taking up their bills in time. We have lived here in the greatest apparent penury. Every day almost, some little comfort has been abridged as a useless luxury; in fact, my master has become a miser in every sense of the word. His only enjoyment in life seems to be in counting over, and over again, a large sum in gold which he always keeps locked up in an iron safe in his bedroom; and this often makes me very uneasy, as I fear every night the old man's life may be sacrificed, if dishonest persons were to know the wealth that is in the house.

"You may ask why I have been in his service so long. I will tell you, sir. When his poor wife was in the agonies of death, she made me make her a solemn promise never to leave him, but to watch over the welfare of her motherless babe; and that sacred trust, sir, I have endeavored to discharge to the best of my poor ability. It is for her sake, chiefly, that I have sent for you this evening. It is in the hope that you may move his cold and unforgiving heart to be reconciled with his daughter before he dies; and also that you may prepare him for death, as a Christian man ought to die.

"He was, in early youth, sir, very attentive to his religious duties. He was his mother's favorite; and her last hours were cheered with the soothing hope of the future virtuous career of her son. But I fear the love of money,—an absorbing, uncontrollable feeling of avarice,—has, for many, many years, rendered him forgetful of his duty to his God, and dead to the holy and consolatory impressions of religion. He cannot last many days; but he will not believe that he is about to die. You will have much difficulty; but I do hope you will succeed.

"And now, sir, pardon me this long narrative I thought it right to acquaint you with the full particulars, that you might know best what course to pursue. I will now see if he is awake."

She was absent about ten minutes. On her return, she motioned me to go up stairs. She whispered that she had not ventured to say I was a clergyman. I must use my own discretion in announcing my errand of mercy.

I entered the bed-chamber. It was a small apartment, miserably furnished. A low truckle-bed, on which lay the helpless sufferer, the bed-clothes, however, scrupulously clean; two rickety rush-bottom chairs; a small, unpainted wash-hand stand; a narrow strip of faded bedside carpet, and a massive iron safe, completed the movables. But from the whitewashed walls beamed many a ray of intellectual beauty. They were covered with gems of priceless value from the Florentine and Venetian schools, with here and there a lifelike and divine specimen of Francia and Carlo Maratti. There was an exquisite "Madonna and Infant Saviour," which hung over the fireplace, and which in an instant realized all my conception of the maternal, sorrowing love of the Virgin Mother, as she bends, with drooping tear-fraught eyelids, over the Incarnate Word, whose little hands and eyes are raised in adoration to His Eternal Father.

These objects I took in at a glance on entering the room, and I gazed with pity on the sick and helpless usurer as I approached his bed, and contemplated the almost unearthly form that lay there. He was exceedingly emaciated; his long white hair was partly covered by an old black velvet cap, and his beard was of many days' growth. The sunken, ashy cheeks gave to the forehead an appearance of almost supernatural breadth; while the grey eyes appeared almost to glow in their dark and hollow sockets as they fixed their stern gaze on me as I drew near his bed.

"Nurse, and you, Mrs. Wilson," said he, "leave the room. Your pleasure, sir?" said the old man, when the door closed on the retreating females.

"I have called, sir," I replied, "to make inquiries after your health, as I hear you are very ill."

"Pshaw, sir! every fool could do that. I thought you came about business; but I now see you are an emissary of that woman who was my daughter: but, curse her, she is no longer a child of mine!"

"Pardon me, Mr. Hamilton," I rejoined, with as much patience as I could assume, "I know not your daughter, have never seen her, and my visit here to-night was solely to yourself, and about your own interests."

"My own interests! " said the sick man. "Have you brought me money? Money is the only thing that will do me good now."

"That depends, Mr. Hamilton. If it is rightly disposed of, then it will not only benefit you in this world, but in the next. You are rich; but I think it my duty to tell you that you are very ill,—may soon die; and, as a Catholic, you should endeavor earnestly to make your peace with God before He summons you from this world."

"You think it your duty!" said the usurer with a sneer. "You think I'm dying! Dying! Pish! pish! people do not die every time they are ill. I have been often ill before, and never died: why should I now? I will not die yet."

And he forced himself upright in his bed. "Who are you, sir, who come to talk to me about dying? It is a lie ; I am not dying."

I gave him my name, and the chapel to which I belonged.

His thin lips were tightly compressed, his stern grey eye shot a keen glance at me for some seconds, when he slowly and distinctly said: "When I want your services, sir, I will send for you. Trouble me no more. There is the door," pointing with his thin skeleton hand; "there is the door. I wish you, sir good night."

Nothing could look more unpromising than my present position; but I was too well used to difficulties to despair. I offered a brief, and I trust a fervent, prayer to Heaven, that His assistance would be mercifully given to win yet this hardened and impenitent soul. My eye rested a moment on the mild, angelic face of the Madonna, and I besought that holy Queen of sorrows to pray for this misguided, dying old man.

My prayer, I think, was heard. The old man's gaze followed mine as it dwelt on the picture and he seemed pleased with the emotion it caused me.

"Fine painting that, sir. Wouldn't take gold for it, if every square inch of the canvas were covered with broad pieces."

"It is indeed a fine painting, Mr. Hamilton; and I almost envy you its possession," said I, glad to have any pretext to open a more lengthened conversation with the irritable old man.

We discoursed some time on the different schools, and he appeared a profound and excellent judge of art. He, too, seemed pleased to have met in me an enthusiast like himself. As I felt he seemed a little softened towards me, and I had gained some little portion of his confidence, I thought I had better not then press further my advantage. I arose to depart, expressing the pleasure it gave me in making his acquaintance, and that nothing would give me greater pleasure than to see his valuable collection of pictures by daylight.

"Well, sir," said he, "come to-morrow; and I think you will like them better by the clear light of day."

The next morning, I again visited him. He was weaker, but more composed. He even shook hands with me, when I had made a few general inquiries after his health. We had a short conversation on art; and each of his paintings in turn derived new value in my estimation from the fine and pure taste evinced in the criticism of the invalid. A sudden thought seized me, that I would turn his love of art to the advantage of his own soul.

"Look," said I, "Mr. Hamilton,—look at that fine 'Madonna and Infant Saviour.' I do not speak of its artistic merits; but of the divine conception it so tenderly portrays. What was the impression that Maratti desired to convey? That of the Eternal Son of God, born of a sinless Virgin, and giving us the sweetest incentive to love, under this His infant form. Turn your eyes to that on the left. It is the same Eternal Son of God, stretching forth His hands to the assembled children of Israel. You may almost hear those words of mercy issue from His blessed lips: 'Come to Me all you that are weary and heavy-burdened, and I will refresh you.' Turn to that scene in the supper-hall of the proud Pharisee.

A young and fair-haired girl kneels, with her golden, dishevelled locks, at the feet of the Son of Mary. You see the full and heavy tears of sorrow streaming down her pale and saddened face; you see her hitherto polluted, but now reverent lips, applied in humblest adoration to the feet of her Redeemer; you see the look of deep, and inmost, and heartfelt grief, saddening her every feature, but a faint and encouraging tinge of hope mantling over all. You see that compassionate gaze of the Saviour; His meek and gentle eyes fixed on her; and that forgiving tone about His divine and parted lips, that opened only to defend her—to pronounce her forgiveness. You see that beautiful embodiment of the Last Supper,—the divine energy and love in the countenance of our Saviour, in the fulfilment of this His dearest wish, to give us His own body and blood in the Eucharistic Sacrament. Look at that picture on the right: you see the same Redeemer, bound, scourged, and bleeding; the thorny crown on His ensanguined temples; the ragged purple robe but ill concealing His lacerated form; the mocking sceptre of a reed;—but the same meek, and heavenly, and uncomplaining look of tenderness, that again says, 'Come to Me all you that labor;' and the troubled, guilty look of Pontius Pilate, as he utters those mournful, deprecatory words: 'Ecce homo,—behold the man!' View again that 'Crucifixion' in the earlier, purer, and more devotional style of Christian art. Its artistic details, perhaps, not so striking as those of a later school; but how suggestive—how truthful—how mournful the eexpressio! The dying eyes of the martyred Lamb of God are upturned towards heaven. He seems regardless of His own sufferings: His parted lips, already livid with approaching death, are uttering His dying prayer, 'Father, forgive them, for they know not what they do.' And if He could forgive that immense and congregated mass of deicide Jews, ravening for His blood, hurling bitter taunts and execrations in His dying ears, how much more the repentant, contrite sinner, who, before his last hour, appeals to Him for mercy? And again, regard that 'Last Judgment,' in all its wonderful and appalling details. He, the arisen, the ascended, has come, after this world's agony and dissolution, to render to every one according to his works. See the unutterable despair, the undying agony of the wicked, as they sink into the gulf of eternal torments; the rapturous upturned look of heavenly joy which animates the immortal countenances of the blessed. You, my dear sir, must shortly appear before the judgment-seat of God; perhaps a few days only intervene between your present moments and eternity. And now, let me ask you to think very seriously on this all-important change. Are you prepared to meet your God?"

The old gentleman had listened to me very patiently, more so than I expected. As I proceeded, he became more interested, raised himself gradually to a sitting posture, his eyes alternately wandering from mine to each picture in succession. When I finished, he uttered a deep sigh, and exclaimed in a softened, tremulous tone: "Why have I not thought of this before? For years I have daily gazed on these pictures; but these thoughts never struck me— I regarded them as mere works of beautiful art. It is now only I read aright the holy and instructive lesson they convey. Seventy-six years have I lived. I am now—I feel it is no use to deceive myself—on the brink of the grave: and, O my God! how much have I offended Thee! Alas, I am a sinful and lost old man!"

He bowed down his head, pressed his hands over his closed eyes, the tears flowed down his sunken cheeks like heavy raindrops, and he sobbed aloud. *Deo gratias!* was my fervent aspiration to Heaven, for this first manifestation of contrition,—for this consolatory triumph of Divine grace.

"Say not so, my dear friend," I rejoined. "Say not that you are lost, while time is yet given you to repent and make atonement to God."

"Ay, sir, there is the grief that now overwhelms me; there is the great fear that oppresses me. I may repent; I feel that I do, I trust most sincerely; and oh! if I had my years to live over again, what a very different life I would lead. Oh! curses on that fatal money, which I do fear will be my eternal damnation. Fool! miserable fool! that I have been. But, sir, although I may repent, yet I am not so ignorant as to forget that confession must be made of my long, long life of sin; that restitution must be made to those whom I may have wronged—I fear, many, and deeply. All this, sir, must be done, before I have the least hope of mercy and forgiveness. Sir, there is no time for all this: I am dying—dying; and I am, I am a lost, and miserable, and sinful old man!"

Again he sobbed more fearfully than before.

He gained more calmness and self-possession, as I gently and soothingly laid before him the many motives of consolation; the high and holy hope of Heaven's mercy, arising from the one, great, and infinite atonement, which our blessed faith so abundantly supplies. And Heaven's gracious and abundant mercy aided my efforts. It was the fierce struggle of an untamed heart, indurated by a long career of uncontrolled self-indulgence, hitherto sustained by a stern defiance of future retribution,—of a mind hitherto blinded to a sense of its future fearful peril. It was a contest hitherto indomitably sustained, unapprehensive, which left that heart stilled and calm in its apathy. But that struggle with the mercy of Omnipotence was now happily at an end: the rebellious creature now bowed himself down with the lowliest contrition,— a grey-haired, dying penitent, before the cross of his crucified Redeemer; and that appeal, I trust, was not made in vain.

His confession was made. That duty over, "Now, sir," said he, "accept my grateful thanks for all your patient kindness with a wayward old man; and pray for me, that my late return to God may be an accepted one. You have prevailed over my long-cherished feelings of resentment. I will indeed see my daughter. I have much to ask her forgiveness of. I wish, indeed, once more to embrace her, and to give her my poor blessing before I die. Not now, sir: I am too weak, too much exhausted; but to-night, sir,—to-night. And you will be here?

I replied in the affirmative; and, with a silent pressure of the hand, and a warm blessing from my heart, I left him to his repose.

I had, in the interim, several other sick calls to make; and they were of a varied nature. Some to the rich man's abode, where pain and sickness were alleviated by all the soothing appliances that wealth or easy circumstances can bestow. Others were made to those lowly habitations where the miserable outcasts of humanity are, from stern necessity, compelled to congregate. And yet, in the poorest, the most squalid of these, it is heart-cheering to see the compassionate sympathy of the poor to each other; and the patient, uncomplaining submission to the will of God, with which they support their grinding lot. What would the poor man be without religion? Religion alone sheds her bright and beautiful gleam of comfort over and irradiates the dreary gloom of his toilsome pilgrimage. Religion sustains him in life; imparts the peace of God to his dying pillow; and with a seraph's smile, and a seraph's voice, points out a brighter, a happier world beyond the grave. Happy, thrice happy, are the poor, when they comply with its soothing, consolatory dictates "Blessed are the poor in spirit, fox theirs is the kingdom of heaven."

In the evening I went again to Mr. Hamilton. The old man was carefully propped up by pillows; his toilet had been attended to; a fire was lit in the small grate, and the room had a much more comfortable appearance than before. He received me with a tranquil, happy smile; and his eye had lost its restless, haggard look.

"I have been very busy, sir, since you left me. I have commenced the great work of atonement, I have sent for my friend, Mr. J—, of the Inner Temple. I have put my affairs in his hands. He is an honorable and just man: and, after my death, will do strict justice, and more, to all whom I have dealt hardly with. I have also," said he with a faint smile, "seen a physician; but I know his aid, at best, can only prolong for a few hours this worthless life of mine. I have also, sir, sent for my daughter: but I fear she will never, never forgive my harshness, cruelty, and neglect. But I will humble myself before her; and the tears of her dying old father may perhaps cause her to relent. And now, sir, if it be not too great a favor for such a sinner as I am to ask, I would indeed wish to receive before I die the Holy Sacrament. I can, indeed, now look to Him who died for my transgressions, with trembling hope,—with humble expectations of mercy. And, if you think fit, I should also wish to receive the last sacrament of anointing."

I knelt down by his bedside, and, in a low, distinct tone, read some of Gother's beautiful prayers for the sick. He accompanied those prayers most fervently; his thin, white hands clasped together, and his eyes fixed on the mild and tender countenance of the Madonna, which hung opposite his bed. It seemed to me that picture now gave him great consolation; that he was now fervently supplicating her blessed aid and prayers; and it was my strong and consoling hope that she was praying for him. I then called up his housekeeper, to assist me while I gave him the holy viaticum and the last anointing.

She came, the tears streaming down her aged cheeks; but they were tears of joy and thankfulness. She lit a wax taper, and knelt down while I recited the preparatory prayers of the Ritual.

He would then be raised to a kneeling posture, to receive his Saviour and his God. He repeated with me, in tones trembling with contrite earnestness, that solemn confession, and supplicatory prayer, the *Confiteor Deo omnipotenti;* and bowed his head in humblest reverence to receive the subjoined absolution.

I stood by the bedside with the ever-adorable and holy Sacrament.

"Ecce Agnus Dei, ecce qui tollit peccata mundi:"

"Behold the Lamb of God; behold Him who taketh away the sins of the world."

Thrice, with deepest humility, he struck his breast at those self-humbling words:

"Domine, non sum dignus ut intres sub tectum meum, sed tantum dic verbo, et sanabitur anima mea."

"Lord, I am not worthy that thou shouldst enter under my roof; say Thou only but the word, and my soul shall be healed."

Then I communicated him in the venerable words of the Ritual:

"Accipe, frater, viaticum Corporis Domini nostri Jesu Christi, qui te custodiat ab hoste maligno, et per ducat in vitam aeternam. Amen."

"Receive, brother, the viaticum of the Body of our Lord Jesus Christ, who may keep thee from the malignant enemy, and bring thee to life everlasting. Amen."

In the solemn pause after the communion, he remained for many minutes in silent prayer. I then prepared him for the last anointing. Telling him again to renew his contrition for every sin, for every frailty of his past life, I repeated the beautiful, consolatory admonition of St. James:

"Is any one sick among you, let him call in the priests of the Church, and let them pray over him, anointing him with oil in the name of the Lord; and the prayer of faith shall save the sick man, and the Lord shall raise him up; and if he be in sins, they shall be forgiven him."

After the solemn words of the Ritual, the consecrated oil of the Church was applied to his eyes, to his ears, his nostrils, to his lips, his hands, and feet, with the traditional apostolic prayer

"Through this holy anointing, and His own tender mercy, may the Lord pardon thee whatever sins thou hast committed by thy sight, etc. Amen."

The subsequent prayers of the Church were then read over the sick man, commending him most fervently to the mercy of God, and praying that this holy anointing, ordained by Him, might heal the soul and body of the sufferer. I ended with the last blessing.

He took a restorative, to strengthen him for his approaching interview with his daughter, for he now gave unequivocal signs of approaching dissolution. In a quarter of an hour she arrived.

I went down stairs to receive her, and to prepare her for her visit to her dying father. She was dressed in deep mourning, and was naturally very much agitated. Her face was pale, and exceedingly beautiful; and the tears flowed fast down her cheeks, as she thanked me again and again for what I had done for her father.

"Oh, sir," said she, "I fear that he is now dying; but it is a great consolation for me to know that he is now prepared to meet his God. I have so long, so often prayed for him, that the Almighty would mercifully turn his heart to religion; that I might once more see my father before he died, and receive his last blessing. It would have broken my heart, sir, if he had died without seeing me,—without forgiving me any uneasiness I might have caused him. I have endured much—much bitter sorrow; but this would have been worse than all."

Woman's gentle heart is ever self-forgetful and forgiving.

"And may I see him now, sir? Do not keep me from him."

We went up stairs. She entered the room, and silently knelt beside his bed.

He stretched out his burning, fevered hands, and, laying them on the head of his daughter, earnestly and solemnly blessed her. Then, after a few moments' pause, he hurriedly said: "The light,—bring the light nearer; let me look at her. Not that way," he cried; "there, that will do." And placing his hands on the shoulders of his daughter, he earnestly looked in her face, while his own worked convulsively with deep emotion, Then, drawing her nearer to him, he cried, "Emily, my child—my child!"

At her father's relenting tenderness of tone her young and patient heart was quite subdued. She affectionately flung her arms around his neck, and kissing his wasted cheeks, while her tears fell fast upon them, she exclaimed, in a low, and gentle, and sobbing tone,—"Yes, dearest father, your child—-your own Emily! Father, forgive me, if ever I have offended you. I fear I have caused you much unhappiness."

"Forgive you, my own dear child! It is I who ought to ask forgiveness of you. How many years of sorrow have I occasioned you! And you too," said he, glancing at her mourning dress, "poor, innocent lamb, you have been sorely tried : but God's holy will be done. And may God Almighty, my own dear, dearest child, eternally bless you; and may His infinite goodness make amends to you for all that you have so patiently suffered from your father's neglect and unmerited cruelty."

"Do not talk thus, my dearest father; it pains me to hear you speak so. I have nothing to forgive, but much, much to rejoice at; for this one hour of happiness is almost more than I can bear. And yet, dear father,"—and she sobbed again—"you are very, very ill: do tell me what I can do for you?"

"Pray for me, my daughter. Life, to me, is well-nigh over; I am going, my child, soon to the presence of an all-seeing, but, I hope, all-merciful God. And do Thou, O Lord, when I am taken from this dear child, do Thou watch over and protect her; and oh, grant that we may both meet in heaven."

They all knelt down, while I read the prayers for the dying. At those hope-inspiring words,—"Depart, Christian soul, out of this world, in the name of God the Father Almighty, who created thee; in the name of Jesus Christ, the Son of the living God, who suffered for thee; in the name of the Holy Ghost, who sanctified thee. May thy place be this day in peace, and thy abode in holy Sion,"—he raised the small crucifix I had given him to his lips, and reverently kissed it.

"Emily, my child, I am going fast: I cannot see you now; but, with my last breath, I bless you." She arose from her knees, sustained his drooping form in her arms, and pillowed his cheek on hers. He faintly whispered, "Jesus, sweet Jesus, receive my soul!" and the next moment that soul was with its God.

It was long before they could separate the child from the dead body of her father. She was carried, fainting, down stairs from the room of death. It was long before I could soothe her tranquility. Her grief would have its way, in a protracted and convulsive fit of weeping. But she mourned not without hope: she had seen him die, happy and resigned—penitent, and she hoped, forgiven; and the tearful prayer from her innocent heart for her father's eternal rest was I trust, heard and accepted in heaven.

The Hospital

THOUGH our English hospitals are deficient in one essential quality so admirably developed in those of Catholic States, viz., the ministration of Sisters of Charity, yet they stand deservedly high for the humanity and high professional skill gratuitously bestowed in the alleviation of the many ills that flesh is heir to. But for their existence, the lot of the suffering poor would be pitiable indeed. The bills of mortality would be swollen to an infinitely more calamitous extent. The industrious artisan, the poor seamstress, the sick widow, the Irish laborer who falls from the scaffold, and every other class of almost penniless sufferers, would soon find their scanty means exhausted by paid professional attendance; and, if not attended gratuitously from motives of humanity, might soon exchange their sick bed for the pauper's shroud and parish grave.

All honor, then, to their generous and philanthropic founders, and to those good Samaritans, who bind up the wounds and heal the infirmities of others by their annual subscriptions and donations. Money was never given for a more righteous purpose, and it is gratifying to think how well those funds are managed, and the enormous amount of real, practical good that is accomplished in the hospitals of England. They give the first medical and surgical skill in the land; every comfort that can soothe or mitigate the sufferer's pain; and the kind and patient ministration of nurses, whose zeal for their patients never flags for an instant. By night and by day, the slightest wish of the pained and, perhaps, fretful sufferer is attended to, and all his capricious longings gratified, if not prejudicial to his health. Luxuries, when he is convalescing, to which he had been all his life a stranger, are given with a generous, ungrudging spirit; and the pool man when cured, leaves that hospital to which, under God, he owes his restoration to health, with every feeling of warm and fervent gratitude that such blessed institutions exist for the relief of the suffering poor.

Reader, take then with me a walk through the wards of an hospital—no matter which, they are all good; but let us choose the one to which my sick calls most frequently lead me. Let us take a melancholy, though reflective, stroll through its wards, and there contemplate poor human nature stricken in infirmity. It may be saddening, but the wise man truly says, "It is better to go to the house of mourning than to the house of feasting:" it will teach thee to be more grateful to that Divine Providence who hath dealt more mercifully with thee than with them: more, perhaps, than thy own shortcomings have deserved. You are, perhaps, a stranger to these asylums of suffering humanity. Be it so. They do not open their gates for the curious to enter easily in and speculate with cool indifference on the poor inmates of the sick-beds. Unless thou art a dear and welcome friend, a relative, or spiritual adviser and comforter of the patient, thou hast no business there—wilt be jealously excluded. They love not their poor inmates to be disturbed by idle and useless visits. But come with me through the medium of these pages, and see what an hospital is, and how it fares with the patients.

You enter, then, with a very solemn feeling, the lazar-house of pain. You are struck with its vast dimensions; its lofty, well-ventilated corridors, and the clean and well-appointed arrangements of the place. An air of quiet and repose prevails throughout. You are sharply scrutinized by the porter. He knows your conductor well from his frequent visits; gives his short civil bow of recognition, and retires with burly stateliness to his den.

We will not, as yet, enter the accident wards: they are on the ground floor, to prevent unnecessary pain to the sufferer in ascending to a higher story. We will take for our inspection one on the first floor. You admire the construction of the staircase, so easy to ascend, so well lit and ventilated. You enter a room sixty feet long by thirty feet wide, and proportionately lofty. Beds are ranged on each side; there may be twenty of them, and each is occupied. The nurses are gliding to and fro with noiseless activity.

Observe how various is the expression of the patients' countenances—how strikingly apparent the diagnostics of their disease. You are told by the attendant that you are in a fever-ward—a shuddering sensation and fear of contagion at first unmans you, if you are unused to the personal inspection of that fearful malady. Curiosity, or it may be a better feeling, prevails. You make a survey of the beds, and their suffering occupants, walking in a straight line through the extensive ward, and keeping as much as possible equidistant from the contagious beds. The atmosphere is heavy, almost overpowering in its faint and sickly odor. An acidulated taint predominates, from the numerous lotions kept day and night on the burning brows of the patients. It is the women's ward that you are perambulating. In the restless, haggard countenances, that are lying uneasily on the pillows, endeavoring in vain to seek a cooler place, you discover every variety of age, from grey-haired decrepitude to the slender girl of twelve or thirteen. Hands, parched and dry, with restless anxiety are tossed to and fro upon the snowy coverlets—for every thing in and about the hospital is kept scrupulously clean—some of those wasted hands are at times joined as if in prayer, though the intellects of the sufferer are quite astray. The red and angry flush of fever is stamped and burnt upon the features of nearly all; the skin of the forehead tight, and shining like burnished copper. The eyes of some are closed, but their lips are moving rapidly; mothers holding imaginary converse with their children, who are far away: wives deprecating the inhuman violence of a brutal and drunken husband, or mingling in plaintive tones the recollections of long-passed love and affection.

One poor attenuated creature, whose wasted, though still beautiful, countenance tells that twenty summers have scarce matured her form, is piteously exclaiming:—

"William, dear—don't strike me; don't, dear—pray don't. Oh, William—you were so kind to me before you married: you were then so good, so affectionate. Mother told me you would change, but I would not believe her. And now we have been but two years married, and, O God, what have I not gone through? William, you will kill me if you beat me so. William, you shan't hurt the baby. Oh, my God, he has killed the child!"

Here the poor sufferer utters a long and piercing scream. Her clenched hands are tossed widely in the air, and it is some minutes before the attendant nurse can pacify her.

You inquire her history. The nurse is communicative, and gives it briefly, but in a feeling manner; for habitual contemplation of human suffering by no means deadens their sensibilities, or renders them less compassionate to the sufferings of the patients. I have repeatedly witnessed the most humane and touching feeling evinced by those good nurses to the poor inmates of the hospital; kindness, to which, in all probability, they had been years and years strangers. This kindness, too, is entirely disinterested, for they are forbidden, under pain of instant dismissal, to receive the smallest gratuity from any of the patients or their friends.

"That poor young woman, sir, married a journeyman painter, about two years ago. Her mother, who is a clean, respectable old body but whose heart is almost broken, was for a long time opposed to the match. 'Better, Nancy,' she said, 'remain single all your life, than to marry a man who drinks. I am sure you won't be happy if you marry him.' 'Oh, but, mother,' she said, 'William has promised me he will give up drinking; and you know what a good workman he is. I am sure we shall be happy.'

"Well, sir, the upshot of it was that they were married. The poor fond old mother could hold out no longer; so she gave her consent, though, she has told me since, most unwillingly.

She said she never knew any good to come of a man who was a drunkard. He might reform for a bit, but sooner or later was sure to break loose, and then become worse than ever.

"For the first year he was steady enough, earned a deal of money, and spent his evenings always at home. After the birth of his child he changed sadly. The infant was sickly, and he said he could not bear the squalling of the brat; so, after his tea, he used always to walk off to the public-house, and was seldom home before midnight. Poor Nancy had soon a hard time of it; what with the illness of her baby, her husband's savage, morose temper,—for he now showed himself in his true colors—his continued drunkenness and brutality, and the frequent want of the necessaries of life, she began to repent that she had not followed her mother's advice and remained single. If it had not been for her poor old mother, she would have starved; for that brute Hardnett would leave her for the week together, and spend every farthing he earned at the public-house and worse places of profligacy.

"She was at length obliged to wean the child. Her milk, from fretting and want, dried up, the poor little creature was always crying for the breast, and Nancy would pace the garret floor the whole night long, endeavoring to pacify its cravings. When Hardnett was at home, which was but seldom, he used to curse most awfully at this. One night, about a month ago, he came home late, much the worse for drink, and very savage. He had lost all his money at dominoes, at some low public-house; had accused the man he played with of cheating him, and was well beaten and kicked out of the house. He insisted on poor Nancy going out for more gin; and, when she said she had no money, that she had pawned her shawl the day before for food for herself and baby, he said it was an infernal lie; that she had money, and money he would have, or it would be the worse for her.

"The poor thing looked round the room, but there was nothing else left to pawn: clothes, furniture, chimney-ornaments, all her treasured articles of the slightest value, had long since disappeared—all sold or pawned for food, for rent, or to supply the drunkard with drink; but one solitary relic of happier days remained, her wedding-ring. The soddened eye of her husband rested for a moment on that sacred memorial of wedded love, and, with a volley of execrations, he told her to go and sell her ring before the shops were closed for the night.

"She burst into tears. 'Oh, William! For God's sake, don't make me sell my ring. It is my wedding-ring; the only thing I have left but my baby to remind me of happier days. Stay till to-morrow, and I will work my fingers to the bone; I will beg or borrow, sooner than part with that.'

"'Give it me this instant, or by—, I'll brain you.'

"She got frightened, turned pale, and was on the point of fainting. A dizziness oppressed her sight; a loud singing in her ears prevented her hearing what followed. The brute waited a moment, again demanded the ring, and, because she was insensible to his request, struck her a heavy blow on the head. She staggered back with the force of the blow—was saved from falling by clinging to the bed-post. She had her child in her arms. Again the ruffian's arm was uplifted, when she frantically exclaimed,—'Oh, William, William, kill me, but don't hurt the child!'

"Blinded, maddened with drunken rage, he cared little where the fell blow descended.

****

"A widow woman who lived in the next room had been awakened by the uproar. After a while, all was still. Then she heard the heavy step of Hardnett descending the stairs. In a short time, finding he did not return, she gathered courage to tap at Nancy's door, and asked what had been the matter. There was no answer. She pushed the door open, and, by the light of the rushlight—which was still burning dimly on the table—she beheld the fearful sight. Mrs. Hardnett was extended on the floor in a state of insensibility, her face livid and swollen from contusions. By her side, with one arm thrown round it for protection, was the innocent baby, Its little face dabbled with blood, and its delicate features almost obliterated by violence. It had been foully murdered by its unnatural father, and its mother had better have been in the grave, than to have awoke from her insensibility and beheld that sad spectacle. She did however awake, by the kind appliances of the weeping widow. When her eyes gazed on the mutilated form of her child, she bent over it with frantic dismay. She could not believe it was dead—clasped it to her bruised bosom, kissed its pale lips, fondled its cold tiny fingers in hers, and then, finding the little limbs grow rigid and colder, burst into a loud and hysterical fit of laughter. The old widow told me, sir, she will never forget that dreadful laugh: if she could have cried, it would have saved her. But she could not shed a single tear; nor has she from that day to this. Her brain was turned; a raging fever set in, and in a week's time she was brought here. But she will never get over it, poor thing; and it will be a happy release for her when it pleases God to take her."

"And what became of her husband?"

"Oh, sir, he is now in jail, and I hope the villain will be hanged for it; the unfeeling brute!"

Again you look at the poor sufferer whose days seem evidently numbered. A serene and placid expression now lights up her girlish and innocent features. A sad smile plays around her wasted lips; and, on your departure, she is murmuring a lullaby to her child.

The Wanderer's Death

CHAPTER I

WHILE a country missionary, my duties led me one day to the jail of the county town, to prepare a convict for transportation. It was late before I returned home, and I retired to rest, fatigued and exhausted with the labors of the day. Sleep visited my weary eyelids, and I wandered free and unconstrained in the happy land of dreams.

The scenes of my childhood were revisited. Friends, long since dead, conversed with me, with their old familiar faces, their ancient smiles of recognition, and I wondered not at their reappearance. Old attachments were revived, and the friendly intercourse with the dead seemed to me as precious as the unexpected gush of the fountain to the thirsty traveller of the desert.

Anon, my dream changed; I was engaged in some perilous enterprise. My life, my liberty, every thing I held most near, was at stake. I was betrayed by the villany of one nearest and dearest to me. Tried, condemned, I was left alone in a dark and dreary dungeon, to prepare, as best I could, my desponding, agonized soul for execution.

But seven short fleeting hours intervened between the present midnight hour, and the place of doom, the headsman's axe, and the grim and fearful paraphernalia of death. I sank exhausted on the stone bench, appointed, as if in mockery, for the last sleep the condemned criminal enjoys before the stern and sad realities of life are over,—before his soul is wrenched from his quivering, palpitating frame.

Anon, the thought struck me that I would escape. I would not die. I would crawl through life, the meanest, most abject, despised, among my fellow creatures,—suffer poverty the most pinching,—drink the bitter cup of misery to the dregs,—rather than thus expire unpitied on the scaffold.

I had read in good books of the resignation of holy men in their last moments: the serenity of martyrs in the midst of fiery torments, that soon wafted their enfranchised souls to heaven. I had read and wondered at the indomitable courage and unbroken patience of tender virgins. The rack, the executioner's sword had been powerless against them; neither molten lead nor boiling oil could extort from them a single groan or murmur; and I, a strong man, wrung my hands in despair, and wept like a child.

But I would escape! I would yet baffle the malice of my persecutors. I would revenge myself—no matter how, at what time, or by what means. I would inflict a deep and dire revenge upon those who so unjustly thirsted for my blood. Pale phantoms, with batlike wings, flitted around me, and whispered, "Escape! escape!" I flew, with a tiger's spring, to the high and strongly barred casement, shook its iron stanchions till the blood spurted from my fingers. It was in vain; they stood firm and immovable.

I fell back on my stony couch exhausted, chilled with despair, the agonizing sweat of incipient death gathering fast on my brow; while around me hovered those hideous phantom shapes, and from their fleshless jaws screamed those ominous words, "There is no escape for the wicked!"

I pressed my bleeding fingers over my eyes, to shut out forms so ghastly, which filled my mind with more than the agony of death. Suicide, the last refuge of cowardly, guilty men, was then whispered into my ears by those unclean tormentors; but no weapon of self-destruction was within my reach. "Strangle thyself!" murmured a low, seductive tone, that strangely fascinated me with its insidious command. "Brave men, and true,—true to themselves, their own dignity, have thus freed themselves from the shame and horrors of a public execution—have thus gained the quiet rest of the grave."

My hands instantly clutched my throat with a convulsive gripe, and a laugh of fiendish exultation rang through the vaulted cell. In ten brief seconds I should have been in eternity. In ten brief seconds my guilty soul would have been in the presence of its Maker, with the last and deadliest sin of suicide to be atoned for by eternal torments, had not the mercy of God stepped forth instantly to my deliverance.

The words of the Psalmist, "Hope in God," seemed whispered to me in tones of sweet and holy confidence.

"Hope in God, for He is merciful, and kind, and forgiving," thrilled through my heart, and stilled its tumultuous beatings. My guilty, bloodstained hands relaxed their grasp; they joined in prayer for forgiveness for the great crime which I meditated, and which, from sore temptation, I had so nearly perpetrated. Tears of sorrow in a quick and ceaseless shower fell from my eyes, as I prayed fervently that my heavenly Father would forgive me this great sin. A feeling of resignation, calm and devout, gradually hushed my wearied soul to peace, and I felt the bitterness of my approaching death was passed.

Hours passed away in prayer and devout communion with God. The prison clock, with its sullen clangor, no longer wounded the sensitive organ of my ear with the stern admonition,—"Prisoner, thou hast one hour less to live!" The grey dawn appeared, and dimly lighted up my cell. My eyes wandered over its narrow confines. Soon a ray of bright sunshine stole slanting through the grated window, and revealed the names of former prisoners, traced by their own hands, as a strange and quaint perpetuity of fame, before they were led to the scaffold.

My name too, I thought, may be held in everlasting reproach; but to God, and His infinite mercy, do I commend my soul. Man may judge unrighteously; may execute with refinement of cruelty iniquitous decrees; but in Thee, O Lord! most holy, most merciful, do I place my trust. *"In te, Domine, speravi, non confundar in aeternum!"*

But, hark! a footstep echoes through the winding corridor that leads to my cell—it approaches: the ministers of justice, the executioners of its sanguinary decrees are at hand. My hour, then, is indeed come. A key is applied to the huge lock of the iron-barred door. It turns with a harsh and grating sound. My heart throbs with breathless, sickening anxiety. I awake, however, with a start of horror, and some seconds elapse before I am conscious the well-remembered tones of my ancient house keeper, telling me there is a *Sick call.*

Chapter II

"A sick call, sir," again pealed from the lips of my housekeeper, before I returned to a full state of consciousness, and the horrors of my dream were dispelled. I dressed hastily; and, on inquiring where my services were required, was informed that a poor man was ill at the lone house on the edge of the moor, about five miles from my residence. A pale, attenuated girl, of twelve or thirteen years of age, was to be my guide.

It was a bitter winter's night, or rather morning, for it was considerably past one. The girl was scantily clad; looked faint and weary with her long walk, and I gave her some refreshment before we started. My kind old housekeeper supplied her with an old, but warm and comfortable cloak; and when she was sufficiently rested, we commenced our journey.

As I had lately arrived at my mission, and knew but little of the surrounding country, I should have soon got bewildered in the pathless intricacies of the moor; but my little guide seemed to thread her way with intuitive sagacity. The moon, at times, gave out a fitful, watery gleam, but was often shrouded by dark masses of hurrying clouds, that drifted across the wintry expanse; and the tangled fern and shadowy dells, through which we plunged, were at times veiled in profound obscurity. A startled hare would spring with quick and timid bounds, and again hide herself in the neighboring thicket, as our approaching footsteps aroused her from her warm and sheltered form. The shrill whir of the blackcock, as he skirried off, impatient and fearful at our intrusion into his wild domain; the plaintive note of the peeweet, as we faintly discerned his long and delicate wings, skimming a few yards above our heads,—told we were journeying through places seldom trodden by the foot of man.

It is at such an hour, in such wild and desolate scenery, that the stern grandeur of nature makes so deep an impression upon the human heart. It is at such an hour, in such a locality, that the ways of God appear to us more holy, more profound, more stamped with divine goodness and infinite wisdom, than when we mingle in the feverish, crowded haunts of men. The fearful dream of the last hour; the agony unutterable; the overwhelming sense of shame and disgrace, he had held my faculties captive in the sleep of midnight—gave an additional tinge of solemnity to my reflections, as I journeyed on to the lone house at the edge of the moor. And now, if my readers will forgive me an episode, I will a preliminary tale unfold.

There had been always an air of mystery attached to that solitary and ancient house. Traditionary rumors among the peasantry said that, a century ago, it was inhabited by an old and wealthy family. Their prosperity, however, was suddenly dimmed, the lustre of their fair fame tarnished, by the foul excesses of the last heir of Hilton Grange. Fearful tales were yet chronicled by grey and ancient men, of the sinful doings of the last heir of his race. When the yule log blazed high and bright on the wide hearth of the substantial yeoman; when the old amber ale had done its best in cheering the hearts of the merry guests; when the Christmas carol had been sung, and the mummers exhibited their clumsy antics, the cheek of the youth or maiden would pale, and their hushed breath declare the interest they took in listening to the downfall of that fated race. They had been stout adherents of the house of York, in the wars of the Roses. By apostasy they saved their lands in the reign of Elizabeth; but lost more than half of their vast possessions for siding with the first Charles against the parliament. In the reign of his profligate son, they still further wasted their possessions by a too faithful imitation of the vices of the court. But in the last heir were centred all the sins of his ill-starred progenitors. It was even said, that he made a compact with the dread enemy of man;—sold his soul to Satan, for the miserable fee of a present supply of wealth, and a few years of unchecked indulgence in his career of crime and debauchery. That, at the appointed time and hour, during the midnight orgie, when the wine and ribald mirth flowed fast and furious, he was torn from that impure throng of atheist revellers by an unseen hand, and hurled with supernatural force against the dark wainscot of the room, and that his blood and brains lay mingled on the floor. Others, however, less credulous and, certainly, more intelligent, supposed that he was slain in a drunken brawl.

This much, however, is certain, that, after his mysterious and untimely end, the old mansion was deserted. The remnant of a once large estate was sold, to pay long-accumulating debts; but no one was found hardy enough to reside in that house where crime and bloodshed had been so fearfully perpetrated. Time, which makes inroads into every thing left exposed to its ravages, soon told heavily on the gabled roofs, the quaint Elizabethan turrets, and the embattled gateway. The casements, once filled with a rich and bright array of stained glass on which many an ancestral deed of piety and heroism was recorded, had been in a great storm shattered, and the free winds and rain of heaven poured through unresisted, and completed the ruin of the interior.

Ten years before my narrative commences, it was currently reported that the old manor-house was haunted. A poacher, laying snares in its vicinity, was scared from his midnight and illicit occupation, by hearing loud shrieks issue from the deserted building: a blaze of light, blue and unearthly, quivered for a few minutes in the old banqueting hall, then expired, and left the dark mass of building in its previous gloom.

Tim Wallace (for so the poacher was called) took to his heels immediately, and ran without stopping, until he arrived, pale and breathless, at the village inn. Fortunately for him, a club of cricketers had been celebrating their final game for the season, with a supper and other convivial enjoyments. They were singing, in chorus, the popular jovial ditty,

> "We won't go home till morning,"

when Tim, with dishevelled hair, his ferret eyes gleaming with excitement, burst into the room.

At first, each of the amazed cricketers thought that his barns, homestead, and sundries were on fire, and that Tim was sent to announce the appalling fact. "Fire, devils, ghosts!" was all that poor Tim could articulate, until a glass of hot punch restored him to consciousness. He then narrated his nocturnal adventure, from prudential motives omitting all mention of the wires he had laid for poor puss; and embroidered his tale with so much of the marvellous, that the worthy farmers remained in solemn conclave, until they literally fulfilled their boastful threat.

> "We won't go home till morning,
> Till daylight doth appear."

After six more bowls of strong punch had been discussed, and the wits of the party somewhat muddled, the following resolutions were voted, *nem. con.:*—

That the old manor house was haunted.

That the ghost of the bad Squire Hilton, who was carried away by the devil, was then and there tormented.

That a deputation, after breakfast, should wait on the rector, and request his reverence to lay the said ghost in the Red Sea, or any other place convenient.

The next morning, accordingly, four of the club, headed by the parish clerk (whom they had pressed into the service by the bribe of half a crown and a jorum of ale), marched in a body to the rectory. They had not long to wait, for the kind rector had finished his breakfast, skimmed the *Clerical Guide,* and was donning his ample great-coat, as the weather was cold, previously to visiting a sick pauper in the almshouse.

"Good morning, gentlemen," said the rector, with a smile mantling on his comely and rosy face. "What has happened, Mr. Stubbs?" turning briskly to the parish clerk, as that respected functionary was smoothing his thin grey hair, and giving two or three preparatory hems before making his speech.

The parish clerk was a little, dried-up man, with a face like a frosted pippin, and was usually habited in the cast-off clothes of the rector's wardrobe. The rector was stout and portly, a man of commanding presence. Mr. Stubbs was the reverse; but his reverence for the Church extended to the garments of his patron, and he never suffered them to be profaned by the altering shears of the village tailor. Consequently, the figure which he made was remarkable. It captivated the eye, and irresistibly led you to draw certain comparisons between the worthy Mr. Stubbs, parish clerk and sexton of Stedley-cum-Lea, and the misfitted objects placed in a field to frighten the birds away from the standing corn.

"What has happened, Mr. Stubbs?"

"Why, your reverence, summut most awful. A ghost has been seen in the old grange at Hilton, and we wishes your reverence to lay him in the Red Zee."

"Pooh, pooh, my good fellow," replied the rector, "you have been dreaming about ghosts, and so have your friends here, or you would not have come to me on such a foolish errand."

"Na, na, doctor," said a fat, doubled-chinned farmer; "we be n't dreaming. Tim Wallace seed the ghost hisself last night—seed him covered with fire and brimstone, and squealing for marcy like my old sow Bess when they are sticking her young uns. He seed it; true as gospel. Take his Bibel oath on't."

"I know Tim Wallace well," said the rector. "He is, I am sorry to say, a man of too loose character for me to place much reliance on his word. However, tell me this strange story, and as briefly as you can; for I want to visit a sick person."

Hereupon, Mr. Stubbs made a full, but not very accurate statement of what had occurred; delivering his narrative with that nasal twang, and marked, though ludicrous solemnity of voice, peculiar to parish clerks. The rector, Dr. Howard, was sorely puzzled. Not that he believed for an instant in the intervention of supernatural agency; but that some deep plot had been laid and executed for the purpose of scaring any murder from the ruins, he felt convinced was the case.

He knew it was a hopeless task to disabuse his present ignorant and superstitious auditory so, assuming a grave and solemn cast of countenance, he assured little Mr. Stubbs, and the four stout deputies of the old cricket club of Stedley-cum-Lea, that he would take the subject into his immediate and serious consideration. They departed, highly gratified with the good rector's prompt acquiescence, and Mr. Stubbs enlightened his friends as to the important task which he himself would play in the approaching proceedings.

Dr. Howard, as soon as he had fulfilled his visit to the almshouse, mounted his horse, and rode off to consult a brother magistrate in the neighborhood. The result of their deliberations was, that a strong body of constables, headed by the two magistrates, marched the same evening to the ruined mansion of Hilton, and commenced a thorough search of the interior.

For a long time their perseverance was baffled. No sign of occupation appeared. All bore the dreary, desolate mark of long-continued solitude. The floors of most of the rooms were thickly covered with large fragments of the stuccoed ceilings. The walls were stained and blackened with trickling damp mildew. The dry rot had made fearful ravages. The boards crumbled and sank beneath the pressure of their footfall. Large spiders' webs trailed pendent from the corners of the cheerless rooms, and were speckled with the exuviae of myriads of summer flies. A faint and earthy smell, as of the grave, pervaded those apartments which were unventilated; and every thing around bore silent testimony that many, many years had elapsed since the solitude of Hilton House had been disturbed by the occupancy of man.

Baffled, but not convinced, Dr. Howard proposed that the extensive vaults of the Grange should be examined. This was acceded to, though with reluctance, by the men. Their pale and anxious countenances had long since told they were on an unwelcome errand. Against the visible things of this world they were stout and courageous; and, in many circumstances of trial and danger, had proved their nerve to be of unflinching quality. The undefined horrors, however, of the supernatural world though they felt, they scarcely dared to acknowledge their fear and reluctance to encounter them.

Cheered by the encouraging voice and firm demeanor of Dr. Howard and his colleague, they lit their lanterns and proceeded to examine carefully every nook and cranny of the vaults. Nothing however appeared to justify the suspicion that any one or more persons were concealed.

The last that remained to be searched was a large vaulted chamber. In the civil wars, it had been used as a powder magazine; and its walls were of prodigious strength and thickness. It had only one entrance built of oak plank about five inches thick; that, too, had a massive covering of sheet-iron, and was crossed and recrossed with iron bars. The lock was of equal strength, and so complicated in its construction, that it defied every effort to pick it.

"Force the door, men!" said Dr. Howard. Crowbars were used, and vigorous efforts made in vain, by the strongest of the party, to lift the door from its massive hinges.

"Give me the tool," said a bow-legged, brawny blacksmith, whose hairy chest and herculean arms showed a frame indurated by toil, and capable of sustaining the severest exertion that human bone, and brawn, and muscle could contend with. Applying the crowbar between the lintel and the door, and taking a long and deep inspiration, he exerted the whole of his gigantic force, till the veins on his throat and brow were distended almost to bursting, and his strong frame heaved under his respiratory efforts, like the huge bellows of his own smithy.

Thrice he had to pause and wipe the sweat from his swarthy brow with his broad and horny hand. At the fourth effort, into which he threw the whole of his immense strength, the door was driven in with a crash, and the smith was precipitated headlong into the vault. Oaths and execrations and the sound of a death-grapple rang through the dark vault. The constables, headed by the two magistrates, poured in, and, by the light of their lanterns, beheld the stout smith in a deadly encounter with two stalwart, determined-looking ruffians.

The smith's left hand had clutched, like a vise, the throat of one; and, with his right, he was warding off with his crowbar several furious blows which the other ruffian, with a heavy bludgeon, was aiming at his head. They were both speedily disarmed, before the honest smith had received any more damage than a smart contusion on his head; a blow sufficient to have fractured the skull of an ordinary man, but which he regarded with indifference.

The vault was then examined. A complete set of coining apparatus was discovered; furnace, moulds, and a store of base coin, in shillings and half-crowns, to an immense amount, neatly folded in packets, and so well executed as to defy a casual or hasty inspection.

Thus was discovered the source of those nocturnal apparitions, those supernatural horrors, which had scared the muddled wits of the good folks of Stedley-cum-Lea. The two culprits were tried, found guilty, and transported for life. Before they left England, they made a full confession, and explained the various means by which they had terrified the ignorant and timid peasantry from approaching the Grange. The burning of blue fire; blazing tow, saturated in spirits of turpentine; uttering fearful yells, which reverberated through the dismantled ruins, and echoed again in accents of pain and despair, were some of their favorite devices; and, but for the prompt and energetic interference of Dr. Howard, would have been sufficient to retain for them, many years to come, the quiet possession of their usurped domain.

Chapter III

The excitement produced in the little quiet village of Stedley-cum-Lea by this nocturnal foray and capture of the coiners, gradually subsided. However, many of the wiseacres, such as Mr. Stubbs, the parish clerk; Tim Wallace, the poacher; and his patron, the doubled-chinned farmer Hodgkin, shook their wise heads, and declared it to be their never-to-be-relinquished opinion, that the ghost of Squire Hilton still haunted the Grange, and that it was not safe to be in its neighborhood after nightfall.

The schoolmaster, a thin, ramrod figure with a whity-brown complexion, many freckles, and sandy hair, puffed his pipe in solemn silence during these discussions. When appealed to for his opinion (for there were several dissentients in the village— among the most pugnacious, a little radical cobbler, who was strongly suspected of being an infidel), he would slowly puff his pipe, and then say that Scripture and history were both in favor of ghosts; and if so, why should not the old Grange be haunted as well as other places; especially, considering the foul end of the last squire. "But seeing, gentlemen" said he, with a smile of quiet humor "seeing is believing."

Since that memorable event, the old Grange remained in its usual quiet and desolate state. The weeds and wall-flowers sprang up yearly in its deserted halls and court-yards,— grew and flourished in their brief holiday of existence,—then drooped and decayed. The ivy mantled more thick and luxuriant on the massive flint walls, gradually creeping upwards with its stealthy approaches, and spreading literally its clasping tendrils, and beautifully contrasting, with its deep glossy green, the grey and ancient stone-work of the ruin. A pair of old white owls, that had for many years whooped a sorrowful lament for the frequent loss of their young, torn from their warm nest in the gateway turret by the marauding schoolboy of the village, now reared an annual brood unscared by prying eye or clambering foot, and whooped and whooped their vesper ditty in grave and undisturbed serenity.

The dried-up moat, luxuriant in brambles, on which the calm misty morn of October revealed a goodly crop of ripened blackberries, seductive to the unsophisticated taste of village boy or maiden, now remained unvisited; its choicest fruit unplucked, untasted. The old fish-pond, that in the bygone time supplied the numerous household with Lenten fare, and where, in later days, many a lusty pike had been caught by the night-lines of Tim Wallace and his poaching fraternity, was now guiltless of intrusion, and the finny tribe increased and multiplied in peaceful security. The old orchard, which yet contained a few antique specimens of apple, pear, and blooming plum-trees, gnarled and riven in their trunks, dismantled by many a wintry storm of half their branchy honors, brought forth their blossoms, produced their ripened fruit, which quietly dropped into the lap of mother earth, and returned to its ample bosom the nourishment they had imbibed. The stately terrace, with its fence of yew, once high, and thick, and trimly kept, now looked forlorn, neglected, and choked with weeds and sedgy grass. The eye might wander round, pained with the universal squalor and ask, "Can this be the once pleasant and beautiful abiding-place of the proud Hilton family? Can it, can it be?"

On winter nights, the old postman, who conveyed the letter-bag to a neighboring market town, and whose road lay within a short distance of the Grange, would, as he passed, whip and spur his broken-kneed, spavined pony into a shuffling, spasmodic gallop, and never relax his speed until he had left the haunted ruin far behind him.

Great, therefore, was the astonishment of the quiet and secluded village of Stedley-cum-Lea when, about a fortnight previously to the opening of my tale, the news was almost simultaneously discussed in the servants' hall of the rectory, and the snug and cosy parlor of our only hotel, the "Chequers," that the old Grange of Hilton was at last inhabited.

A poor family of homeless wanderers had taken shelter in its ruined walls. They were too miserable, too much broken down by poverty and its many attendant ills, to fear the approach of ghost or goblin. The stern realities of life, the want of daily bread, the clamorous cry of famishing children, the pinching cold of bleak December nights, and the failing health of the father, induced these poor and travel-worn wayfarers to tarry and rest awhile, and recruit their exhausted strength by appealing to the charity of the village.

And that charity was not appealed to in vain. Blankets were sent from the rectory: the fat cook walked down herself to see after the sufferer's accommodation, and broth and other nourishing things for the father (who, the cook said, "was worn to an atomy, and far gone in a decline") were also contributed in the good spirit of the Samaritan.

I, also, contributed my humble mite, and intended to walk over and see of what assistance I could be to them. A journey, however, to a distant part of England, to attend the last moments of a dying relative, unhappily prevented me.

It was on the night of my return that I was summoned, after my visit to the jail, to give spiritual consolation to the poor father of this helpless family: for I knew not till then that he was a Catholic. It was his eldest girl who was my guide.

About three o'clock, we came in sight of the ruin. The night, which had been stormy, had now lulled to a profound calm. The moon was high in the heavens, and near the full. A flood of light, clear and beautiful, revealed every object around. The grey ruin stood sharp and well defined against the moonlit sky. On a near approach you could trace every stone, every quaintly-devised ornament, of its Tudor gateway; the exquisitely proportioned entrance arch, with its frowning grotesque heads on its corbels,— its deeply embayed windows, now tenantless of glass, and their stone mullions draperied with ivy, were as well revealed to the eye, as if beheld by the light of day.

A drawbridge, now ruinous and tottering from decay, was passed in safety. I entered the gatehouse, where the sick man had taken up his temporary, but what proved his last, abode. I climbed up with difficulty a spiral staircase, which wound its steep ascent around a slender column. The steps were worn and broken. When my little guide and myself arrived breathless at the top, a woman, whose sharp and haggard features bore the stamp of famine and long-continued hardship, met us with a rushlight; yet there was a gentleness of mien that won your sympathy. She might in her days of youth have been beautiful, but years of suffering had traced indelibly their withering lines on her pale and anxious face.

"Is that you, Aleen?"

"Yes, mother, and here is the priest for father."

"Glory be to God, and thanks to your reverence for coming so far on a winter's night to see my dear, dear husband. Oh, may the heavens be your bed, and glory await you hereafter!"

I interrupted the current of her blessings spoken with the softest Irish accent and a low and gentle tone, to inquire where her husband was, and how he fared.

"He is there, sir," pointing to an open door. "God and his blessed mother help him. He is not long for this sinful, miserable world and a good husband and a kind father he has been to me and mine. O pitying Queen of Heaven, do, do pray for him! pray that God may spare him a little longer to his poor broken-hearted Kathleen."

Tears flowed down her cheeks, and a convulsive sob worked fearfully on the muscles of her thin, white lips. I entered the room, and accustomed as I was to scenes of misery, the one before me surpassed all I had yet witnessed. On a scanty heap of straw, rendered damp by the driving rain and mist which often poured in through the shelterless casement of that large and dreary room, lay a man apparently about eight-and-thirty or forty years of age; his countenance was of Galway stamp, and had been eminently handsome; of Spanish outline, but with true Milesian features. The high, broad forehead told of powerful intellect; the deep corrugations about the brow, the stamp of fierce, yet now subdued passions on the large and eloquently-formed mouth, showed that his was repose like that of a spent volcano, which was slumbering from exhaustion. He lay before me the wreck of a most powerful man : he slept the deep and heavy sleep produced by opium. His broad and fleshless chest heaved with a rapid and gurgling respiration, and his hands were clutching the blankets that partially covered him. The death-sweat gathered fast on his hollow temples; a hectic red dyed his cheekbones with the flush of consumption, and his nostrils were pinched by approaching dissolution. Death, the universal homicide, was indeed making rapid work, and I saw would in a few hours claim his own.

I stood, and gazed around the room: chair or table, or furniture of any kind, there was none. A fire of damp sticks and furze had been enkindled on the ample hearth; but it smouldered away in smoke, and gave neither flame nor warmth. Two children of infant years, and a boy about eight, lay upon a few rags in a corner, wrapped in a sleep that rarely refuses to visit the young, however wretched their lot may be.

I looked again on the bed of approaching death, and requested the wife to awaken her husband, as I wished to impart to him, before it was too late, the last consolations of religion. I felt there was a soul before me, which might yet be saved—that, however steeped in misery, tinged with frailty, aye, even polluted with crime, his past career might be, still, God was infinitely merciful, and might yet extend forgiveness to the sight and tears of a contrite heart. She stooped over his dying form, and with a countenance on which unutterable anguish and affection were mingled, and a voice tremulous with grief, whispered, "Alick, mavourneen! wake, dearest; the priest has come to prepare your soul for heaven."

How beautiful and tender a summons!

The sick man opened his eyes, glazed with the film of death, and wandering, as if from a recent troubled dream.

"Mary, asthore! is it you? I thought I was gone far—far from you and the children."

Their eyes met, and mingled in a long and earnest gaze of mutual love. He turned to me with an inquiring look; when his wife again fondly whispered, "Alick, dear, this is the priest you wished me to send for. Oh! for the love of heaven, make your peace with God; and put your trust, Alick, in your heavenly Father, who will never abandon or forsake you. We must all die Alick, and may the pitying Queen of heaven hear my prayer for you, my dear husband, that we may both, and our poor helpless babes, meet in heaven."

The poor man meekly joined his hands together, cast his dying eyes upwards, as if in earnest entreaty that the prayers of his sorrowing wife might be heard: then motioned her to leave him, while he made his confession. She withdrew with the children to an adjoining room, and I prepared myself for the solemn duty of hearing a death-bed confession. Over this, of course, hangs the ever-impenetrable veil.

Time flew; but I heeded it not. But oh, what a change took place in the dying Christian, as, in the beautiful words of the ritual, I imparted to him the solemn absolution of his sins. His countenance had lost its haggard and restless appearance. A settled calm, peaceful and holy, on its fading lineaments gave me the encouraging hope that he had made his peace with God,—that his sins were indeed forgiven,—that he was about to quit a world which had dealt hardly with him, and to enter those eternal regions of happiness, where "the wicked cease from troubling, and the weary are at rest."

I then called in his weeping wife and children, and bade them kneel down and pray for his departing soul, while I administered the last sacraments of the Church. These he received with fervent, unaffected piety; no murmur, no complaint, escaped his lips, about the hardships of his dying lot. He said, it was good for him thus to suffer. He would be raised on his trembling knees to receive the body of the martyred Lamb of God; and his prayers, after the viaticum, showed that his faith was accompanied with the most fervent love of God,—with a profound resignation to His holy will; and that the consolations of His holy Church had removed from him all the terrors of approaching death. I had attended many, many dying beds; I had seen the infidel dying in his unbelief, wretched and undone; I had seen the hoary profligate stunned and maddened at the fatal summons which, like an unexpected thunder-clap, announced that he must die; I had seen the young man cut off in the budding spring-time of life, who had vainly hoped for many years' indulgence and after-repentance. All these had put off the day of their repentance, and found the futility of their hopes in their dying hour. Apathy or despair is the general, I might say the too-constant, state of those who neglect their preparation for eternity and put it off to their last hour. But the pool dying Alick had long since learned true wisdom in the bitter, though wholesome, school of adversity. He had long since lived as a Christian ought to live, who would die the death of the just. No earthly calamity could shake his confidence in the kind and ever-merciful providence of God. In sickness, cold, and famine, his constant prayer was, "Thy will be done;" and that same all-merciful God, whom he had served faithfully in adversity, did not abandon him in his utmost need. In the solemn moments which intervene between time and eternity, He more than compensated for all His poor servant had so patiently endured,—for the heavy cross which he had so meekly borne. He had loved and practised religion in life, and he found her consolations in death.

When all was concluded, the anointing, the prayers for the dying, the last blessing, and plenary indulgence given,—he beckoned his wife to approach. She arose from her knees, seated herself on the floor beside him, passed her arm tenderly round his neck, and rested his head gently on her bosom. Her right hand was clasped in his; their eyes again met, to take a last, long, and lingering farewell. My little guide now brought her infant sisters and brother, to receive the last legacy which their poor father could bestow. His dying, powerless hand was guided, and placed reverently on their heads. Looking gratefully at me,—turning upon them a wistful gaze,—his lips moving in silent prayer,—he gave one sigh, and his soul was in eternity.

Lowly as he was, which of us might not safely wish that our last end should be like unto his?

The Dying Shirt-Maker

ONE Saturday morning, about a year ago, I was busily employed in preparing my Sunday's sermon. I was aroused from my meditations by a knock at my door.

"Come in."

The door of my study opened, and a young woman entered. She stood trembling for some seconds: her lips quivered, and it was with difficulty that she made her errand known. Her dress was poor—miserably poor—and much worn; but there was an air of neatness about it that bespoke respectable poverty; there was also a quiet propriety of manner about this young person, that showed she had seen better days. Her age might be three or four and twenty. Her countenance was pale, and very thin; but of that mild and gentle cast of features, that intellectual expression, which wins a kindly feeling ere a word be told. She stood before me, her eyes downcast and sobbing.

"What do you want, my child?"

"Oh, sir," she said—when she stopped suddenly, and the heavy tear-drops coursed their way rapidly down her cheeks—"pardon me for troubling you;—but my poor mother is very ill, and confined to her bed,—would you have the kindness to see her?"

"Certainly," I replied. "Where do you live?"

She gave me her direction, which was in one of the many labyrinths of courts that environ the Strand.

"Is your mother a penitent of mine?" I asked.

"Oh, yes, sir; we both belong to you."

I looked at the poor girl more narrowly, and then recollected her. She had long been a weekly communicant; and I had always been much edified by her gentle and fervent piety, and submission to the will of God. During our brief conversation, I was concerned to see this poor child suffering from a most distressing cough. She evidently looked not long for this world; consumption had laid its dread impress on every feature. Yet she thought not of her own sufferings; her sole anxiety was for her mother.

In a short time, I was in F— Court, one of those unhappy localities that swarm with dirty, ragged, noisy little imps, whose sole enjoyment seems to exist in stunning the wretched neighbors with screams and shouts the live-long day. It was with some difficulty that I found out the house I was searching for; a few doors had the numbers scrawled in partly obliterated chalk; but a friendly old Irishwoman, who sold sweet stuff on the corner, soon put me on the right track. I had to ascend three steep and winding flights of stairs before I arrived at my sick penitent's room. It was at a back attic. I entered, and beheld one of those mournful sights of virtuous, uncomplaining poverty, too common, alas! in this metropolis; where the extremes of want and wealth exist, with an impassable gulf between. The room was large; and, though almost entirely denuded of furniture, was scrupulously clean and neat. A truckle-bed, curtainless; two chairs, a small deal table, and a bandbox, seemed its only accessories, save a few pious prints, which were carefully arranged over the low mantel-piece. In the grate, though the weather was bitterly cold, there was an exceeding small fire of coke, which gave little warmth to that large and cheerless room. The daughter who was busily employed at work when I entered, rose, approached her parent in bed, and whispered that I was come. I looked at her work: God help her, she was a shirt-maker!

On her retiring, I approached the bedside of my aged penitent. I looked, and saw a wasted and pallid face, turned towards the pillow, as though to drown the hoarse murmur of the crowded court without. Her eyes were closed; and her wasted hands lay upon the coverlet in the relaxation of debility.

"My dear friend," I said, "you seem very ill. You sent for me from the chapel?"

She unclosed her sunken eyes for a moment, and gazed on me with that earnest expression, which those, who have seen it in the countenance of the dying, can never forget. She tried to speak, but a quick, hollow, and continued cough for a time impeded her utterance. Her face flushed with anxiety, and the perspiration stood thick on her sunken brow as she faintly tried to thank me for coming.

"Thanks—thanks—sir," was all she could utter.

The half of a lemon was on the table by her bedside. I squeezed a few drops of the grateful acid in some water, and held it to her lips; for her hand was too feeble, and trembled too much to hold the glass. This revived her; and, in a low, tremulous tone, she told me how grateful she was to God for affording her the consolations of religion in her last moments.

"I am dying, sir,—dying fast. I shall not live many—many more days. I would gladly, most gladly, and thankfully, quit this weary world; but oh, father! what will become of my poor child when I am gone? She has killed herself with work since I have been ill; and though I have begged and prayed her not to work so hard, she would do it. She would ever say,— 'Mother, I cannot see you starve.' She has gone, I fear, often hungry and famishing to bed, that I might have food, and the shelter of this poor roof over me, and that I might not die in the workhouse."

A gush of irrepressible tears choked her utterance.

"But why, my good friend," said I, as soothingly as I could, "why did you not send for me before? Why did you make known to me your distressing situation?"

"Perhaps, father, it was pride; but I and my child would have rather starved than begged. She, my darling Mary, would never think of it while she could use her needle, and the work, poor as it was, was to be got. But I have not sent for you, sir, for temporal relief, but I do wish most earnestly for the consolations of religion before I die, that I may be prepared to meet my God."*

Her confession was soon made. Oh, how different to that of many unhappy beings whom it is my melancholy duty to attend in their last moments!—a life of sin, with the miserable and insulting mockery of a death-bed repentance—a death-bed confession, unprepared for, with despair, overpowering fear, and most terrible alarm, pressing heavily at the heart, and filling it with unmitigated anguish! But my present duty was one most consolatory. A poor fervent Christian, making a most Christian end. Years of toil and hardship most patiently borne, a past life sanctified by religion, now bore their blessed fruits, as the good works of the dying Christian were about to be garnered into the heavenly heritage of the saints. Her confession was soon made, and most happily ended; for the confession of a good Christian,

---

* This, from long knowledge, I know to be the case with thousands of the industrious classes of London. They will endure the greatest privations, rather than beg, or apply to the parish; and I have often grieved to think how these poor, honest, hard-working creatures are overlooked in the distribution of charitable funds. The clamorous, and, in many cases, unworthy, applicant gets relief again and again—perhaps spends the proceeds in debauchery; while the uncomplaining artisan, who is out of work or sick, or slowly recovering from wasting disease, is left to pine and starve—neglected and overlooked—because a feeling of honorable pride prevents him from assuming the importunate guise of the mendicant. It has frequently happened in my sick visits, that it was only by dint of persevering inquiry that I knew the terrible state of destitution into which an honest tradesman's or mechanic's family was plunged—the father sick, a large family faint and silent from hunger, and almost every article of necessary and daily use pawned for food and medicines,—the landlord clamorous for his rent, and a most dreary prospect for ensuing days. A little timely relief on these occasions has shed the bright sunshine of happiness upon these uncomplaining beings, and elicited grateful thanks, almost too painful to receive. If the immense sums that are annually given in indiscriminate charity were devoted to the necessitous poor, a vast amount of human suffering would be alleviated, and thousands of broken-hearted creatures would be rescued from the crushing miseries that are driving them with headlong speed to the grave.

though tears of heartfelt sorrow may flow most plentifully for past offences, yet the sorrow is not a new sorrow—it is not of to-day, nor of yesterday; it is of ancient date; it has long preceded the hour of death; it has been succeeded by a true and lasting amendment of life—by a return to God, never violated by after permanent transgressions. The great work of confession,—of reconciliation,—of atonement, was commenced long ago, when its sincerity was tested by no immediate fear of death; it was accepted: and its effects were durable. Not like the pretended repentance of those carnal-minded beings, who only repent, or rather pretend to repent, when sickness causes a revulsion of fear of God's judgment upon sinners; but who, when their sickness leaves them, return, as a dog to his vomit, to their former sensual and criminal courses. But peace, heavenly peace, calmed the dying features of this exemplary woman as my hand was raised to give her pardon and absolution of her sins. Her fervent "amen" showed that a devout hope existed in her heart, that her repentance was accepted,—that her sins were indeed forgiven.

And then followed that consolatory rite of our holy Church, the last communion for the dying. Beautiful was the heartfelt welcome the penitent gave our blessed Saviour. She remained silent for a while; and then murmured, in scarcely audible accents, the most loving and tender thanksgiving that ever proceeded from a grateful heart. She was not then tormented with those anxious doubts and fears as to points of faith and ritual observances, that afflict the minds of so many dying Anglicans; but she then enjoyed, in their magnificent fulness, that sweet repose, that heavenly calm, that freedom from all anxiety, which alone is enjoyed by those who worthily receive the last sacraments of the One Holy Catholic Church. No misgivings; but perfect faith, enshrined in hope, and perfected by charity.

And beautiful, too, was the devotion with which she received that venerable and apostolic sacrament, the Last Anointing. As the sacred unction was applied to her several senses; as those tender and mercy-breathing words of the Church were recited, imploring God's forgive- ness for all past frailties, sins, and transgressions, committed by these senses, her lips moved ceaselessly in prayer; her thin, wasted hands were joined reverently in supplication to the Most High, and a light, as it were from heaven, stole over her fading lineaments.

Exhorting her to patience, resignation, and an entire submission to God, I prepared to take my leave. Happily, I then remembered that a good lady had called upon me that morning, and left with me two sovereigns for the poor. These I pressed into her trembling hand when I bade her farewell. A crimson flush mantled on her face and neck, as her eyes followed me she was speechless from gratitude.

On the Monday morning following, the daughter called to let me know how her mother was. All the painful and distressing symptoms of her malady had left her—a not unusual event after receiving extreme unction. I have witnessed again and again the most miraculous alleviations, the entire suspension of pain, and sometimes an immediate convalescence from a deadly disease, when the last anointing has been received and administered with entire faith in its saving and healing virtues. Protestants, especially medical men, attribute this wonderful change in the patient to the exciting effects of a vivid imagination; Catholics look to the express words of St. James: "The prayer of faith shall save the sick man, and the Lord will raise him up." Be this as it may, my poor penitent was evidently better, though still extremely weak. God permitted her to live a little longer, that she might make a more fervent preparation for heaven—might merit a brighter and happier crown hereafter.

Nothing could exceed the gratitude of her daughter. My kind friend's benevolence had been timely bestowed, and on most deserving objects. It appeared they were in arrears for rent; and a harsh landlord had threatened to turn the sick woman and her children into the streets, if the rent were not speedily paid. Thirty shillings of my donation went to stop his clamorous and insulting threats; the remainder had been spent in getting a warm blanket and other little necessaries for the invalid.

I wished to know something of their past history; and, from her simple narrative, interrupted at times by many tears, I gathered the following:—

They had not always been in their present poor and precarious situation. Her mother, Mrs. Faulkner, married in early life a respect- able merchant. Not satisfied with the ordinary gains of commerce, he plunged recklessly into the many speculative schemes that were so rife in the years 1824 and 1825. At length the crash came. He was a ruined man. Bankrupt, he felt himself dishonored; and he never held his head up afterwards. From a state of great affluence, he was at once reduced to extreme poverty. Nothing was saved from the wreck, and had it not been for the compassion of one of the principal creditors, they must have starved. This kind-hearted man, though a severe sufferer from Mr. Faulkner's reckless folly, exerted himself in their behalf, and got Mr. Faulkner a junior clerkship in an insurance office; and, if they were not happy, they were at least contented with their lot.

But, after the first year, Mr. Faulkner's spirits drooped daily. He could not bear to meet his former associates in wealth and speculative enterprise, who, more fortunate than himself, had weathered the storm, and looked with cold disdain on the bankrupt merchant. Every slight he received sank deep and corrodingly into his inmost heart; and at night, in the bosom of his family, when he recounted the daily mortifications he endured, fearful paroxysms of irritability ensued. His wife, and his innocent child Mary, in vain endeavored to soothe his grief. The ban of poverty, the keen sense of disgrace, ate like a consuming fire into his mind, and eventually turned his brain. He became imbecile; was dismissed his employment, and they were again assailed by the horrors of want.

Mrs. Faulkner's health had always been delicate; but she now exerted herself to the utmost to provide bread for her helpless husband and child. She was a good embroideress; and, by dint of working early and late, managed to keep things together. But her sight soon began to fail, caused by excessive weeping; and she was obliged to have recourse to commoner and coarser work for subsistence. Five weary years the patient creature struggled on; tending, with unruffled sweetness of temper, the wayward fancies of her childlike, imbecile husband. At length God took him to Himself; and all her energies were bent upon educating the little Mary, her sole stay and comfort in a world of sin and sorrow. And Mary, when she was twelve years old, began to ply her little fingers busily at the needle, to make herself useful in the house; and in many little ways helped her now declining mother: for grief, anxiety, toil, and privation had sadly reduced her strength; and the infirmities of old age rapidly stole upon her, and diminished her powers of earning bread for them both.

Some few years before my visit, a sad calamity befell them. A dress of rich and costly material, given them to make up, was stolen from their room during their temporary absence at chapel. Their employer disbelieved their pitiful tale, and threatened to prosecute Mrs. Faulkner, unless the price were made good. To avoid the disgrace of a prosecution, and perhaps consequent imprisonment, Mrs. Faulkner was obliged to give up the money she had laid by for her rent, and to sell every disposable article in her possession.

Quarter-day came, but there was no rent forthcoming. A month passed, and then another; an execution was put in—her scanty stock of furniture sold—and Mrs. Faulkner, sick and penniless, with her child, was turned into the streets on a cold November night.

For hours and hours, until the grey dawn, they wandered about, drenched to the skin with a drizzling sleety shower, and resting occasionally on a cold, wet door-stone, until driven off by the surly command of a policeman. About seven o'clock the next morning, when both were fainting from fatigue and exhaustion, a good Samaritan, in the person of a bustling Irish washerwoman, took them to her humble dwelling, and gave them food and shelter until they could turn themselves round. But this, though a much-desired, was not a speedy event. Acute rheumatism struck deep into Mrs. Faulkner's feeble frame; for months she lay helpless on her bed, dependent on the charity of the warm-hearted washerwoman, and the slight, though willing, exertions of her child.

"Musha thin, Mrs. Faulkner, don't be aggravating me with talking the likes of obligation. Sure it's proud and happy I am in doing anything for yees. And see the darling Mary, the purty colleen, how quick she is with the needle, and how handy she is in making every thing tidy for us both. It's my opinion, ma'am, that I've had better luck since yees both come into my little place: so don't say any thing more about it, good, bad, or indifferent, or ye'll offend me mightily." And then the good, honest creature would smoke away vigorously, for an evening pipe of tobacco was the only luxury she allowed herself after her hard day's work was done; and then she would stroke affectionately the little black pusheen that nestled in her lap, purring and blinking its green and half-closed eyes; and then she would take her three cups of well-brewed tea with infinite relish and satisfaction, and look at all times with motherly tenderness on the little shirt-maker, Mary.

Yes, little Mary was now a shirt-maker the horrors of this white-slave system have of late years been freely exposed. Mary felt them not in their most stringent and grinding force, while she and her mother were under the sheltering roof of the kind Irish washerwoman. But, when partially restored to the use of her limbs, Mrs. Faulkner's innate sense of rectitude forbade her to be a burden any longer to such hard-earned hospitality. She took the poor room in which I found her; and mother and daughter struggled on, as they best might, in the wretchedly-paid employment of shirt-making.

By working hard—as hard as willing fingers could work—for twelve, or sometimes fourteen hours a-day, they realized the sum of ten shillings per week. Out of this they had to find needles thread, pins, &c. In winter, their miserable earnings were terribly encroached upon by the additions of fire and candle. Fire they frequently did without, save lighting a little modicum twice a day to boil the kettle for their trashy tea; for tea and a little dry bread were their chief support. Then the rent of their room was three shillings a-week; and then clothes, at rare intervals, had to be purchased—second-hand of course, but which the neat-fingered Mary soon altered and shaped surprisingly. And then an occasional doctor's bill had to be paid, by small weekly instalments; for illness would come, when human nature and energies were thus taxed so severely; so that it was no wonder that hunger, and cold, and privation of every kind, were the frequent inmates of Mrs. Faulkner's lowly home.

But still they were contented and resigned. They struggled on, submissive to the inscrutable designs of Divine Providence, knowing that, if they patiently bore their cross in this life, their future happiness was much more certain. It was their strong and fervent attachment to religion that enabled them to do this; and, in the midst of every trial, of every privation, impelled them to say, with heartfelt sincerity, "Thy will be done." They both, as I before mentioned, received weekly the most holy sacrament; and I am sure that was the chief cause of their heroic patience, and of the blameless sanctity of their lives. And here let me observe, how edifying it is to see the crowds of poor penitents that surround our confessionals on the nights devoted to that holy purpose. A poor man's or poor woman's time is literally their money—their all; yet they freely sacrifice that, wait patiently many of them for hours, until their turn comes to confess; go fasting the following morning to communion, though worn out and exhausted from the week's previous toil; and deny themselves the poor man's luxury, a long rest in bed on the Sabbath morn. Again, I repeat, this is very edifying; and God will assuredly bless them for their piety, and the sacrifices they make in proof of their love of Him, their desire to be reconciled to Him, and their earnest wish to be united to their Divine Saviour in the holy sacrament of the altar. God bless the virtuous, struggling poor; for theirs assuredly is the kingdom of heaven.

But "the lines" of the unfortunate shirt-makers were not destined "to fall in more pleasant places." Competition came: speculating Israelites, by purchasing at exceedingly low rates the refuse of stock, at the forced or fraudulent sales of tradesmen anxious for a temporary advance, soon gained the monopoly of this indispensable garment. They undersold every competitor, and ground down the poor victims who worked for them to the extreme limits of ceaseless toil, and almost unendurable starvation.

Five farthings per shirt was the splendid remuneration received by Mrs. Faulkner and her daughter, when the new Israelite tariff was established! Five farthings of good and lawful coin of the realm for several thousand stitches, and running, and sewing, and hemming, and basting; with needles and thread, and fire and candle-light, also to provide; and the utmost promptitude, and subservience, and gratitude expected. Truly, it was a grand and noble remuneration; and the authors of this ingenious scheme of human extermination deserved a civic crown for their philanthropy!

Thousands, however, of unhappy women are eager claimants for this villanous employment; for villanous it is on the part of the blood-sucking tradesmen who thus grind the poor starving, helpless women of London.*

By working sixteen or eighteen hours a day—and that every day in the week—after deducting expenses in the shape of thread, needles, and candles—from three and sixpence to four, or at the utmost five, shillings remain to the poor overwrought sempstress for her six days' deadly toil. Out of this magnificent sum, rent is to be paid, fuel to be procured, a little food to sustain life, till the welcome grave receives its toil-worn, weary occupant. No wonder that so many of these poor creatures, if young and pretty, or even tolerably good-looking, and especially if not sustained by strong religious principles, go astray and become the most abandoned of their sex.

But what cares the Jew, or the Christian (?) salesman, who finds a ready market for these cheaply wrought shirts, if every seam were stained with the life's blood of its unhappy worker? What sympathy has he for the tears, and groans, and sweat of agony, with which the making of these vile shirts was accompanied? What cares he for the starvation, the premature old age, and the ruin of body and soul to which it impels so many of the unhappy tribe of shirt-makers? I fear that the hunger and thirst after filthy lucre has deadened every manly—not to say Christian—feeling in the hearts of these wholesale butchers. They know that the

---

* "Thirty-three thousand five hundred women are engaged in this one trade, (needlework), of whom twenty-eight thousand five hundred are under twenty years of age; and of these, a large portion living, or attempting to live, on sums varying from 4½d. to 2½d. a day."—See *Times,* Dec. 6, 1849.

market of human flesh is inexhaustible—that fresh victims are crowding daily in the shambles of shirt-making, clamorous for employment, and hunger-driven, too anxious for work, to cavil at whatever remuneration they receive. God help them, poor things, and sustain them in their meek, and patient, and uncomplaining endurance of much and pitiful wrong!

But the rascality does not end in shirt-making. Every kind of garment that man or woman wears—from the dress-coat or Albert wrapper to the leggings or jacket of the navigator—from the braided riding-habit, to the servant-of-all-work's dowdy garniture—all bear the foul impress of cold-blooded, grinding exaction—of pitiless cruelty to the starving artisan. In the rage for a cheap article, humanity is forgotten—is trampled underfoot. But who is chiefly to blame for this? Not so much the seller of the over-cheap article, but the grasping public, who beat down the price, and who will purchase at a rate that no tradesman can fairly or conscientiously compete with. It is the careless, indifferent public, who are chiefly to blame for the misery, the degradation, and the starvation that so plentifully abound in London; and not the time-serving shopkeepers who supply the cheap but ill-made, bad-materialed article—dearest by far in the end.

Reader, whatever you purchase, buy it not at these cheap and unholy marts: the money you give in payment is the price of blood. Far better deal with a respectable tradesman, who asks a fair price for his article, but who sells it to you well made, and of good material; who pays a fair remuneration to his workwomen; who enables them to live, not at death's door, but in decent comfort and respectability; who frees them thereby from the terrible temptations that beset the path of the starved and oftentimes reckless sempstress.

How often in my daily walks to visit the sick, when plunging fearlessly, with the sagacity of long-tried acquaintance, into the intricacies and bewilderments of the netlike courts and alleys about Drury-lane, the Strand, Fleet-street, and Holborn, I have gazed and speculated upon the crowds of meagre, pinched-up featured women, whose years, save those of the grey-headed, no one could guess at; for, though in reality young, the advent of age appeared grim and indurated upon every famine-worn feature. Carking cares had long since destroyed every budding trace of juvenility. It is probable they never looked young. They may have been dragged up the steep hill of life, with all the terrible cares of existence too palpably developed, too rigidly ascendant, to permit the slightest gleam of youthful happiness to irradiate their gloomy path. Mendicancy and starvation are sad initiations to premature decay in the childish age of our London poor. God pity them! But how do these crowds of wizened and poorly-clad women exist? How do they live? What trade or segment of an occupation do they pursue? They must consume a few ounces of food per diem, however coarse that food may be; or at least their involuntary abstinence may not be continued beyond an intervening banyan day. But how is that food procured? from what source is the purchasing coin obtained? Again, where lodge they? how is their nightly resting-place of shelter paid for? It is a mystery. The majority seem so helpless, so miserable, so in inefficient, that no lucifer manufactory would employ them, no cat's-meat establishment tolerate their carving the savory slices for the eager expectants of the feline race. Whence come they? How do they live? How do they die? Perhaps they are shirt-makers; and if so, that would solve the problem. But to return to my tale.

A few months before my visit to this struggling mother and child, Mrs. Faulkner met with an accident in taking home some work. She fell down a steep flight of stairs leading from the warehouse in which the work was cut and distributed to the needlewomen, and received a severe internal injury from which she never eventually recovered. In addition to this, her right arm was broken, and several of her ribs. She was carried to St. Bartholomew's Hospital.

This was a sore trial for poor Mary, who loved her mother most tenderly, and had never been separated from her. In wealth and poverty, they had never been divided. She went daily to the hospital to see her parent, and to whisper loving words of tenderness and endearment by the bedside of the suffering woman—and oh! how precious to the hospital patient are those acts of filial affection! How eagerly looked or—how every moment is counted until the darling, trembling child appears and gladdens those aching eyes of the mother. The world may forget her, but her child—never.

Mary had now to work harder than ever. For the six weeks that her mother was in the hospital, she scarcely had two hours' rest at night. And she told me, with many gushing tears, what a sore trial, what a grievous temptation it was to her, when, as going or returning to the hospital, a hoary miscreant would continually waylay her, and offer her wealth and every luxury to consent to his evil wishes.

"For myself, sir, I would rather have starved, or begged my bread from door to door; but when I thought of my poor sick mother, and what was to become of her when she left the hospital infirm and unable to work, I trembled exceedingly, and was more moved by the temptations that bad man held out to me, than I thought would have been possible. God forgive me if I harbored the temptation for a moment: but oh! sir, it is a sore trial to poor girls in like situations; and I have learnt from my own trials to look with pity on those who have fallen. No one knows, but those who have tried it, how hard it is to bear the hunger day by day; never to have a sufficient meal,—to spend your youth in thankless, ill-paid toil, and no prospect when old age comes on, but the workhouse and the parish grave. I do not wonder that so many go astray; I only wonder that the number of unfortunates is not infinitely greater."

In six weeks', time Mrs. Faulkner was discharged from the hospital as incurable. She was taken home in a cab by her affectionate daughter, who redoubled her attentions, and lavished the rich treasures of her warm, affectionate heart upon the helpless invalid. She was henceforth confined to her bed, and Mary had to work harder than ever.

At the end of a month, she grew rapidly worse, and I was sent for. My first visit I have described.

When I went again, I found Mrs. Faulkner free from pain—her cough had left her, and she complained of nothing but great debility. She was very cheerful, resigned, and full of heavenly hope.

But hard work, privation, want of rest, now told fearfully on the debilitated constitution of her daughter. At times her chest would heave, and a hard and painful cough, again renewed and long continued, would shake her feeble frame; the blood rushed to her brow, and tears of bodily anguish started to her eyes; and with her slight back quivering with the struggle, she would bend forward for a few moments exhausted on the table before her. But brief was the pause of rest she allowed herself. Bread was to be earned for her poor bedridden mother. The tears of pain and exhaustion were soon wiped away from her bloodshot eyes; the sob of hysterical languor was finally repressed; the feeble hands were once more in motion; and the penny-farthing labor of the unfinished shirt was again renewed.

"Mary, my poor child," said I, "you work too hard."

A sorrowful look of entreaty flashed from her tear-fraught eyes; and a deprecatory shake of the head told me how unwelcome was my interference.

Her mother complained of thirst. She bent over the helpless form of her parent, took the cup of tea, already prepared, and held it to her lips. The sufferer drank eagerly, and blessed her child. Mary took the cup from her trembling lips, and looked upon her with a gaze of heartfelt love and commiseration. Her own sufferings, her own rapidly-approaching death, were forgotten, as she gazed upon her kind and bedridden mother. The tears again sprang to her eyes as she stooped down gently and kissed her parent. The muscles of that parent's face slightly quivered, as, with an incredible effort, she threw around the neck of her daughter her wasted arms, and feebly clasped her to her heart.

Sacred embrace of mother and child!—but to one it was an embrace of agony. Slight as it was, it had caused a pang, sharp as a dagger's stab, to the side of her daughter. She turned aside her head, and groaned aloud.

"My child," said the mother, "what ails you?"

"Nothing, mother," she feebly answered; but her quick, labored breath, and the convulsive shivering of her frame gave an unmistakable contradiction to this venial departure from the truth.

"Mary," said the mother "I am sure you are very ill; you confine yourself too much: you are killing yourself, my dear child. Do, my love, get a little fresh air, it will revive you."

Her child answered her not. The bright hectic flush that now mantled upon her cheek, the involuntary shudder, slight, though incapable of being concealed, that ran through her limbs, the closed eyelid, the tremulous movement of the lips, the beadlike sweat that gathered upon her brow, the ashy paleness of her complexion, and the drooping neck that bent under the weight of the fainting head, put to flight even a mother's sanguine hopes. In a few moments the poor girl sank insensible on the bosom of her mother.

* * * * *

The mother soon died, and died most happily. And Mary's turn, too, soon after came to die. Fortunately, I was enabled, by the assistance of a kind friend, to provide sufficiently for her daily wants. A skillful physician, whose name is held in benediction by the poor, saw her almost daily at my request, and did his best to alleviate her now increasing sufferings. She was soon past all work, or the slightest exertion of any kind, and she never touched a penny-farthing shirt again.

She slept but little, for her friendly doctor could not subdue the violence of her cough which was rapidly hurrying her to the grave; but she never murmured, never complained, prayed much, and meditated often on the passion of her Redeemer. This, she said, gave her the greatest support and consolation under all her sufferings.

I need not here relate with what touching fervor this good and dear child received the last sacraments. She received them with angelic piety; and then she longed most ardently, though very submissively, to die and go to God.

One night, the good Irish washerwoman came and told me her darling Mary was dying.

As I entered the room, her large blue eyes were turned earnestly towards me—her thin white hand held out to welcome me; but the pillow beneath her head was spotted with blood. In a paroxysm of coughing she had ruptured a blood-vessel.

"I am dying, father," said the poor girl in a faint tone, "but I shall die happy now."

She looked so sinless, so much a child of God about to wing her flight to her heavenly home, that it was with no ordinary feelings of hope that I read over her the consoling prayers and last benediction for the dying.

She spoke much and movingly of her poor departed mother, and hoped to be soon happy with her in heaven. She appeared exhausted by what she had spoken; her eyelids drooping and closed, and but for the trembling of the bedclothes, they seemed to have closed in death.

The wind of a December night howled without, the rain beat heavily against the casement, and the distant sound of a street brawl were alone heard in that room, as I watched and prayed by the dying-bed of the young shirt-maker. Towards midnight, she opened her eyes once more, gazed on me long and tenderly, and with a look of infinite gratitude—a smile, seraphic in its expression, played upon her lips;—her lips parted, a slight quiver, a faint sigh, and the solemn stillness that ensued told me that all was over:—her gentle spirit had fled to her Father and her God.

The Broken Heart

A CATHOLIC priest has unhappily frequent cases of extreme sorrow and desolation to witness;—not only to witness, but to alleviate, assuage, and console to the best of his power and ability. Why do the Catholic poor love their clergy, reverence them so much, and fly to them in all their troubles, send for them on instant when pain or infirmity has touched their frames, when grief or anguish has laid prostrate their mental energies, when despair at the icy apathy of the world has seized their darkened minds? It is because they trust in his sympathy, in his fatherly love to them, though mean and squalid and ragged, though abiding in haunts of fetid squalor and wretchedness that effectually keep far from them the delicate and sensitive and more favored of their fellow-creatures, but into which they well know the Catholic priest never shrinks from entering. They well know that he cheerfully, aye, most kindly, remains by their loathsome bedside in cholera, in fever, in the other terrible and infectious maladies which afflict poor human nature—remains there for an hour or two, and more if necessary, to hear the long confession, to probe the conscience, and extract a good confession from a poor agonized and departing soul, so that he may make, even at the last awful moment, his peace with God; remains there without showing any outward manifestation of disgust, though his whole frame may be trembling and stricken with the incipient attack of contagious disease:—the poor dying Catholic knows this well—often beseeches his pastor not to come too near his infectious bed for fear he should catch the fever:—but what priest ever shrinks from his duty? Aye, though he knows that by every inspiration he is inhaling the morbid poison of infection, though his life may be the sure sacrifice of his missionary attendance on his sick penitent,—thanks be to the great God of heaven, no instance has yet been proclaimed where he has neglected a dying penitent in this land of most miserable apostasy.

Some twenty years ago a young priest left college and was appointed to a London mission. He had never attended a sick bed, and had a natural terror of infective disorders. His first sick call was to a case of fever. The young priest turned pale, a sickness of the heart stole over him, and he felt an extreme reluctance to attend the penitent—he felt that if he went, he was a dead man. He felt convinced that if he went, he should catch the fever and die. He went in great trouble to his brother-chaplain, told him his fears, and begged him to attend the case, as he felt sick at heart and was terribly afraid. The older priest was inured to such cases, and thought the sooner his young confrère was broken in, the better; joked him about his fears; told him to throw himself boldly and unflinchingly upon the fatherly protection of his good God—said he would go if he wished, but that he had better attend the sick call himself, and go fearless of infection: God would protect him. But God called him to Himself. He went in fear and trembling. He stayed a long time by the bedside of a poor dying Catholic—caught the fever before he left, staggered home, and died at the end of the week. But he died a martyr to charity, and his death was enviable.

In my own case I have been often similarly situated; have been summoned in cases of typhus, gone with fear and an almost certain conviction that I should catch the fever, and most probably die. Six years last January I was called to attend a poor Irishwoman in Brewer's-court, Great Wild-street. She was in the last stage of typhus. The court had a most unhappy name. It had only five houses, was three feet wide—and that blind, and squalid, and miserable court was always overflowed with noxious filth and slush. The stench was intolerable, and for two years previous it had never been free from typhus. It was my first essay in that perilous locality. I went with a heavy and despondent heart. I knew that I must go; there was no flinching from the call of missionary duty. I offered, as fervently as I could, the sacrifice of my life at the shrine of duty, and humbly, resignedly committed my life to God's holy and all merciful keeping. I knew that if I indeed died in the discharge of a call of missionary duty, it was God's holy will, was the best thing that could happen to me, and the surer was the prospect of my eventual happiness in heaven. I would not (though I felt strongly that sinking of the heart at the thought of impending fever) ask any of my brother-chaplains to take the sick call. I went:—but the events, and the after-consequences of that sick call, are burned in letters of fire upon my memory. I attended that poor dying Irishwoman three times that day. Never had I before inhaled so fearful, so pestilential a stench as I endured those three perilous visits. It seemed to percolate throughout my entire frame; but I soon forgot the annoyance in my anxious desire to reconcile this dying woman to her God. Her sufferings were terrible. She had been scorched up with fever—delirious—raving,—but now consciousness was restored; the lull of the tempest, before death shattered the frail bark of life. I knew that ere many hours she would die, and I improved those precious fragments of time to the utmost. She had been the most miserable of the poor, and had suffered much and heavily. She had been so chafed and miserable from privation, from sufferings, from pity and relief too long withheld, that she had become desperate and despairing. She thought that no human heart in this wide world could feel the least pity for her. The fever came, and her sufferings and her despair were at the climax. One of her poor neighbors sent for me when her feeble intellect came round. As I have stated, I went, though with most heavy misgivings as to my own eventual safety and health. I found her completely prostrate in mind and body—the wild and ghastly and staring look—her shrunken brow glowing like burnished copper, her lips black and crusted, her poor wasted, dried-up hands clutching and picking the bedclothes, which were raised momentarily with the rapid heaving of her chest.

"Come to me, all you that labor and are heavy burdened," was the blessed admonition of Christ. I went to this poor dying creature as His representative. Thanks be to God, when I entered this pestilent den, all thoughts or fear of infection left me. I was only anxious to lead that poor dying soul to God, and effect her peace with Him. A few kind, pitying, soothing words, and the effect was marvelous. Her poor eyes, that per- haps for years had not shed a single tear of sorrow for her sins, now rained in passionate weeping for her past offences. And then, as I laid before her, in the intervals of confession, the strong and abiding hopes in the merits of her Redeemer, those tears of sorrow were changed to tears of hope, and love, and much and joyful thankfulness. When I told her to offer up the sacrifice of her life with all its attendant pains, and whatever might be the agonies of her death, in union with the sufferings of her Redeemer, and in penance for her past sins, her resignation was extreme. She was anxious even to suffer more. There was no more restlessness, but perfect and assured peace. There was no longer despair, but assured and Christian hope. She knew well the power of the keys, committed by God to His one true Church; and most reverently and thankfully did she receive the blessed pardon of her sins. I then anointed her, and promised to bring the blessed sacrament within the hour.

And when I went again with that most touching and consoling of all God's sacraments, I found in my patient a marked and blessed change. She was perfectly resigned, repentant, and hopeful. The love of God, though late, through His singular and tender mercy, now held full possession of her departing soul. And, as I leaned over that miserable bed of rags to give her the Holy Viaticum, I felt a chill and sickness at my heart! I knew that I had caught the fever. But the poor thing wished to see me again before she died. I went to see her the same evening. The death-rattle then gave unmistakable notice that her parting moments were at hand. Her dying eyes were fixed upon me as I entered, but how changed their expression! I knelt down by her bedside to hear her last wishes, for she was all but speechless.

"Father," she whispered faintly, "I die so happy—I go now, I hope, thanks be to God and your blessed ministry, to join my husband and my children in heaven. Pray for me, father, when you say Mass;—remember me in the holy sacrifice of the altar."

I held a little crucifix to her dying lips; she kissed it reverently;—a tear fell upon that sacred emblem of her Saviour's sufferings; a slight quiver convulsed her features for an instant; and then all was over.

I returned home, thankful for the happy and consoling death of this poor destitute Irishwoman, but before midnight I became partially delirious. I went to bed wretchedly ill, got up the next morning worse, managed to say Mass, then sent for the doctor, was told that low fever had set in, took again to my bed, and was soon in a state of strong delirium. For weeks I hovered between life and death, lying insensible, and like a burnt-up log upon my bed. Through the goodness of Almighty God, through the prayers of my flock, and the skill and unremitting care of my medical attendants, Dr. Arnott, and Mr. Edward White of Lamb's Conduit street, I at length happily recovered. When my strength was tolerably restored, I returned to my duties. Since then, I have had almost weekly, sometimes daily, similar cases of typhus to attend; sometimes thought I had caught the fever, but, thank God, have hitherto escaped.

But now the cholera is come. This, however, is dangerous only to the patient, not to the medical or clerical attendant. It is most certainly not infectious, so I have not the slightest fear in attending. But terrible are the sufferings of the poor cholera patient; those who witness them will never forget those agonies to their dying day. In the early part of this week, I received an urgent summons to attend a poor woman in one of those numerous and filthy purlieus that branch forth like pestilent arteries from Gray's-Inn lane;* a labyrinth and net-work of courts and alleys

---

* In this court under notice, from twelve to twenty, or even more, of the poor Irish reside in one room. There is rarely any ventilation; no wonder that epidemics consign so many to the grave.

one within the other, into which fresh air never enters, in which fever and other fatal maladies are ever rife and prevalent to this densely-crowded locality I immediately repaired. In a little back closet, about eight feet square, dark, dirty, and miserable, with no fire, no bed, but a piece of sacking, no sheets nor blankets, but an old worn-out coverlet, lay a still beautiful young woman groaning and shrieking with pain. She had gone through the previous distressing stages of this singular malady, and collapse was now supervening. A cupful of miserably cold tea, without either milk or sugar, was the only sustenance she had, and with which she vainly tried to alleviate her thirst, and applied continually to her cold blue lips. I sent a good woman who attended her immediately for a glass of hot brandy and water from the nearest public-house. This warmed and revived her, and mitigated her tortures. I saw a ring on the fourth finger of her left hand. I asked her if she was married:—

"God help me your reverence," said she, "I am. More's the misfortune."

"How so?" I inquired.

"O sir," she replied, "it is a long tale, and a sad tale to tell, and I have not strength to tell it now. My husband is living, but I am separated from him now. Your reverence, do you see these scars on my forehead? Do you see this mark on my throat? My unfortunate husband was given to drink, and when the drink was in him, he cared little what he did; and when he came home tipsy at night, he used to beat me and knock me about most cruelly. Last Easter he came home as usual, roaring mad with the drink, and because I was in bed, and the fire was out.—I had no money to buy coals, and I had gone hungry and fasting to bed—he dragged me out of my bed by the hair of my head; and when I screamed with the pain, he snatched up a knife from the table, and cut me with it in the throat, and three times in the head, and he then kicked me in the back till it was all but broken. I was eleven weeks in the hospital after that, father; and since then, I have been afraid to live with him. I then went into service; but the weakness in my back prevented me doing hard work; and how I have lived since then I scarcely know."

It appeared, from further questioning this unhappy creature, that she had had several children, but that they had all died in their infancy, chiefly of starvation, and from ill-treatment from their drunken father.

"Oh, father," said she, with many a gushing tear, "I could not believed, when I married him, that I should have gone through so much hardship, nor that he would have treated me so cruelly. I did not mind so much what he did to myself, but to the poor children, when they were screaming for food, and with scarcely a rag to cover their poor little limbs; and when he was spending his earnings at the public-house, and then came home swearing, and blaspheming and beating not only me, but the poor babies for crying;—it broke my heart, sir, to see all this, to suffer it day by day, night by night; and then to see the poor little innocents pine away for the want of food; and then to die off one after the other, until my last, little blue-eyed Nelly, was laid, poor innocent, cold and dead, in the parish coffin, I then felt, sir, that I was childless, and my heart shed bitter, scalding tears; and in the midst of my grief, when I lay awake praying to God, and thanking Him that my poor starved children were now with the saints in glory, where they will never feel the hunger any more,—that was the time, your reverence, with the coffin of my dead child in the room, when my husband came in, and cut my throat, and stabbed me in the head, and broke the back of me. He did more than that, sir; he broke my heart. All the bright and beautiful love that I vowed for him on my marriage day, and which no ill-treatment could ever drive from me, then vanished entirely; and I felt a bitter hatred arising in my heart against the father of my dead child, who could not respect the presence of her cold remains, and who then could treat its mother and his wife so cruelly.

"But you forgive him, my dear child, you forgive him from your heart, do you not?"

"Oh, sir, I do indeed forgive him, as I pray God to forgive me my sins against Him. I used to lay awake in the hospital night after night thinking of him—thinking on the early days of my marriage, when we were so comfortable and happy together, and so wishing he would come and see me. But he never did, sir. I sent to him twice, but he never came. When the pain of my wounds lessened, all my old love for him returned, and I shall never die happy until I see him again. It was the drink, sir, that made him a bad husband and father to his children, for he was as good and kind-hearted a boy as ever broke bread before he took to the drink and went to the bad."

And as she told me this touching tale of woman's suffering, of woman's magnificent forgiveness for most cruel outrages and wrongs, her beautiful countenance was lit up with an unmistakable look of entire affection to the degraded brute so unworthy the name of a husband. She prayed most fervently to God for his conversion from his sinful life, that she might see him yet before she died, and might impart to him her entire forgiveness.

I have often, in my other "Sick Calls," narrated the fervent piety with which so many of the sick and dying Catholic poor receive the last sacraments of the Church. This poor young woman's reception of them was all I could desire. I was never more deeply impressed with their sanctifying, comforting, and sustaining influence in preparing a Christian soul for a happy death, and endless felicity beyond the grave.

While I was yet reciting the prayers for the dying, a hasty and heavy step ascended the creaking stairs. A hand was applied stealthily to the room-door—I turned my head—the door slowly opened—a rough, shaggy head, and a countenance soddened and inflamed with drink, was thrust, horror-struck, forwards,— the eyes of that hideous countenance glanced rapidly round the room—fell spell-bound on the bed. The husband,—for it was he,—in that glance of inquiry recognized his dying wife. In an instant he was at her bedside—prostrate, grovelling on the floor, beating his head, his breast, and groaning aloud, and with choking sobs, proclaiming himself her murderer.

"James, darling, don't take on so," she faintly murmured; "look up, dear, and kiss me before I die."

"Oh, Mary asthore, my darling, much injured wife, how can I look up, how can I dare to kiss your pure and innocent lips when your blood is on my hands, when I all but murdered you in my drunken rage."

"Oh, James dear, don't say any more about that; I have long since forgiven you from my inmost heart. I shall die happy now I have seen you once more. Come, darling, kiss your poor Mary before she dies."

The poor, wretched, and all but homicide husband arose from his knees, bent, with many a choking sob, over the form of his dying, loving, and forgiving wife—clasped her with a gush of returning fondness to his heart,—and in that moment of forgiveness and reconciliation she expired.

The Destitute Poor

IN MY frequent visits to the sick, I am continually edified by the meek, uncomplaining patience and entire resignation to the will of the Almighty, with which my poor suffering penitents bear their trying lot. If Shylock, with poetical license exclaimed, in the immortal lines of Shakespeare,

> "Sufferance is the badge of our tribe!"

the poor destitute Catholic of London may in solemn verity proclaim the endurance of the same miserable heritage. It is far different with the Protestant poor; of whatever religious denomination they may be. The numerous Anglicans and dissenting visiting committees seek out zealously and unremittingly their brethren and sisters in affliction. They have ample means placed at their disposal for mitigating the crushing evils of poverty and disease; and to their praise be it spoken, when they confine their ministrations to the members of their own peculiar tenets, they do a vast amount of real practical good. But the desire of proselytism carries them frequently astray. In the squalid courts and filthy lanes, where the poor do congregate, they meet with abundance of Irish

Catholics. They assail the poor natives of Erin with grievous temptations. Coal-tickets, bread-tickets, the white shilling in hand, and education and clothing for their half-naked children, present a climax of temptation to the poor destitute creatures, little inferior to that which was propounded by the great enemy to our first parent in Paradise. "Only let me pray by you—only let me instruct you in the saving truths of the gospel—only send your children to a Protestant school, and we will take care of you—you shall never want." And this unctuous, all-but-irresistible appeal to a poor sick mother, and famishing, ragged children, clamorous for food! But the faith that is in them generally, almost universally, prevails. "Oh, father," they have often told me, "I would rather suffer death sooner than leave my faith; but I felt terribly tempted, when I thought of the children! But, glory be to God, I held out firmly when I thought what a sin it would be to leave the blessed faith of the Church, and take to that which I know to be wrong." Poor things, they know it to be wrong, they feel it to be wrong, but they in general argue poorly upon its hollow pretensions. I lately pounced, in a back garret, upon a sturdy Irish fish-wife, an old penitent, of mine, seated by her chimney-nook, with her short pipe in her mouth, in grave and earnest disputation with a black-coated gentleman from the Anglican Visiting Committee. The old lady had evidently the best of the argument, for when I taxed him with unauthorized intrusion, he assured me that no harm was done; that old Biddy M'Gallaghan defended her religion well, and would not listen to his prayers or exhortations.

But sometimes, nay, too often, sore temptation succeeds. The sick woman is relieved, and that most abundantly; her children are well clothed, sent to a neighboring district school, and her husband is recommended to immediate employment. Poor Paddy, his wife, and seven chubby children, are immediately entered upon the books as converts to the Anglican persuasion. In extreme cases, and at rare intervals, some unfortunate wretches so far trample upon their consciences as to attend the Protestant service, and outrage every feeling of their desolate hearts by an outward conformity to the delusive forms of heresy. But let their

Judas bribe cease, and the mockery of their conversion ceases also. These are happily rare and extreme cases. All praise be to the Irish poor; their faith is miraculous, considering the grievous temptations by which they are surrounded. His faith is the last thing on earth that an Irish Catholic surrender. He may sin to the lowest depth of iniquity, but faith still dimly shines in the drear abyss of his poor sinful heart, and its feeble flicker, by God's ineffable grace, still survives though everything else be lost; and when contrition haply intervenes, that still existent faith moves him to a most glorious repentance and a hearty amendment of life.

Often and often have I grieved, on witnessing the extreme privations of the Catholic poor, at the many cruel snares that beset them; often have I wished that the influential Catholics of London would bestir themselves and take a leaf out of their brother Anglican's book. The brotherhood of St. Vincent of Paul has done much; but how crippled its means, how limited are its resources! The Sisters of Mercy have also done much, in their humble, zealous, noiseless way; and God eternally reward the angelic women for their useful and untiring ministrations among the poor. But the great bulk of the Catholic poor, and especially those who have the least thought of religion, are thrown entirely upon the hands, and extremely limited means of the clergy, who, however willing, have only a mere fraction of charity to divide among them. This I frequently and acutely feel. Last week I attended seven destitute creatures seized with typhus fever; I had to provide cab-hire, and a change of linen to get them to the hospital, besides present comforts of which they were sorely in need. I attended a poor carpenter, who, in his work, had ran a chisel into the lower part of his thumb. He was attacked with that terrible malady, lock-jaw, and for three nights and days was in strong delirium and the most frightful convulsions; every nerve and muscle quivering, and every limb beating the air with violent and involuntary movements. His wife was penniless. I attended a poor bricklayer, who caught cold from over exertion, and who was then delirious, rushed out of bed and ran in his shirt repeatedly into the street, whose poor wife was worn out with daily and nightly watching—who was famishing—and who had spent her only penny for the obtainment of a cup of miserable tea for her husband. I attended a young man in the last stage of consumption, "the only son of his mother, and she was a widow;" poor, desolate, and brokenhearted,—still tenderly devoted to her dying son—and who had spent her last halfpenny in the purchase of a few flowers, which she placed beside his dying head on the pillow. All these I make comparatively happy by a small donation. I attended also last week, in a little court that branches out of Gray's Inn Lane, a poor young woman, who, with her husband, had lately come over from Ireland, driven from the land of their birth by drear starvation. Her husband had vainly applied for work, and he scorned to beg. They had been for some time in extreme want; he had that morning walked far into the country to seek employment in haymaking. I found the poor thing, a mere girl in appearance, in a wretched back room, lying on a few rags upon the floor, furniture there was none, save a little stool. She had suddenly been taken in labor of her first child, and, after the doctor had safely delivered her, I was sent for. I found her very weak and exhausted. I think that she had no sustenance that day, and it was then evening but she thought nothing of herself; her sole care was for her child, and she begged of me to get a little flannel for the poor little innocent that lay nestled and sleeping by her side. Never shall I forget the look of gratitude she gave me when I put three shillings into her trembling hand: one for her baby, and two to get nourishment for herself: it was all I had,— little enough,—and in an ecstasy of gratitude she heaped every blessing and prayer upon my head. She never once complained or alluded to her privations. In my sermon on Sunday night, I mentioned this case as one illustrative of that spirit of patient fortitude existing among the Catholic poor. Several of my kind parishioners have visited her since, and, with great humanity have relieved her necessities.

My dear reader, I have had an object in writing this brief and hurried sketch. It is this:—think sometimes of the sufferings and destitution of your poor brethren and sisters in Christ; and when you go to chapel to pray for the forgiveness of your sins, and to adore the God of all mercy, make your way, before you leave, to the poor-box, and let its silent appeal—"Pray remember the poor," induce you to drop into that custodium whatever you can afford for the sick and destitute poor. Believe me, reader, the prayers of these grateful creatures in your behalf are worth acquiring at so small a sacrifice. By doing this, you will be the happy means of reconciling many souls to God. The poor sinner's heart is melted and subdued when the priest's offering of charity has first unlocked that tabernacle of sorrow, and shows him that charity exists not in name only, but in deed and verity. It is then, and often then only, that the saving voice of religion is listened to and obeyed. Happy for the donors! God speed them.

The Cholera Patient

IT IS the 27th July, 1849,—and it may be a memorable day for the future health of cholera-stricken London. Wise and learned men tell us that when the lightning and the thunder comes, the cholera ceases its ravages, or, at all events, its train of victims is sensibly diminished. I sit down to write this sketch at half-past two, P.M. The sky is darkened, so that I can scarcely see to write. A deluge of hail and rain is pouring heavily down. The paved square before my window is covered with a flood of rapidly flowing water. The crushing thunder is hurling with loud reverberations overhead, and the vivid, and quickly repeated flash of lightning blazes, for an instant, in my room, and then leaves it in dim and sepulchral obscurity. It is a most terrible and awful storm; and yet, God be thanked, most humbly and gratefully, for it. I have now most cheering hopes that the dread pestilence will soon abate; that the half of a million of the wretchedly-lodged, and poverty-stricken poor, will yet be spared the decimating influences of this fell antagonist of life.

At every minute's pause, I am half-blinded by the electric stream of light—half-stunned by the crashing, booming peals of thunder; weak and exhausted from a long attack of the premonitory symptoms of this fearful malady, I have hovered between life and death, in daily expectation—not to say fear—that it would terminate fatally, and, I may truly say in daily preparation for that awful judgment, to which each of my readers most assuredly will be called. I have preached a thousand and a thousand times, to my flock, the imperative necessity of being well prepared for death. God forbid that I should forget my own, and, perhaps, soon approaching end. And it is when the lightnings of heaven are flashing fearfully above us,—when the dread thunders of the Omnipotent are rolling and crashing in the dark and lurid sky,—when the mind of man is subdued, softened, and turned inwards to a true sense of his lowliness and dependence on the protection of the all-good, all-merciful Supreme,—it is, at such a moment, that I would give utterance to a few thoughts, and indite a few reflections upon what I have lately witnessed in my sick calls, among my cholera-stricken penitents.

On Sunday week last, a poor, starved, and gaunt-looking Irishman came to me crying, and begged me to go immediately to his wife who was dying of the cholera. He lived in that focus of disease, Pheasant's court, Gray's Inn Lane.* It was six o'clock in the morning; and I went immediately. The heat at that early hour was most oppressive, and when I entered this foul and squalid court, the faint and mephitic odor that steamed from the densely peopled houses was all but stifling. A crowd of barefooted women at one of the doors,—a hearse-like machine with two bearers from the workhouse, who were cooly smoking their pipes, and seated upon the shafts,—told me, at a glance, in what habitation the poor cholera-stricken creature resided.

"Up stairs, yer reverence,—she won't be taken to the infirmary till she sees the clargy."

---

* Pheasant's court consists only of nine small houses, and yet contains nearly three hundred inhabitants—almost entirely the poorest of the Irish. Two or three large families live in each of the wretched rooms, and sleep huddled together on a few rags of straw upon the boards. The filth and stench of this horrible locality are indescribable, and, for a long time back, it has never been free from typhus and cholera. It sadly wants a visit of inspection from the Sanitary Commissioners.

The feeble old men from the workhouse had been patiently waiting more than an hour, until I was sent for and arrived. The woman's life was sacrificed by the delay.

I groped my way up the dark, slimy, and filthy staircase, until I arrived at the first landing.

The door of the front room was open, and a crowd of heads were peeping through.

"Where is the sick woman?" I asked.

"There, father," said an old crone; "there she is, poor sowl. Glory be to God! I hope we shan't catch the cholera."

I looked in the direction to watch her skinny finger pointed, and beheld, through the dim obscurity, at the end of the passage, a woman doubled up on the floor, and a small tub beside her. She had been turned out of the room to live or die upon the stairs.* As I could not, in such a place, either with convenience or propriety, offer the last consolations of religion to this poor dying woman, I made a strong effort to get her into the back room. Without any ceremony I opened the door, and told the inmates, who were in bed, to get up and leave the room, while I heard the confession of their dying neighbor. They all promptly obeyed. The poor thing was then dragged into the apartment by a powerful young fellow, who turned deadly pale as he performed this charitable action and made his exit as speedily as possible. The poor woman was propped up against the wall, and when I gazed upon her, I felt that I had no time to lose. She was in a state of collapse; the features shrunk and ghastly, and with that terrible blue tint which shows that cholera has done its worst—that death, with hasty strides, is rapidly advancing. The hands were blue, the finger nails black, and the fingers bent and twisted from the previous cramps. She opened her eyes—gazed on me so mournfully, and with faint and husky whisper said something in Irish.

How was I to act?—how was I to hear her confession? I spoke to her; but she knew not one word of English.

---

* Such treatment is, happily, excessively rare among the poor Irish. They are uniformly most kind and devoted in their attention to their sick relatives and friends. In this instance, they were paralyzed with fear.

"I solved the difficulty by calling in an interpreter. A good woman, though exceedingly terrified, at length consented; and with great humanity, for which in my inmost heart I blessed her, sat down beside the dying creature, suffered her languid agonized head to recline gently upon her bosom—wiped the death sweat from her clammy brow—and spoke kindly and encouragingly to her. I heard the word "Sog-garth"* repeatedly uttered, and the dying eyes of the sick woman were upturned reverently to heaven, and a more tranquil expression stole upon her convulsed features. So situated I could not act as I do in ordinary circumstances. I was satisfied with getting my kind interpreter to tell her of the infinite mercy of God, the all-atoning merits of her Saviour, the consoling thought of the all-powerful prayers of Mary, the mother of God, and refuge of the penitent sinner. As my words were slowly translated to her, I was edified with the piety which beamed on her dying countenance, and the ejaculations of assent, which, though low and broken in their tone, were fervent and heartfelt. I got her to make an act of contrition for the sins of her whole past life, and absolved her in the name of the Father, and of the Son, and of the Holy Ghost. She could not receive the adorable Viaticum of the most Holy Sacrament—nature was too far spent for that consoling rite. But I anointed her; I knelt down beside her, and applied the sacred unction, and recited over her those magnificent prayers of the Ritual which accompany the anointing. I then finished my ministry by giving her the last solemn blessing of the church, and a few earnest words of hope and consolation. Her last look at me was wonderfully touching and tranquil. The smile of true Christian hope lit up every feature, and seemed triumphant over the power of death.

She was then taken to the infirmary, but died that morning.

Before the end of the week, her broken-hearted husband was seized with the same malady, and died also. I trust their souls are now with God.

---

* Priest.

The Drunkard's Death[*]

SOME years ago, on a fine summer's evening, when the sun was setting, and, even through the dull atmosphere of London, there was poured a flood of golden light which gave a tinge of mellowness to its brick-built and sombre streets, a sick call awaited me after a fatiguing round of visits. An elderly woman brought it, and was urgent that I should go immediately.

"Oh, sir!" said she, "my neighbor, Mr. Symmons,[†] has stabbed his son. I am afraid the poor young man will die. Pray, sir, do come as soon as you can."

After taking down the address, I promised I would go immediately. Within five minutes, after recommending the unfortunate object of my visit to God, I went forth on my sick call.

---

[*] Although this story is truly appalling, it is retained it here lest modern people forget what life was like for women before a Godly finger in the last several decades pointed out what was hidden in plain sight, that attitudes that contribute to the domination and oppression of women—endemic to many societies and thus also poisoning members of the Church—are SINFUL. —*The Publisher, 2022.*

[†] The names of persons and localities are, of course, altered.

Half-an-hour's smart walking brought me to the neighborhood. It was one I was not much acquainted with, lying on the outskirts of my parish. After several inquiries, and going astray three or four times, I encountered, in a little dingy court, two sweeps, whose separate ages might vary from forty to sixty. They were, with all the playful buoyancy of youth, engaged in a warm contest of battledore and shuttlecock. Interrupting for a moment their scientific recreation, I inquired of them the way to Duke's-court.

"Lor,' sir," said one, "you can't miss it. Take the first to the right, then the third to the left, the second to the right again, and you will be sure to find it."

"My good friend," I replied, "I am going to a sick person, and have already lost my way. If you would show me where the place is, I should feel much obliged."

"Duke's-court," said the elder sweep, with a musing air. "What number?"

"Bless my soul and body, Bill, it must be young Symmons, who had the knife whipped into him by the old 'un."

"Never you mind that, Jack. Least said soonest mended,— that's my maxum. I'll show you directly, sir."

The venerable sweep, who was humpbacked and bandy-legged, trudged manfully before me, whistling a fashionable waltz with no mean skill; and, with this strange escort, I soon reached my destination.

I entered an alley, where cast-off clothes and faded finery wooed the pockets of the poor and economical. A marine store, with a flaring black doll, graced one corner of the entrance; on the other stood, with all its pomp and pride, a resplendent gin-palace of *more* than Corinthian architecture, and whose gaudy show of plate-glass, brass rails, and French-polished mahogany, contrasted strangely and sadly with the squalor around and within. The court was long and narrow. The houses were old, bulging in every direction, and only kept from crushing each other in a deadly embrace of ruin by transverse beams. The cheerful light of the sun never visited the pavement of this wretched locality. The air seemed thick and stagnant, loaded with foul and greasy vapors from two cookshops, a cat's-meat establishment, and a depot for fried fish. The flagstones swarmed with a dirty, unwashed brood of ragged children, many of whom looked prematurely old and careworn. You might look in vain for an innocent, unpolluted face, in that little wretched tribe of humanity. Nurslings lisping with indifference the deadliest oaths and blasphemies; girls, whose tender years might lead you to think them unacquainted with guilt, bandying from one to another the foulest expressions of obscenity. Matrons, too, whose gray hairs told that death would soon number them his own, reeling about in helpless intoxication, hurling curses at each other; and some, finishing their quarrel by a pugilistic encounter.

Two drunken men were staggering towards the half-open door of a low public-house. A young half-dressed woman, with famine stamped on her pale cheek, with a little puny child hanging at her breast, had hold of the arm of one of these tipplers. He might have been her husband: alas! I fear not.

"Come home, dear Jem: don't spend any more money to-night, I've had nothing to eat all day. I'm quite famished. Do, dear, come home."

"Go to h—ll, you—!" said the ruffian, disengaging his arm, and striking the poor girl a heavy blow on the left temple.

She fell to the ground insensible. In an instant, every quarrel in the court was hushed. A crowd of women raised the poor victim of man's drunken brutality, and carried her to an adjacent dwelling. I had no time to stop, as my case was urgent, but hastened to the house pointed out by my friendly sweep.

Three weary flights of stairs I had to climb. The banister and rails were for the most part gone; perhaps burnt for fuel by some of the needy, thrifty lodgers. On reaching the landing on the third floor, I found congregated a little knot of Irish women, who are ever ready to fly to the succor of those who are in affliction. They were confabulating in a loud and eager whisper about the wounded man within. As I toiled my slow and painful way up the broken stairs, I heard the following pithy expressions jerked out with every variety of brogue:

"Musha, then! glory be to the heavenly Father, I hope the poor boy won't die."

"Ah, then, Biddy! it's the fine corpse he'd be making. Mrs. Symmons, though her husband's a Sassenach, is of the rale ould stock: it's a fine wake, may be, she won't have. Glory be to God. Amen."

"Hould yer whisht, Nora avourneen; sure the bouchal isn't dead yet; the moulds and the coffin havn't got the boy. She is a good creatur, and has, to my knowledge, had her heavy crosses to bear. God send her grace to bear them; and may His holy angels make her bed in heaven."

"Whisht! hould your tongues, yer vagabones. Don't you see the clargy coming?" said a little fat woman, with a laughing, merry blue eye, whose brightness no hardship or suffering had ever dimmed.

"Hould yer tongues, every one of yez! here's his blessed reverence!"

Such was my greeting, as my head appeared on the level of the landing-place where these hard-working, good creatures were assembled. Their welcome was most cordial; such as a Catholic priest ever receives from the Irish poor, such as makes him often pour forth to God a grateful prayer that his lot of life is cast among them. True, very many of the Irish poor are chargeable, perhaps justly chargeable, with numerous vices. Look to the temptations by which they are surrounded; the corrupt and profligate localities in which, from poverty, they are condemned to live; the vicious scum of Protestant (say infidel) population with whom, not from choice, but from stern necessity, they are compelled to congregate. Tell me, then, ye cold and calculating moralists, whether the poor Irish, in this great Babylon of iniquity, may not justly plead the excuse of great and sore temptation? Place an individual, of the most refined and delicate sensibility, the most sensitive conscience, the most earnest desire to save his soul,—place him, I say,—compel him to live, with poor and scanty means, in the very heart of one of those many rookeries, which long experience has made me familiar with,— and a twelvemonth's residence will not alter him for the better.

The very atmosphere he breathes is loaded with curses, tainted with immorality, and deadening to every sense of previous piety. Each locality of this kind is an incipient hell. Far from wondering at the vices of the poor Irish, I only wonder at their many and splendid virtues. Their generosity, their charity to each other in distress and affliction, is beyond all praise. I speak from repeated personal experience. I have often seen the poor Irish laborer, after a hard day's toil—(and who works harder than the Irish laborer, when he has work to do? who puts, as he humorously says, "more power to his elbow?"),—I have seen these fine fellows,—aye, thinking nothing of it, deeming it unworthy of a moment's comment, a moment's praise,—sit up two nights successively with a sick and dying countryman, attending to his every wayward wish, with that rare and delicate feeling which nothing but true charity could inculcate or foster.

Is there a Catholic church to be built, no matter in what part of London it may be, the poor Irishman gives his hard-earned shilling with pride and pleasure—he gives it with grace too, so as to make it plain that he is the obliged person, not you who receive it. And he gives it again and again, without grudging, or a long tirade of his poverty. I appeal to my reverend brethren—I ask them, in all their appeals for the erection of chapels, schools, and convents, for any religious or charitable purpose for which the aid of the Catholic public is and has been solicited,—whether, in all their applications, they have not found the poor Irish subscribe most nobly and promptly, considering their scanty means? God bless them—they will have their reward!

And again, the heart of the most cold and indifferent must kindle when he thinks of the faith of the poor Irish, as they are often sarcastically called. How rare it is that an Irish Catholic loses his faith or betrays it by apostasy, notwithstanding the grievous temptations which his frequent poverty makes him familiar with!

How often, when out of work, when sick, when penniless, and no refuge offered but the work-house—when, at those trying moments, that at times almost shake his trust in Divine Providence, who has promised "that the children of the righteous shall never lack bread,"—how often, at these gloomy, despairing moments, when a famishing wife, when starving children are clamorous for that bread without which they die, the tempter comes in the shape of some well-dressed, kind, conciliatory lady or gentleman with a religious tract in one hand, money in the other, promises the most flattering on their lips—work for himself, employment for his wife, clothes for his half-naked, shivering children, schooling for them, and the affectionate solicitude of the whole of the dissenting or evangelical body lavished on him and his *in sempiternum!* All this mighty and inestimable boon to a starving, famishing wretch, if he will only join—become an attendant at their conventicle! And yet, thanks be to God! all praise to the faith, the steadfast faith of the poor Irish, how few, how very few are the exceptions of those who, in their deadly struggle with poverty and affliction, fall under the fascination of the serpent!

Kind reader, excuse—pardon this digression. I have been led into it from that intense love which I feel for the noble and heroic qualities which in many years' missionary experience I have ever found in the poor Irish of London. Again do I fervently say, God bless them! and the warmest prayer of my heart is, that their holy religion may be their guide in life, their solace in death; and that their great patience on earth, their humble, their fervent piety, amidst so many sorrows and trials, may be eternally rewarded with a bright and glorious crown in heaven.

Need I remind any English lady, whether Catholic or Protestant, of the pain they excite, of the solecism in good taste, in good feeling, they exhibit, when, in their advertisements for a servant, they so often add this insulting postscript, "No Irish need apply"?

But to return to my tale.

On my knocking for admission, the door was opened. I beheld a sad sight. On a bed near the window, half reclining, partly supported in his mother's arms, lay the body of a fine and handsome young man. His bust was uncovered, and I rarely beheld one that exhibited greater symmetry or more muscular power. A wide and apparently deep wound below the right breast had been stanched, and the edges brought together by strips of adhesive plaster. He looked, thus recumbent, pale, wounded, apparently dead, like a young gladiator who had fallen in the Roman circus. He had fainted under the probing and dressing of the wound. A surgeon was applying some strong salts of ammonia to his nostrils as I entered. A slight shudder, a twitching of the muscles of the mouth, a low gasping sob, and he recovered.

"Mother," he faintly whispered, "where am I? What has happened?"

"Hush, darling! don't speak; you'll be better soon."

"Keep him quiet, my good woman," said the surgeon. "If he is not kept perfectly quiet, I will not answer for the consequences. He must be removed immediately to the hospital. I am going there now, and will send you a proper conveyance."

I beckoned the surgeon to another part of the room, and asked him in a low tone if he thought there was any danger.

"No immediate danger," he replied; "but it is impossible to say. As far as I have examined, no vital organ has been touched; but inflammatory symptoms may come on, and then"—with a shrug of the shoulders, and an almost imperceptible elevation of the eyebrows—"I am afraid it will be serious."

He bowed and retired.

The young man had been laid down gently and tenderly on the bed by his mother, and a clean sheet placed carefully over him. I took a chair, seated myself by the bedside, and looked around. The room was tolerably large, and though poorly furnished, exceedingly clean and neat in its arrangements. A few pious prints, and a rude representation of the crucifixion in plaster, adorned the low wall over the mantelpiece. I looked at the mother as she sat on the other side of the bed near the window, rocking herself to and fro with an intense but wordless grief. Her lips moved convulsively, as if in prayer for her son. Every now and then she gave him a quick and searching glance of agonized affection, and the big tears coursed each other heavily down her furrowed cheeks. Her appearance was very prepossessing: a kind, and motherly, and intelligent cast of features. If a mother's prayer could prevail with heaven, hers would save her son.

As I gazed and meditated on the scene before me, not venturing to break the silence, and disturb the restless slumber into which the wounded man had fallen, I was startled by a loud groan and a muttered imprecation from the farther corner of the room, now somewhat hidden in shadow from the increasing gloom of the evening. I made out the outline of a very tall and heavily-built man, seated at a table, over which his body was bent; his head and face rested on his hands, which had crushed his hat in the grasp of his muscular fingers. His powerful frame every few seconds shook convulsively, so as to make even the tea-cups on the mantelpiece rattle. His iron-grey hair seemed damp and matted with the agony of repentant sorrow. He was the father who had stabbed his son.

I went up to him, laid my hand upon his arm and whispered to him for the sake of his poor boy to be quiet. With an impatient jerk he threw my hand aside, raised his bloodshot eyes to mine, and hoarsely muttered, "I have murdered him, and by— they will hang me. No matter, it will serve me right."

The poor afflicted mother crept with a noiseless step to his side, threw her arms round his neck, kissed him, and burst into tears.

The powerful homicide wept too; and long did this sorrowing couple mourn together. A faint groan from the bed arrested their grief. The mother was by her son in an instant. The father, whose right hand and sleeve were still stained with blood, reared himself to his full height, and gazed with heavy and drooping eyelids on the bed. He was a man of herculean proportions, and of vast strength. The face was bold in character, and showed the remains of once handsome features; but the bloodshot eye, its glassy appearance, the swollen, blotchy countenance, the puffy, ashen lip, showed the confirmed and habitual drunkard. He stood the very image of despair. His remorse and agony had sobered him; and by the quiver of his lip, the tremulous tears that gathered and fell from his eyes, I could well see that he would have given worlds to have undone that night's calamity.

"Father," said the poor boy faintly, "father come here."

The man staggered to the bedside, for his limbs bent beneath his trembling frame; threw himself on his knees, and hid his face in the bedclothes.

Father," said he, "dear father, don't take on so; it may not be so bad with me. I hope I shall get over it. But they shan't harm you, father, whatever happens. I'll say it was an accident. And I am sure it was, for you never intended, father, to hurt me; it was the drink, father; I'm sure it was."

The man Symmons groaned, and exclaimed, "Oh, that cursed d—d drink, it has made me a murderer!"

"Oh, Willy dear!" said the mother—"*Cushla ma chree*—(pulse of my heart)—God spare you, my child, and may His blessed mother in heaven pray for you!"

I now interposed, prohibiting any further agitating converse, and requested the parents to retire to an adjoining room while I heard the poor wounded lad's confession.

That holy consolation was soon over. He had lately been to his religious duties. He and his parents had been residents only a few weeks in my parish, so I was sent for instead of his former director. Happy for him that he had been thus attentive, thus prepared. I left him fully resigned and obedient to the will of God. He thought not of his own sufferings, but grieved over the anguish his unhappy father must feel; and after his confession had been made, prayed me earnestly to do what I could to soothe his parent—to make him leave off drinking and attend to his religion.

I was exceedingly edified by the great and consolatory influence which religion possessed over the heart and mind of the sufferer.

I found his parents in the next room—the father still on his knees, and wringing his hands in apparently heart-broken anguish. It is a fearful thing at any time to see a strong man weeping; the very effort he makes to subdue his grief causes the tears at length to gush forth with irrepressible violence, even as the pent-up waters dash through the dyke when a breach has been effected. I endeavored to soothe his grief, and turn his thoughts to a better and holier channel. I made him promise solemnly to abandon drink for ever, and to prepare for the speedy confession of his sins; I held out to him the consolatory effects of repentance, and that his sins, though very great, though very calamitous, would of a certainty be forgiven if he repented, confessed them, and amended his life. I left him in a more tranquil frame of mind. We shall see if he redeemed his promise.

On going down stairs, the landlady of the house invited me to enter her room. I was glad to have a few minutes' quiet and rest, as my nerves were somewhat shaken by the appalling scene I had gone through. I asked her how this melancholy affair took place, and what sort of character the father of the wounded lad bore.

"Oh, sir, I am sorry to say he is a sad drunkard, and uses his poor wife most cruelly. He spends, I believe, all his earnings in drink; and He would have starved long ago, if it had not been for that poor boy up stairs: he has been the good son to his poor mother. God bless him and bring him safe out of this trouble. Tonight his father came home drunk as usual, and the first thing he did was to dash the tea-things under the grate. Mrs. Symmons began to cry; and then he damned, and cursed her for crying. And then, because she could not leave off crying, he snatched up a knife from the table, and swore he would have her heart's blood if she did not leave off whimpering. Poor William jumped up to protect his mother: there was a scuffle between them, and, as you have seen, sir, the poor boy got stabbed. He deserves hanging, sir; and if it wasn't for his wife, I hope he may be hanged; and I think I'd go to see it! She's too quiet for him. Oh, if he was my husband, wouldn't I give it him—oh no!"

Here the good woman turned pale with suppressed rage, and her fingers worked convulsively, as if she desired nothing better than to give the unhappy drunkard a manual proof of her virtuous indignation.

The next day I went to see my patient at the hospital. Happily he had passed a good night; the profuse discharge of blood had saved him from feverish or inflammatory symptoms, and the calm and religious tendency of his mind aided wonderfully in promoting his cure. In a week's time he was out of all danger. In a month, he was discharged as convalescent.

He came to me, for about two years, regularly once a month to confession. The father never came at all. His repentance was as short-lived as his sorrow. He continued the same drunken, unfeeling brute; insensible to the sufferings he inflicted; intent only on his sordid self, and the indulgence of his own foul and sensual inclinations. To drink and revel; to be the taproom orator,—for he could speak well and fluently; to herd with the vile and reprobate; and then to wind up his night's debauchery by ill-treating his patient wife, seemed the only purpose for which he toiled and lived.

I met him at intervals: but he ever shunned my approach. His attire, every month, seemed more squalid, though still carefully patched and mended. Whose active needle darned those unsightly rents? Whose tears of meek uncomplaining sorrow fell on that needle, and dimmed its brightness for an instant's space? His wife's! But this stalwart ruffian little recked whose heart was breaking at home, while liquor was to be had to pour down his ever-parched and thirsty throat, until insensibility or partial delirium relieved him from the sense of its burning, destroying influence. No fear of the awful judgments of God ever outwardly seemed to disturb, for an instant's pause, that terrible apathy into which long-continued and increasing excesses had plunged him. Yet, if that heart were analyzed, how fearful, at times, would be the portraiture of its workings! An overwhelming sense of guilt—a most bitter self-accusing thought of ruined hopes, of fair purposes laid waste and desolate—and the deadly fear of future punishment, though not always acutely felt,—are ever the inmates of the drunkard's heart: like scorpion whips, they lacerate that heart; aye, even in this life, inflict on him some of the anticipated woes of that miserable eternity—that dread abyss into which he is madly plunged. Alas for the drunkard! Angels in heaven are weeping—if angelic spirits can sorrow—over this pitiable ruin of an immortal soul; hearts, too, are breaking on earth: hearts, bound to his, like the living chained to the dead. Alas for the drunkard! Is there none, the faintest hope of rescuing him from that most miserable of all slaveries, the thraldom of drink? Listen to the midnight prayer of expectant wife and children! breadless, fireless, awaiting in tearful, shivering expectation; listening for the staggering footsteps of the home-returning drunkard. Their prayer of agony, their cry of heart-rending supplication, has ascended again and again to the throne of the Omnipotent. Whose prayer can equal theirs in intensity of purpose? Whose heart-scalding tears can flow longer, more perseveringly than theirs? But how often are those prayers and tears poured forth apparently in vain!

Pause, reader! before you blame—you execrate. Pray, rather, for yourself, that you be not led into temptation. Pray, rather, that your own innate weakness may be so strengthened by God's grace, that you may escape the rocks, the quick sands, on which the drunkard's bark has struck, and made shipwreck of his happiness. No one knows the extremity of his own frailty until he is tried by great and sore temptation.

Return we, though, to our tragedy, for it is no longer an ordinary tale.

Three years after the commencement of this narrative, the monthly visits of young Symmons to my confessional were all at once discontinued.

After a short time had elapsed, I went to their lodgings to know the reason, as I feared he might be unwell. I found, to my sorrow, that such was the case. He had been always delicate since his wound, and had worked beyond his strength, to procure his mother those comforts so necessary for her now declining health. He had caught a violent cold, which unhappily he neglected. He would continue his employment, which was in an iron foundry, and very laborious. He would not lie by for a single day, though his mother begged him to do so; but, over-anxious for her, he neglected himself. The consequence was, that, at the close of a more than ordinarily hard day's work, he was seized with a violent fit of coughing, ruptured a blood-vessel, and was soon in a dying state.

I attended him daily. He suffered much in this his last illness, but he bore those sufferings with unshaken fortitude, with the most humble and Christian resignation. He died happy and resigned; and I almost envied him as he lay on his bed of death.

His weeping mother gazed sorrowfully on the face of the dead, but his soul, I devoutly hope, was with God. His last prayer was for his unhappy father. Where was that father then? Drunk and insensible in the cell of a station-house.

I cannot dwell on the grief of his afflicted mother. Used as I was to scenes of sorrow, I rarely witnessed mental affliction to equal hers. Her child—her only child—the support of her old age, was taken from her. Her comfort, in her daily and nightly sorrows, was removed. Her protector, the intrepid interposer between her and her husband's frequent brutality, was gone, was buried in the grave. She was alone, happiness seemed to have fled from her for ever.

In a month's time her hair grew white as silver; but religion, the balm of the wounded heart, soothed her sorrows, and gradually calmed down the agonized feelings of her now childless heart, to a devout submission to the will of God. Her only care was so to live, that she might hereafter meet her beloved child in heaven. She communicated weekly; and, though not a penitent of mine, I visited her often, and some charitable ladies of my acquaintance settled on her a small weekly pension,—enough, however, for her humble wants.

One day, having called on her to see how she was (for no professional motive brought me there—indeed, I never heard her confession in my life), I asked her for some particulars of her past life, and how it was her husband fell into such degrading habits. She gave me the following interesting narrative, which, as the reader may suppose, I have not wholly anglicized.

"You may not think it true, sir," said she, with a sad smile, "but when I was a colleen, I was a laughing, fair-haired girl, that loved, to my shame be it spoken, the music of my own footstep at the dance, better than saying my beads, or going to the house of God. I was young and foolish, and, may be, thoughtless; and I fear, much too fond of a smart word, a kind glance of the eye from the roving boys of our barony. No one could tire me down in the dance, and I often won the pattern-cake, to the envy of my neighbors' daughters. I was then as happy and as merry as the little lark that sings its innocent song of joy, and mounts up higher and higher in the blue and purty sky, as if he would sing his way quite up to heaven. But though thoughtless and lighthearted, I was serious sometimes; may be, never so much as when I knelt at Father O'Rourke's knee, and confessed my sins at the station. Lord be merciful to his soul; it was he that gave me the good advice; happy should I have been if I had followed it. But I know not how it was, the next dance, the next wake or fair, put all those good thoughts and resolutions clean out of my head. And it was the old father and mother that were proud of their girleen; and my brothers would have laid down their lives, and died to have saved me from harm. Oh, those were happy, happy days! and I was not thankful enough for them. They came and went, like the beautiful sun that shines on my own Wicklow mountains. The clouds rise from the hills, and his brightness and glory is seen no more. Dark and gloomy has been my after lot: but God's holy will be done. He has comforted me in my many troubles.

"When I was about nineteen, my destined husband, with many other workmen, came to Ireland, to arrange some difficult machinery in the opening of a copper mine, in my neighborhood. Harry was then the finest boy I had ever seen; when I first saw him, I felt I must love him for ever. He was a very clever workman, and much respected by his employers. He was a Catholic too, which I was glad to hear; and I am afraid, on Sundays, at chapel, my eyes used often to stray from my prayer-book, to see how steadily he prayed, and how handsome he looked. Many's the penance I got for that. He was the best hurler, the best wrestler within ten miles round and when he had been with us awhile, none of the boys, though they often tried, could beat him in a jig or a hornpipe. And then he was so good, so steady, so kind-hearted, that no one could help loving him, notwithstanding he was a foreigner. He was nothing more than civil and kind to me, till one day, when walking home alone from a neighbor's house, I met in the little lane a squireen who was a great cockfighter and a bully to the fore. I saw, by the way he walked, he had drank more than was good for him; so I stepped out, and tried to get away as fast as I could. He ran after me, when my foot slipped. I thought I should have fainted. I know not what he said, but he frightened me with his horrid looks. I begged him to let me go; but he would not, till I had promised to become Mrs. Dimsey. I refused; when he swore he would force me to be his wife. He was going to lay hold of me, sir, when I screamed. And oh! how light my heart became, when Harry dashed through the hedge, sprang down the bank, and with one blow of his blackthorn laid the coward insensible on the ground.

"I thought at first he was killed; but he soon rose, shook his fist at Harry, and swore, with terrible oaths, that he would be revenged on us both. Harry laughed at his threats, and asked him if he wanted another taste of his blackthorn. The villain left us, swearing as he went, and I heard the next day that he had gone to Dublin—at least I never saw him again.

"My heart was in such a flutter, that I could hardly thank Harry for the great service he had done me; but I suppose my eyes thanked him more than my words, for before we reached my father's—and we were a long time getting home—I had promised to become his wife if my parents consented.

"At first my father shook his head; he could not bear the idea of my marrying an Englishman and a foreigner. He said none of the family had ever so demeaned themselves. But my mother's looks and tears—for Harry was a great favorite of hers—and I suppose my looks also of sorrowful entreaty, soon won his consent. He could not bear, though, the idea of my leaving him and settling in a strange land. But Harry showed him what high wages he earned in England; that he had saved up two hundred pounds, and that with my hundred, after he had saved more, he would go into business on his own account and make a lady of me.

"So all was agreed to, and ours was the gay and happy wedding. Three neighboring parish priests, besides Father O'Rourke and their young reverences, the curates, were at the head table in the barn. Such lashings of turkeys and geese and rounds of beef were, I think, never seen before. There was port wine for the clergy, and I don't know how many gallons of whiskey for the boys: and maybe the lasses looked rosy, and their eyes grew brighter, when they tasted the hot punch; and didn't they dance the better for it! The barn was cleared, and the piper and the two blind fiddlers kept them at it till daybreak. Oh! sir, never shall I forget the look of affection that Harry gave me when he put the little ring on my finger. It has sustained me in many long and weary years of sorrow. Often in my dreams I have seen him just as he then looked, the kind husband for whose happiness I would have walked the wide world barefoot. And then when I look on him as he now is—so changed! my heart feels as if it were breaking. But it was the drink, sir, that changed him for the bad.

"In six months, we left Ireland. My father and mother, and two of my brothers, would see me to Cork, from whence the ship sailed, that the last objects I might look upon on Irish ground might be those who loved me so well. And when the ship was ready and I could no longer stay, I fell upon my knees—I did not heed the crowd—and begged my parents' blessing. My father—he was a fine old man, sir, took off his hat, joined his hands together, raised his eyes to heaven, as if he saw the Almighty's throne there, and prayed fervently for my happiness. The big tears were in his eyes, too, and when he took me into his arms and kissed me, I felt it was the last parent's kiss I should ever receive—I felt that I should never see him more. And oh! sadly my poor mother looked, sadly she felt when her parting tears fell like rain on my face. Little do we think of a parent's love till we lose them for ever.

"We settled in Birmingham, where my husband got constant employment and very high wages, for he was always inventing some new improvement in machinery, and his masters placed great confidence in him. All things went on well for five years, when my three poor children were at once attacked with the measles; and oh, sir, they all three blessed innocents, died and are now spotless angels in heaven. It was a sore, sore trial; but God was good, and enabled me to bear my cross. I wish I could say my husband bore his patiently. He was a long time frantic with grief, and I then perceived with sorrow that he began to take to drinking for consolation. He was before this a very sober man, no one more so. But now he would come home late at night, and all the worse for what he had taken. It was my sorest trial. But in a year's time my poor William was born, and then Harry was the same kind and sober husband that he was before.

"We went on thus for ten years more. We had our trials, but God enabled us to bear them. And then, sir, a terrible calamity befell us. There was a strike among the workingmen at Birmingham. My husband unhappily joined them; and as he was a good speaker, and had great influence among them, he was chosen one of their delegates. That was a black day to me and mine. We had saved about a thousand pounds, and my husband was thinking about going into business on our own account, and of becoming a master himself in one of the smaller branches of the hardware line, which does not want much capital. But this unhappy strike put an end to all those schemes for our advancement.

"My husband was now out late and early, speaking at every meeting, haranguing the people for what he called their rights, though what those rights were I could never clearly make out. They had as good wages as the masters could afford, considering the times were bad for trade; and when things mended, their wages would mend too; so I used to tell them, when my husband's brother-delegates used to meet at our house, and colleague together to bother the brains of the poor people. And it's not a trifle those delegates ate and drank at our expense; not that I was such a nagur as to begrudge them the bit and the sup; but I was vexed to see our substance wasted upon such thieving villains, who were setting the country in flame, and themselves only profiting by it. I told them a bit of my mind; but they only laughed at me, and asked me what right a woman had to bother herself about politics, of which she knew nothing.

"Sometimes Harry would be absent for three weeks or a month, visiting all the neighboring towns, and making the poor workmen join the strike: many, I am sure, sorely against their will. One day he came home with a tall black-whiskered man, whose name I will not mention; and when my eyes first got sight of him, I turned entirely against him. I felt as if a fairy blast had struck me. And sure, my presentiment was right. He was with my husband night and day, he slept at our house, took his meals with us, and Harry seemed infatuated with him; nothing was too good for him. His look, sir, had the cunning of the fox and the cruelty of a wolf. I cannot bear to think of all this now; but it ended in his persuading my too-confiding husband to intrust him with our thousand pounds. In a short time, he said, he could realize with it a little fortune, and then he and Harry would enter into partnership, and in a few years they would be wealthy men.

"He lent him the money. The next week he had absconded to America. But that is always the way with those scheming villains when they have served their own turn, they will leave you to perish in the ruin their treachery has caused you. But this man was an infidel. He used to sneer at all religion as nothing but cant and superstition. But what can you expect of such men who deny their God, think that their soul perishes with the body, who have no restraint of conscience to guide them, and are only governed by motives of self-interest and the indulgence of their own desires?

"We were thus all at once plunged in poverty. The strike had continued for six months. The funds of the unionists were almost exhausted but a miserable pittance was given, not sufficient to keep soul and body together. One of our masters' wives was very kind to me, or I should have starved. Many were indeed starving. Large bodies of hungry men went round the neighboring villages, and laid violent hands on all the food they met with. The soldiers were called out, and many poor misguided men were wounded and taken to the hospitals. We were in a dreadful state of alarm at home, for my husband would go with them. He became a marked man, and I daily trembled for his life. At length the union, like a snow-drift on a warm spring morning, melted away. Every day hundreds abandoned the strike, and took work again at the new prices, so that it soon came to an end. But Harry could no longer get work: they refused to employ him. They said he was a dangerous character, and I believe it was through pity for me and my boy they would not prosecute him.

"We had to go to London, and there, after a long and anxious search, my husband at length found employment. But he was no longer the same man. His kind, good heart was entirely changed. He seldom or ever went to chapel. Easter came again and again, but he never attended his duties. His Sundays, his evenings, were spent in the public-house, and Monday was generally a black Monday with him. I have knelt to him, sir, and prayed, as I think never yet woman prayed to man, that he would leave off drink, attend to his duties, and spend his evenings in his own little home. But no—the bitter curse, the hard blow—terrible and heart-breaking from a husband's hand—such were the answers I got for my entreaties.

"I will not weary you, sir, by telling much more of our sad downfall. Every year brought its increase of poverty and misery. My parents were happily long since dead. God be merciful to their souls! It would have broken their hearts if they had known what their poor Kathleen had to go through. My husband often lost his work by absenting himself from his employment, but he always got it somewhere else, as he was such a fine workman. But all his earnings were spent on drink; and if I had not worked early and late at washing and needlework, and if poor Willy had not worked hard too, we should have been badly off indeed.

"And then, O heavenly Father! the worst of all my sorrows— the loss of my son! O God! grant me patience that I may never murmur at Thy chastisement! He was the pulse of my heart, the light of my soul, my only earthly comfort, and I used to think he was too good for this world: and God in his mercy has taken him to Himself. Since his death, sir, I have often remained awake at night, expecting my husband's return, and when he has been asleep by my side in the heavy sleep of intoxication, my heart has turned cold as a stone. I felt that the murderer of my boy was sleeping beside me, and then I have prayed to God that all such wicked thoughts might be taken from me, and that I might never forget that, though a sinful man, he was still my husband,—still my dear Harry who had won my first love and been the kind and good husband to me. And now, sir, it is my only wish that my husband may repent. Pray for him. sir, I beseech you; God is infinitely merciful. I know that I have not long to live; and oh! if I could but see him reconciled with his God, I would then lie down in peace and rest my weary head in the grave."

Such was the touching narrative given me by this excellent woman—this humble follower in the footsteps of the crucified Saviour. Her tears flowed frequently during her narrative. Mine certainly did—I could not restrain them. The mean and bare apartment seemed to me to have become the very temple of piety, hallowed by woman's charity, long-suffering, and forgiveness. I left her with unfeigned feelings of admiration, and her tale of woe filled my mind with sadness for many days after.

But the last act of this tragedy is yet to be narrated.

On a bitter cold winter's night, when the wind was howling without, and the snow was falling fast, enveloping London with a white and dreary pall, a violent ringing at the bell arrested my attention as I was reciting the closing office of the day. The housekeeper came to me, and said that a woman was below who wished to see me immediately. I went down, and found Mrs. O'Flannagan, the landlady of the house where Mrs. Symmons resided.

I asked her what was the matter.

"Sir," she said, "poor Mrs. Symmons is dead."

I started with surprise. It was but a few days since I saw her—weak and ailing certainly, but with no immediate prospect of being so soon released from her sufferings. "Dead!" I exclaimed; "what did she die of?"

"She was murdered, sir! Murdered by that brute, her husband. I always thought it would be so; but I am afraid I shan't see the villain hanged; he's near dying himself. I am afraid, your reverence, you cannot do anything for him; but I thought it my duty to let you know."

I made her sit down, and requested an account of this melancholy occurrence. I will give it in her own words, as they were interlarded with many an angry expletive. But the substance is the same, and may be relied on as the truth.

Two nights previous, at a very late hour—indeed it was past one—the miserable Symmons reached home, drunk, as usual. He let himself in with a latch-key and staggered up stairs to bed. Contrary to her usual custom, Mrs. Symmons had sat up for him. She said the next day that she was restless when she went to bed at ten o'clock: that she got up, dressed, and employed herself in needle-work and reading her prayer-book until her husband returned. He was in a terrible state of intoxication. His face bore the marks of severe bruises, and one eye was much swollen and discolored. He had evidently been engaged in an affray, and had been severely beaten. This seemed to have irritated to madness his now brutal disposition. Seeing his wife sitting up for him, unmindful of the lingering suspense of the midnight hour, he staggered up to the table where she was at work, and exclaimed, in the thick, hoarse tones of drunken rage.

"What the h—ll are you sitting up for, wasting the fire and candle? D— me if I'll stand such extravagance. You want, ma'am, to be a spy upon my actions, and to chatter to your neighbors at what hour I choose to return from my friends. Curse you—, I'll have none of this d—d nonsense! so to bed, ma'am; none of your whimpering—; do as I order you, or by—"

"You are hurt Harry, dear," she mildly interposed; "let me bathe that swelling on your forehead; I've got some vinegar in the cupboard."

"Curse you and your vinegar! Do as I tell you, or, by all the devils in hell, I'll murder you!"

What followed is almost too horrible to narrate. Suffice it to say that Mrs. Symmons, overcome by weakness and desolation of heart, sank fainting on a chair. A violent fit of weeping relieved in some measure her overcharged spirit. The demon in human shape who stood over her, with glaring eyes and distended nostrils, and whose every feature bore the stamp of hellish passions, howled at her like a wild beast,—sprang at her,—clutched her with his tremendous gripe,—dashed her pale, wasted form on the boards,—kicked her repeatedly with his iron- shod boots, and finally consummated his infernal brutality by stamping on her chest.

Alas! that I should have to record such horrors. He decamped immediately.

The neighbors in the next room were awakened by the scuffle and uproar; but the well-known violence of Symmons's character deterred them from entering until they had heard him descend the stairs and leave the house, banging the street-door after him. They then, frightened enough, crept into the room, and beheld, to their horror, Mrs. Symmons stretched dead, as it were, on the ground, and blood issuing from her mouth and nostrils.

One of them ran immediately for the nearest surgeon. He came soon and tried to bleed her in the arm, from which blood long refused to flow; but at length a few drops came, then a slender current, and the sufferer was restored to a most miserable consciousness.

The surgeon then examined her wasted skeleton frame. It was one mass of bruises from head to foot, few of which were of a recent date, plainly showing that her ill-treatment, which she had never divulged, was of long standing and frequent occurrence. Three of her ribs were fractured,—her left side and breast frightfully injured.

The surgeon was a man of the greatest humanity: he refrained from asking her useless questions as to how this ferocious attack originated, and soothed her with kind and friendly words, administered a strong opiate, and promised to see her again in a few hours.

At an early hour of that same morning she seemed fast sinking. The grey shadow of death crept imperceptibly but surely, over her collapsing features. A cold and clammy sweat stood in beads on her brow; every thing seemed dim and dark to her filmy vision; but her soul was serene and tranquil,—yea, happy, incredible though it may appear. Her helpless form was paralyzed, except her left hand; with one wasted finger she beckoned the good woman who had sat up with her, and in a faint whisper begged her to send for the priest, as she felt she was going fast. A messenger ran all the way, with the speed that an Irishman puts forth on such an occasion. Her director came immediately. In the Holy Viaticum she received Him who had suffered much and died for her sake. In His sufferings, she then found great solace and sustainment.

She was then anointed, and that sacrament calmed every anxious feeling. Her trust was in the Most High. She had suffered much, very much in life, but she now experienced, in their fullest extent, the glorious consolations of her religion. She had served her God faithfully in life, and in her extremity He did not abandon her, but was at once her friend, her father, and her all-merciful comforter. No murmur, no complaint issued from her dying lips. She prayed fervently for her misguided husband, who was thus the murderer of his wife and only child. She prayed that God would have pity on him when she was taken from him; that repentance might yet visit his heart, that no harm would befall him. She forgave him most earnestly and entirely; said she was sure he did not intend it and that it might have been her fault. And she finally prayed, with her thin wasted hands joined together,—her dying eyes swimming with tears, cast reverently and affectionately upon the crucifix,—that He who died for her upon that sacred emblem of salvation, would in His mercy reunite her to her parents—to her children in heaven.

She died the death of the righteous; and may my last end be like unto hers.

Owing to the mistaken feeling of the neighbors and their respect for the last wishes of Mrs. Symmons, no information was given of her untimely death to the public authorities.

She was placed that same evening in her humble shroud and coffin. They heard nothing of Symmons, and it was thought he was hiding to avoid the penalty of his crime.

The following night, however, about half-past ten, the good woman of the next room, who was sitting up watching the dead, and praying with true Irish Catholic fervor for the repose of the departed soul, was startled in her devotions by hearing a heavy yet cautious footstep ascending the stairs. It was a footstep she well knew, and she shuddered. It was the footstep of the murderer approaching his victim. The footstep paused, as if the guilty homicide was in the act of listening in fear of detection: then it approached, stopped again for a few seconds,—and the old woman's heart was nearly throbless with fear. After a long interval, which appeared almost interminable, she heard the latch of the door stealthily raised; the door opened by straw-breadths, about a foot's space was opened, and a ghastly head was intruded, which wore a spectral look of horror and apprehension. The woman said, afterwards, she was too frightened to speak or to scream. The eyes of this deathlike head wandered round the room—fixed themselves on the old woman in the chair, and with a basilisk glance, gazed her into a trance of terror. Then the head was slowly followed by the gaunt and wasted form of Symmons, who strode like a moving statue into the room; so rigid were his limbs, so heavy and stony-like was his footfall.

"Woman!" said he, in a low and hissing tone, every syllable of which pierced like a dagger's point upon her brain,—"where is my wife?"

The trance of terror was over, the spell was broken. Up rose that weak and aged woman, in the might of innocence, sustained by the wrongs of the dead.

"There, murderer! there is your wife!" said she, pointing to the bed.

In one vast stride he was by the side of the once fair-haired Kathleen—the once happy, loving bride of his youth; but now the cold and insensible monument of his brutality.

"She is dead! she is dead!" he exclaimed; "my God! my God! what have I done?"

He gave one long piercing scream, or rather yell of anguish; those who heard it will not forget it to their dying hour. He threw up his hands to their utmost height,—dashed them,—clenched them together, and while he gazed with distended eyeballs, his lips parted in horror, until all his teeth were visible; a ghastly hue of livid white overspread his visage, then a crimson flush, and he fell heavily on the floor.

The poor woman screamed loudly for assistance,—the neighbors ran in and raised the homicide; no sooner was he raised than, like a galvanized corpse, he lunged out his powerful arms, and by tremendous blows struck down two of his supporters.

His face bore still the blank and drear expression of death. He rushed again to the bedside; and then the same awful flush dyed his features. He gazed—and raved a maniac. He was attacked with delirium tremens.

Their first thought was for his unhappy soul, and they sent for me.

I found him on the bed,—the coffin had been removed,—six strong men were holding him down, hanging with their whole weight on his limbs; but every minute, with a convulsive throe, he heaved and shook them as if they had been so many infants. A door-key was placed between his teeth to prevent him biting his tongue, and he ground it with a crunching noise. The veins on his forehead were distended like a mass of knotted cordage, and his dilated eyeballs rolled and glared with a quick and exceedingly tremulous movement. Oh! what an appalling lesson did this miserable man read his fellow-drunkards, in this his awful hour of retribution!

A surgeon came, and as I could do nothing for him then, I told them to send for me the moment he showed any sign of consciousness, as I thought his reason might return an hour or so before he died. It did. I was sent for the following night.

I went and found him terribly changed. All his flesh seemed dried up, and his skin blackened by the intense and deadly fever he had endured. A strait-waistcoat confined his arms. A dark ring half encircled his eyes, the whites were turned to a dull red, the lips were shriveled and covered with a brown crust, death was on every feature. His gaze on me made me shudder; it was one full of consciousness, but was stamped with despair.

"Symmons," said I, "my poor fellow, your hours are numbered; it would be cruel to deceive you—you will shortly appear before the presence of your Maker: endeavor now, my good friend, to make your peace with him. Do not, for God's sake, think it is too late to repent."

"Repent!" said he, with a ghastly look "there is no repentance for a wretch like me. I shall be damned, damned for all eternity. All last night—all this day, I have seen my murdered wife and son standing by this bed and threatening me. Sometimes, they pointed with their shadowy fingers to the corners of the room, and there I beheld the infernal fiends mocking at me, gibing at me. Sometimes, those damned spirits would crowd round the bed, and bend their hated faces over mine: bound as I was, I could not turn from them; then they would grin at me, spit at me, and with hellish laughter, tell me what a welcome they would give me to-night in hell. No, sir, I have sinned beyond redemption. There is no mercy for me. I have abused every grace of God, and murdered those two angels now in heaven. Sir, the sacraments you would give me would only increase my damnation."

In vain I attempted to combat his despair. He was deaf to all my entreaties. He would not confess,—said it was useless; he could not—would not repent. And then the current of his mind changed. He broke out into a torrent of blasphemy too horrible to be repeated; it was as if seven devils and more possessed his soul. Then, his pitiful appeals to hide him from his wife and child, whose spirits haunted and tormented him. Then, the fragment of a ribald song would he sing; and then join in a rambling chorus with the former associates of his debaucheries. Then he would pour forth the most frantic exclamations of fear and agony; shouting as none but a dying, despairing sinner can shout, that fearful devils were crowding around his bed to carry his soul to hell, the blue and surging flames of which he said he distinctly saw.

But why prolong this scene of horrors? I was appalled; all were stricken with fear. At the midnight hour, when the booming sound of the church clock swept dull and heavy through the air, he gave a long, terrible howl—and expired.

The Merchant's Clerk

CHAPTER I

LONDON embraces in its ample bosom above seventy thousand clerks. The greater part of these useful members of society reside in the suburbs, where lodgings are cheaper than in central and more crowded districts. Their incomes varying from three or four hundred a year to the minimum of fifty pounds and under, enabling them to live either as respectably, or as economically, as their means will allow. The sleek, well-dressed denizen of Camberwell in the south, or Maida Hill towards the north, with his matutinal and vesper ride in the 'buss, differs materially from the poor copying clerk of Lincoln's Inn, who vegetates in a back garret in the classic region of Clare market, or Drury lane. The one has an hebdomada saturnalia on his day of rest; a good sirloin, with accompaniment of pudding, and a glass of genuine old port for a friend: the other is thankful for a broiled steak and potato of his own especial cooking, and a pint of mild porter from "the Black jack,"* and a soothing afternoon whiff of the Virginian weed. But the limits are not confined to these two staple representatives of the clerkly grade. There is the little, pert, prying, sharp, and cockney junior, the slip of a lad of fourteen or fifteen, who rejoices in the splendid stipend of twenty pounds a year, which he faithfully puts into his mother's hands in its welcome quarterly payments, and receives in return her blessing and a shilling to spend. For this juvenile tyro of the pen there are transient gleams of happiness, in an expected rise of salary, a rarely acquired holiday, which is religiously devoted to a day's fishing in the Lea, or a fourpenny trip by steam to the verdant park of Greenwich; or, if funds will allow, a magnificent dash at Gravesend, or its tempting umbrageous neighbor Rosherville Gardens, and its wondrous maze, and archery, and what not.

There is also the banker's clerk of high degree, the merchant's factotum, the lawyer's managing clerk with his two-story villa at Clap- ham; there is the stock-broker's clerk, the India House clerk, and the same industrious book-keeper of wealthy and trading emporiums; there is the Government Office clerk, of high and noble lineage, who is not ashamed to earn his bread by close and daily attendance at his office, and who prefers rising in the world by his own exertions to becoming the Will Wimble to his elder brother, a diner-out at other men's tables, tolerated for his wit, his social accomplishments, and connections, but most rigidly interdicted by shrewd mammas from any matrimonial intentions with the fair daughters of his hospitable entertainers: he is a younger brother.

It is, however, with a poor, broken-down merchant's clerk that we have now to do, to relate his decaying fortunes, and his most Christian-like end.

Towards the end of last summer, and about nine in the evening, I was summoned from the confessional by an urgent sick call. A meek-eyed, gentle-looking little girl, apparently nine years old, had brought it. The poor child looked thin and pinched in

---

* An old established hostler much patronized by the quill-drivers of Lincoln's Inn.

feature, and though exceedingly well-bred in manner, was shabbily dressed, and bore the certain mark of having seen better and happier days. I saw her in the sacristy, whither the beadle had summoned me. Her little pale and delicate face was upturned towards me the moment I entered; her poor thin hands were clasped together, and she trembled violently when she implored me to come immediately and see her father, who, she assured me, was very sick and like to die. She shed no tears; but perhaps the fount of sorrow had been prematurely dried up in that innocent bosom by long-continued and most acute suffering and misfortunes.

I had not far to go. Almost within a stone's throw of the Mission-house stands Clare market, that venerable emporium of butcher's meat, fish stalls, and tripe shops. Centuries may have passed over this ancient settlement of the knights of the cleaver, and yet witnessed no improvement of its squalid appearance. The adjacent slaughter-houses, in a little cross-grained street at the fag-end of the market, cause twice a week a constant flow in its puddles of ensanguined and pestiferous fluid. It is the paradise of filth. On one side of the market, verging to the Strand, runs Clement's Lane; a narrow, crooked, and most foul locality. It was once celebrated for its dissenting chapel in the vaults of which were deposited the decaying remains of thousands of human bodies. This horrible chapel proved, in the end, the hotbed of typhus: public attention, and, for a rare circumstance, public indignation, was aroused; the vaults were cleared, the chapel closed, and the nuisance was abated.

Mr.—, the merchant's clerk, resided in the narrowest and darkest part of Clement's Lane, where lodgings were cheapest, and the tenants more indifferent, from poverty, and senses long blunted by hardships, to the trifling ills of pestilence and impending death. No.—, my destination, was one of the most squalid of those black, decayed, and tottering mansions. In a back room on the second floor, I found the poor object of my search. The room was entirely denuded of furniture save the ragged bedding on the floor, a rickety three-legged stool, and a few cooking utensils of the humblest description. A dim light struggled through the begrimed window, and rested with a sickly lustre on the wasted form of the invalid. His little child, who had summoned me, was administering to him with touching tenderness a glass of wine which I had sent to her for his immediate relief. His hand trembled too much to hold the glass steadily. One little arm of hers was thrown tenderly around his face to support his fainting form—with the other she guided the glass to his lips. He drained with eagerness the generous cordial, and it seemed to put new life into him. His eye caught mine as I stood beside his bed, and with a voice tremulous with emotion, he thanked his Maker that I had come.

There was a quiet gentlemanly tone of bearing about this poor man, in a few words he uttered, that formed a sad contrast to his present misery. I begged his little girl to leave the room for a few minutes while I conversed with her father alone. When she retired, I looked more earnestly on my penitent. In age he might be forty-five or sixty; it was impossible to say which. His hair was dark, with but a light sprinkling of grey, but his face and form were shrunken, attenuated, and his eye dim and lusterless. I stood by the bedside of a man assuredly about to die. The quick heaving of his fleshless chest, those other unmistakable signs which are patent to those who minister daily, like the Catholic missionary, by the dying beds of the poor—all told me I had no time to lose in preparing my poor brother in affliction for his last solemn journey to eternity. But here, blessed be God, was true Christian hope, the true and patient child of God, about to wing his flight to his imperishable home in another and a better world, "where the wicked cease from troubling and the weary are at rest." He needed no exhortations to repentance; his heart was full of it. He needed no repeated entreaties to confess—no terrible announcement of endless tortures for those who die without repentance for their heavy and accumulated offences—no earnest endeavors to move his dying heart to the love of God—to a childlike confidence in his blessed Mother. He was all that I could wish. Each succeeding sacrament that

I administered—Confession—Viaticum—and the holy Anointing—advanced him a stage nearer to an indissoluble union with God. His fervor was admirable and most edifying.

After giving him the last blessing, and a few consolatory words, about the happiness of dying in the peace of God, and the great rewards which the Almighty has laid up in heaven for those who serve him faithfully to the end, I allowed him a few minutes' quiet recollection with his God whom he had then received in the adorable Sacrament. He then thanked me most gratefully for the great consolations I had imparted to him.

"Reverend sir," said he, "accept a poor and dying man's thanks for what you have now so kindly done. I shall soon meet my God face to face. If, through His infinite and all-atoning mercy I am saved—I will remember you in heaven. I quit this world without the shadow of a regret, save one—What will become of my child when I am gone? I have neither friends nor kindred here to look after her—in the workhouse"—here his lips trembled, and he burst into tears—"in the workhouse, she will be probably forced to abandon her faith—that faith that gives me now in my last moments such unutterable consolation. Sir, the thought is very terrible that my little Mary should become an apostate."

I felt to my heart's core this pitiable appeal -- this well-grounded fear. I had seen it verified in too many melancholy instances where Catholic orphans were compelled to attend the Protestant service in poor-houses, were forced to learn the Protestant Catechism, and were so drugged with Protestantism and insidious calumnies against their faith that they gave way, and grew up nominal adherents to the Establishment, but with not a particle of religion in their hearts, and most indifferent members of society.

How many hundreds of our poor orphans in London alone do we lose annually by this shameful oppression, by our sad wants of means, *or perhaps the will,* to counteract this crying and damning evil? God grant that it may be soon remedied. Let each parish farm out its orphan Catholic children to *us.* Our excellent bishop, Dr. Wiseman, is most anxious for this. He has even made the application to one board of guardians. While writing this, his lordship's application is under consideration, and if happily it succeeds, the gate of deliverance from most cruel spiritual bondage is at hand for those bereaved little ones of Christ. *We* must then do *our* duty strenuously by them, or our religion will be in vain. The tinkling cymbal of a perhaps over-vain rejoicing for our numerous converts has been too often in our hands and played upon. We forget the black array against us, of thousands perverted from their faith in the Union bastiles—of tens of thousands who wallow in their iniquities—nominal Catholics who never attend their chapel—who never send their children either there, to the sacraments, or to school—who live and die a scandal to their faith or if, in the last dread agony of expiring nature, they do think of God, it is to die in despair, blaspheming His holy name. Place to the credit side of the account, our converts—to the debtor, our certain annual loss from the above- mentioned details, and see then, dear reader, on which side the balance of loss or gain will be struck. Let us glorify ourselves no more. Let us humble ourselves rather before God, and strain every nerve to promote the emancipation of the orphan, the extension of our schools, and the endowment of new missions where and whenever they are wanted most. We shall then have freed our souls from a most pressing obligation, and for the prompt and generous accomplishment of which, according to our means, or its non-fulfilment, God will one day, perhaps sooner than we expect, call us to a strict and most rigorous account. St. Paul wept and prayed amidst his daily instance for the Church's good. Every Catholic priest's heart must be alike sorely tried, especially if he have a large congregation, and with inadequate means to provide for the spiritual weal of every single member of his flock, and for whose salvation or damnation he is responsible to God. He is then of necessity a mendicant, a suppliant at the door of the rich and the well to do, to glean a scanty subsidiary aid for his chapel, his schools, and his poor. His time is broken in upon by these frequent, personal, or epistolary appeals—that precious time, which if devoted to his missionary duties, might win many and many a soul to God.

Again, we glorify ourselves when we build a splendid temple for the worship of the Most High. We contrast, naturally enough, our present grand orthodox display, our rigid compliance with the Church's beautiful ceremonial, with the former mean and squalid state of the Church's worship, and our former non-observance of the Church's ritual. That a better, and more cheering state of things in this respect exists, no one can deny, and the writer of this "Sick Call" is truly grateful for this fresh manifestation of His divine mercy, this fresh proof of His love for us. But the time was, and that within the recollection of many living and aged Catholics, when it was felony to preach the gospel, when Bishop Talbot was arraigned at a felon's bar for saying Mass; when the saintly Bishop Challoner used to meet a few of his persecuted flock at a public-house in Gate-street, Lincoln's-Inn-Fields, hiring the apartment by the year as a club-room, and on the night of meeting, a sturdy Irishman at the door to admit none but the faithful with the appointed watchword; how the same venerable prelate, thus pitifully bowed down by circumstances, under cruel penal laws, came in colored clothes, and preached a little comfortable exhortation—much like his own series of meditations—and, to save appearances in case the Philistines should break in, with a pint of porter before him, which the good bishop never tasted, but which was drank reverently by one or other of the assemblage as "the Bishop's Beer."

Is it yet forgotten that a sedate and good young lad was chosen to wait on that little audience in the olden times,—yet still fondly pondered upon by the silver-haired octogenarian—and that this excellent and trustworthy youth became especially endeared to Bishop Challoner, was sent by him to school from thence to Douay, where he became a priest; in England, a burning and a shining light, known as Dr. Archer!* the celebrated preacher of Warwick-street chapel for more than a generation of years; and how this little man, but most wonderful preacher, attracted many a Protestant bishop in Mufti to hear him; how he hired, when he first came on the Mission, a large workshop in Long Acre to give moral lectures, and cunningly turned them to lectures on the gospel and a hearty amendment of life! Is it yet forgotten how Mr. Berrington, the controversialist, who died some five-and-twenty years ago, was the first priest in England to leave off colored clothes, and top-boots, and assume the clerical black? Is it yet passed into oblivion that about the year 1780, there was a

---

* Dr. Archer was very short of stature; not, perhaps, more than five feet one, or two. But he had a magnificent head; his brow was wonderfully ample and intellectual; his deep gray eye shone with a flashing brilliancy until his seventieth year and upwards. His voice was silvery in its tone, exquisitely musical in its cadences, and wonderfully distinct in the pulpit. He was justly considered as the father of pulpit oratory in England; and his whole missionary career, for nearly half a century, was earnestly devoted to preaching the Gospel on each returning Sunday. I believe he never missed one, through that extended period. In his later years, when I first had the happiness of hearing him, he was much afflicted by a paralytic affection of the left side; and though, at times, he must have endured great agony, his voice never faltered, but the same flow of musical eloquence was heard from the announcement of the text to the final blessing and amen. Shortly after my conversion, in the year 1822, I saw the venerable little man for the first time out of the pulpit. He was busily employed in looking over some books in front of an old shop in Holborn. I stood behind him for more than five minutes, gazing with reverence upon him whose eloquent sermons had been so mainly instrumental in promoting my conversion. His dress was certainly rather slovenly. A long brown great coat, much the worse for wear, nearly down to his heels; an old broad-brimmed hat; and thick-soled shoes, a world too large for his feet, which had evidently been soled a score of times. Though I took in these discrepancies at a glance, I thought not of them, but of the mind and heart they concealed. He found, some years after, a peaceful happy end, in the family of the late lamented Mr. Booker, in whose house he had resided for more than twenty-five years. Alas! how few of those old Douay priests now survive—the solitary connecting links between the iron rule of persecution and penal laws, and the present religious freedom which we so happily, yet, perhaps, so thoughtlessly enjoy. Dr. Lingard, Mr. Wilds, Mr. Bowland, and one or two others, are the sole venerated remains of that college of heroes and martyred saints. A "Requiescant in pace" for those who are gone, and a fervent "God speed" for those who yet remain to join, we fervently hope and pray, their comrades in heaven.

farm-house at Paddington—situated somewhat where now the Great Western station stands—and that in this lone farm-house, then tenanted by a worthy son of the Church, Mass was said at distant and precarious intervals by a priest who incurred banishment or imprisonment for his life in thus braving the laws of this Protestant country; and that the trembling congregation, as they crept heedfully, and watchfully, through by-ways to the surburban and homely place of worship, were stopped at the threshold by a strongly barred and iron-plated door, in the upper part of which was a little sliding wicket, and through which peeped the janitor, a sturdy believer from Erin, who would not suffer them to enter without the pass-word then current among the faithful? Such things were—and yet, in those persecuting times, how many saints lived and died, and went to heaven?

In, and in the neighborhood of Fitzroy square, at the beginning of the present century, the Catholic country gentry, in their annual emigration to town, used ordinarily to lodge. They formed each spring one united colony of the faithful. They affected no Protestant gayeties, Protestant society, or Protestant marriages, but associated with each other. From the east and the west, from the north and the south of merry England, they were thus congregated together for a brief season of brotherly and sisterly love. How happy they were I have heard from many a gray-haired old friend. How good they were, how charitable they were, how solicitous they were for the solacement and alleviation of the ills, bodily and spiritual of the poor London Catholic folk, I have also heard from the same venerable authorities. Fitzroy square and its vicinity was then called the Holy Land, from the piety, the union, the brotherly and sisterly love of its Catholic sojourners. Would that that same edifying title were linked to the habitat of our London-season Catholic gentry now. Then Catholics clung together the more they were oppressed; it was with a more than Masonic sign then to be introduced into Catholic society as a brother, or a sister Catholic. The ready, true, and affectionate hand was held out to grasp that of a fellow-sufferer for the faith. We had few converts then, but they were wonderfully good, wonderfully humble and obedient to the Church's authority, and placed themselves naturally in their proper rank as neophytes; unassuming, grateful, happy and contented with their change from heresy to truth, and thinking nothing of the sacrifices they had made,—and they were many and terrible in those troublous and persecuting days. The heir-apparent of the Duke of Norfolk could not accept a tidewaiter's place, if so inclined, if so reduced, without damning his soul by apostasy. A Protestant rector or curate could not, after previous preparation, be a Catholic priest, without encountering infinitely more degrading and perilous mortifications and untoward circumstances than at present. But those outward mortifications and untoward circumstances were then wonderfully relieved by Catholic union, by Catholic charity, and by the stringent bond of Catholic brotherly love. Then as before said, Catholics clung together—Catholic tradesmen were dealt with to a man by Catholics—Catholic servants were sure to get a Catholic place—a Catholic convert took his right place and was appreciated accordingly—nothing was too good for him or her, both parties rejoiced exceedingly; and there was then no after backsliding. The convert was then cherished, and assisted according to his utmost need, but he was not lifted off his legs, or thrust into perilous offices unsuited to his green and tender capabilities by over-fond and unwise friends. May the same wisdom, at the present day, guide those who have power and influence, as did our predecessors in the faith of the last century, and the still eventful period before the Emancipation. That it is so, we have a proof in dear Mr. Oakley, Mr. Talbot, Mr. McMullins, and several others of our good convert priests, who, by day and night, have braved death in administering the last consolations of religion to their cholera-stricken penitents. How often hath the death-bell rung for them, and never were they wanting? This is heart cheering; they have braved pestilence: they have labored at most imminent personal risk, as good and true men should labor among the poor; as zealous ministers of Christ, and most sparing of themselves, their own health, comfort, and strength.

And to these edifying and zealous convert missionaries, how cheering the contrast must be—what they now do—what they now merit—between the dead and sterile level of their former

Anglican existence? They may have tried before to absolve according to Ritual, in their Puseyite days of parochial dominion, but with what feelings of doubtful authority? When administering the Anglican sacrament, how alarming the doubt, whether they had the power to consecrate, and whether or no, a lie was perpetrated, when they uttered those awful words in the administration of that same juggling and most doubtful Anglican communion? And when good Presbyter Oakley attends a dying penitent, absolves him, gives him the Viaticum, anoints, him, and imparts to him the last blessing and plenary indulgence, and *knows* he has the power, and the right to do so; and knows, moreover, that the poor dying creature dies in the true faith, with every outward and visible sign of benefiting most materially by those last holy sacraments and priestly ministrations—his reflections, I am sure, must be consolatory in the extreme.

But these, perhaps garrulous reflections—pardonable I hope in an old convert—have drawn me imperceptibly from the path of my narrative of what befell the merchant's clerk, and his young and now orphan child. In the next chapter will be made a full and explicit revelation of his eventful career.

Chapter II

My readers will please recollect that in my last chapter, my dying penitent expressed great concern lest his child should become an apostate after his decease. I was then led into somewhat rambling reflections, to show that those apprehensions were not entirely groundless, and that a vast number of cases annually occur in which orphan Catholic children are really and truly dissevered from their faith in poor-houses, and that by the most shameful and compulsory means. What reply could I make to his earnest, pitiful appeal? I could only give him faint, illusory hopes that such might not be the case with her—I could only tell him that God, in His infinite goodness, would assuredly raise up for her some kind and charitable friend, who would shield her in her innocence, and preserve her in her faith.

"God is good—is infinitely merciful," he faintly murmured, and sank back exhausted on his pillow. I then called in his child—gave some silver to a good woman in the next room, to get food for the little girl, and whatever the sick man might fancy. I then left him, with a promise to come and see him the next morning.

Accordingly I went, and was gratified to find that he had passed a tranquil night, and was also much easier in his mind. The good widow in the next room had sat up all night with him, though she had been slaving all day at washing and charing. She had made him some nice savory beef-tea, with a thin slice of dried toast nicely diced, and which he took with infinite relish. But what above all things cheered him was a promise fervently given by the good widow, Kitty Maloney, that she would adopt the little Mary as her own child whenever it should please God to take him. This promise, earnestly, truthfully made, relieved the dying heart of the father from a cruel load of anxiety.

He pressed my hand warmly and gratefully, when I seated myself by his bedside, and thanked me again and again for the peaceful moments he then enjoyed. He spoke with a most humble reverential confidence in the mercy and acceptance of God, in the prayers and protection of His blessed Mother. I have never yet seen a good Catholic die who had not a singular love and veneration for the Blessed Virgin Mary, and it ever seemed to me that the terrors of approaching death were clean banished away by the prayers of that most holy Virgin Mother of the Redeemer. Other priests, good and holy missionaries, have often told me the same. I stayed with my penitent that morning for some hours. I was charmed with his conversation. He looked upon me as his friend and confided in me as such. He gave me a brief outline of his past life, which had been a very checkered career, and gave me also permission to make it known. "It may do good," he said, "it may be a warning to others." I was deeply interested in his affecting narrative, nearly every word was imprinted on my memory, and I will give it, as much as possible in the very words of the narrator.

"I will not trouble you, reverend sir, with any trifling details of my youthful days—they were passed partly at school, partly at home, and when I had received an excellent education, my father procured for me an engagement with a large mercantile house at Bristol as a junior clerk. I labored hard to make myself perfectly conversant with my duties, and by my diligence and attention soon won the good will of my employers. Every third year I had a rise in my salary, and when I was thirty, I felt justified in marrying, as my circumstances were easy and improving. I led to the altar a most excellent young woman whom I had long known and tenderly loved. She had the same affection for me, and we looked forward, with God's blessing, to many years of comfort and happiness. She was a Catholic, sir, and a most devout one. Her life was a constant edification to me—so innocent—so pure—so good. An unkind, or an uncharitable word she never uttered during the twenty years we lived together and I felt that when she died a saint had gone to heaven. God mercifully grant that I may meet her there—never—never to be parted. She had two children, sir—they were both girls. Our first-born was very beautiful. Poor Agnes!—" his eyes closed for a few minutes and his lips were tremulous; he then continued—"There was a long interval between her birth and that of the dear child who is now with the good widow in the next room. I need not tell you, sir, that both my wife and myself were most anxious to train up our Agnes in the path of virtue. Her mother's excellent example was ever before her to imitate—our unceasing prayers were daily and nightly offered to the throne of grace in her behalf, and she was allowed to associate with none but virtuous companions. She grew up every thing we could wish, and I was never tired of gazing upon her innocent, beautiful countenance, and my heart always felt light and happy when I left the counting-house to spend the evening quietly in the bosom of my own happy and united family.

"When Agnes was fifteen years old, little Mary was born. We all rejoiced that God had given us another pledge of affection, and we named her after our blessed Mother in heaven. Another year passed tranquilly, happily, and then another—and then, our troubles began. Agnes was now seventeen and was grown up to be a very beautiful young woman. I trembled sometimes when I thought how passing fair she was, and what snares and temptations such beauty as hers was exposed to. We all, that is, my wife and Agnes and I, used to go to our duty once a month, but now Agnes used often to seek an excuse for absenting herself from the sacraments. Her little practices of daily devotion were neglected, or, if done at all were performed with negligence and apathy. Her innocent joyous look was now clouded with a secret care. At times she would break out into a wild burst of causeless merriment, and then fall into a fit of passionate weeping. My wife and I endeavored, but in vain, to know what ailed her, but she was either obstinately silent, or pettishly declared there was nothing the matter with her. She grew thinner and paler every day. Her appetite also failed her, and my wife and I used to lie awake at night by the hour together, listening to the moaning noise she made in her sleep, and her muttered accents of sleeping sorrow. She slept in the next room to us, and many a wakeful and anxious night she caused us. I called in the best medical advice, but the doctors said there was no bodily ailment, but something appeared to weigh upon her mind. What that was, neither they nor we could discover.

"Four months of misery were thus spent. The bolt of agony was thus long delayed, but it fell at length with a crushing and most terrible effect. One evening, shortly after my return from the counting-house, and after the tea things were cleared, Agnes put on her bonnet, and said she should like to take a walk. 'Do so, my dear,' said her mother; 'it will do you good—you have moped yourself too much at home of late.' In leaving, she held the room door some time open by her hand, and seemed lost in thought. She then closed the door—went up hurriedly to her mother—knelt down, and besought her blessing and forgiveness—she cried much, and said she had not been so good a girl as she ought, and that she felt as if her heart was breaking. Her poor mother threw her arms around her child—embraced her with infinite tenderness and begged her to tell her grief—'Not now mother—I cannot—another time—say that you forgive me—will pray for me: and you too, my father—will forgive your

Agnes all the anxiety she has caused you—and all I trust will be well.'

"My wife and I mingled our tears with hers—but they were tears of returning happiness. Confidence between our child and her parents seemed now on the point of being restored. Brighter, happier days now seemed in store for us all, and many a silent prayer that evening arose from our hearts to heaven in behalf of our darling child.

"The evening wore away, but Agnes did not return. Nine o'clock, ten o'clock, came, and still she came not; I grew very uneasy, but my wife said she had probably visited one of our old friends and had remained for supper. At length I could bear my suspense and uneasiness no longer: I put on my hat and went in quest of my daughter. I went the round of all my friends and acquaintance, but Agnes had not been seen that night by any of them. I grew dreadfully alarmed, fearing some accident had happened to her, and inquired of every passenger in the street if he had seen my child. No one had seen her. I then hurried home blaming myself for my foolish fears—she might have been there all along, and I had needlessly exposed myself to unnecessary alarms. I got home at midnight—but no Agnes was there. I had scarcely released the knocker from my trembling grasp, when my wife rushed to the door, and in an hysteric burst of anguish, asked if I had found her child. I felt ten years older that minute. My heart seemed like a lump of ice—my brain reeled, and but for my wife falling in a swoon at my feet, I think I should have choked with the mental agony I endured. I forgot for a while my own griefs in attending to my heart-broken wife. I carried her up stairs and laid her gently on her bed. It was long before I and our maid restored her to consciousness, and when it came, a poor, miserable and heart-broken couple we were. We clung to each other in our mutual distress. We had no comfort for each other, but mutual fear for our poor lost child. We dreaded the worst. Her late and increasing trouble of mind was not assuredly without its cause. Some terrible calamity must have happened—either death or dishonor. The latter thought maddened me quite. I was beginning to give vent to a torrent of imprecations, when *she*—the mother of our lost child—put her hand gently, but firmly before my mouth, and though big and scalding tears nearly choked her utterance, said—

"'Do not curse her, my husband, but rather let us pray for her to God. Kneel down with me, my dear, dear husband, and let us pray for her to our Maker. He will not be deaf to our prayers.'

"I did so. For a long time we prayed—ay—even till the gray light of a summer's dawn revealed to each other our pale and grief worn faces.

"We thought not of rest. I was out again and early to seek intelligence of my child. No one had seen her, or heard of her whereabouts. That day passed. The next came and went with the like ill-success. I tried to attend to my employment, but made so many mistakes in the ledgers, that the head-partner kindly told me to go home and not to come back till I was better able to attend to business. A month of horrible torture, suspense, and unceasing inquiry passed away. I advertised in almost every newspaper, offering a large reward for her discovery either alive or dead, for it was supposed by many that she had made away with herself. But no discovery was made. I made many journeys to near and distant towns and villages to glean information, but all to no avail. This terrible anxiety of mind, joined to sleepless nights, at length threw me into a brain fever. I became raving mad. I was strapped down on my bed, with a strait-waistcoat around my arms, to prevent me injuring myself or others. Weeks and weeks I lay in this miserable condition; howling, raving mad. My place in the counting-house was in the mean time filled up; the doctors were hopeless of my recovery. My angel of a wife, was, as I was told afterwards, constantly by my bedside. How she lived was a miracle. She took little sustenance, slept less, and was constantly bathing my burning brow with a cooling lotion. To her ceaseless attentions I owe my recovery. I awoke at length as if from a horrid and lengthened dream. For some time I lay motionless, gazing dreamily through my half-closed eyelids. I heard a faint sigh, and then saw my wife, whom I instantly recognized by the light of the chamber lamp, arising from her knees, in which reverent posture she had been doubtlessly praying for me.

"'Ellen!' I feebly exclaimed. Never shall I forget the look of deep gratitude, love, and thankfulness, that beamed in that dear woman's countenance when she heard the whispered accent of returned consciousness. She bent over me, so gently kissed my now cool brow, said she was so happy—I should soon be quite well; and prayed me not to speak more, but to take a composing draught and try to get to sleep again.

"My mind was too feeble to recollect any of my past misfortunes. There was a dull weight upon my mind, what it was I knew not; but I turned on my other side, and sank into a profound and lengthened slumber. It was the afternoon of the ensuing day before I awoke. The dread reality of my past affliction was then made known to me. Memory again resumed its empire over my brain. Nothing had been heard of my daughter. My recovery was slow. Two months elapsed before I could feebly crawl out of doors to breathe a little fresh air; but I was quickly driven in: the commiserating looks of my neighbors; their blunt inquiries for *her*, were too much for my shattered nerves.

"And now a fresh calamity befell me. My employers had kindly sent repeated messages to inquire after my health, and promised, as soon as I was strong enough to work, to obtain another situation for me. But a panic was then in the mercantile world. Crash after crash followed. The oldest houses became bankrupt, and my late employers among the rest. Their influence was gone. They were ruined men; and I was a ruined, heart-broken, and almost penniless clerk. The heavy expenses of my illness had well nigh drained us of our last shilling, when I felt somewhat myself again and able to return to my duties. But in Bristol I could not remain. I had a constant fever on my spirits as long as I remained there. I sold off my furniture, paid whatever debts I owed, and with about fifty pounds in my pocket, departed with my wife and infant child to London, to seek, by honest industry, to gain bread for them and employment for myself. I wanted something to do, to divert the current of restless grief. Sir, it was religion's voice alone—it was going often to confession, and pouring out my grief to the throne of mercy, that prevented me from being a suicide. I had prided myself so much on Agnes's beauty—I idolized her like a fond and foolish parent—and when she fled from me, the pedestal of fatherly pride, to which I had presumptuously clung, was shivered, and I became shipwrecked in happiness, and well nigh divested of all hope in God's saving and protecting mercies. But religion—my blessed and venerated faith, and its consoling sacraments—wonderfully brought me through all these trials. But for them, I should have become a castaway.

"I reached London by the humblest and cheapest conveyance. My wife, and little Mary, then about two years old, accompanied me. I took lodgings in the heart of the city, that I might be near the mercantile world in my daily search for employment. But I sought for it in vain. In Bristol, as in other large and flourishing communities, London had its full share of commercial distress. The muster roll of bankrupts in the Gazette was frequent and full. Hundreds of clerks like myself were thrown out of employment. They stood a far better chance than an unknown provincial like me in getting employment; and after beating about for ten long weary months I gave it up in despair. My money, though I used the strictest economy, was then almost expended. A little rivulet of good fortune then flowed in. The grocer, of whom I weekly purchased my scanty stock of tea and sugar, had heard of my misfortune, and that I wrote a good hand. He employed me occasionally to make up his books and write on his bills. Though the remuneration was small, it kept us from starvation. He also recommended me to another tradesman, who gave me employment of the same kind from time to time. I was just then beginning to hope for better days, when it pleased God to send me a fresh trial. My dear wife began to sicken in the close and confined atmosphere of the court in which we lived. She had taken in needle-work from one of the large city shops, but the payment was miserably small. She had to work hard sixteen hours a day to earn a shilling, and her eyesight now failed her. She soon took to her bed; and I was sorely tried when, doing my utmost, I could hardly supply her with necessaries sufficient to keep her alive. She still pined and mourned after her daughter Agnes, of whose fate we were still profoundly ignorant.

"I was returning home one night, comparatively happy that I had earned a few shillings and was thinking what little delicacy my poor wife might fancy most, and was calculating how far my funds would go in its purchase, when—oh God!—whom should I meet in the Strand but my daughter Agnes! No longer my innocent, my pure, my beautiful child—but a painted, reckless drunken street-walker. I knew her at once. The ribald laugh was on the lips of her—my child—the obscene oath, the staggering gait, the wanton leer—all, all was before me. I shrieked out 'Agnes! my child!'—and I fell on the pavement as if struck by lightning. On coming to myself, I found I was in a chemist's shop, supported by two laboring men, who had kindly carried me in. Some restoratives brought me round, and to a full sense of the damning scene I had witnessed.

"'Was that young woman any relation of yours, master?' said one of them. 'She took on uncommonly bad when you were down in a faint She screamed and yelled like a bedlamite, and was bundling off to drown herself in double quick time, when she was dragged off by two of her pals.'

"'Do you know where she is gone?'

"'Can't say at all, master,' he replied, 'and I don't think its any use your seeking. She will cut her stick from this beat of hers, you may rest assured.'

"I thanked him—staggered home, and trembled all over when I entered our humble abode.

"'John, dear,' said my poor wife, 'what is the matter?—you look dreadfully ill.'

"I could restrain my grief no longer. I told her all. I have blamed myself for it ever since, for it broke her heart. In a week's time, I had to summon her director to prepare her for death. She died, sir, as a Christian mother should die—full of faith and hope, and most entire forgiveness for her lost and wretched child. Oh, sir, how rapturously I could then have died with her; but my little Mary aroused within me some desire to live, that she might not, like Agnes, become a cast-away."

"I sold some of our last remaining pledges of affection—a brooch with her hair, ay, and even her own wedding ring, to provide a coffin for her loved remains. The undertaker came and concluded his sad office of measuring the body. After his departure I was sitting in the next room, meditating in silence and sorrow on her, the gentle loving wife of my bosom—but who was now dead, cold, and insensible to my oft-repeated words of passionate endearment, when I heard a footstep slowly ascending the stairs—stopping at intervals, and then proceeding, as if uncertain or reluctant to advance. A thrill of horror crept over me—I knew not why—but I remained quite still. The door was then gently, slowly opened—I turned round—I started bolt upright—I felt turned into stone—it was my daughter Agnes who then stood before me!"

Chapter III

"Yes, reverend sir, it was my lost, abandoned daughter Agnes who then stood before me, and within a few yards of her dead mother. Had an apparition from another world appeared before me, I could not have been more surprised—more terrified than I was then. Rage, pity, indignation, compassion—scorn for the polluted thing, mingled with the irrepressible feeling of a still lingering fatherly affection, struck me dumb—perplexed me sorely, and caused a whirl-wind of conflicting thought to rush through my astounded brain. I felt awe-struck at her audacity in thus presenting herself, the destroyer of her mother—the heart-breaker of the widowed father—the living scandal to her innocent little sister Mary—into the dread neighborhood of that dead mother's cold remains, slain, as it were, by her abandonment of her home, and her after most terrible misconduct.

"Merciful God! I yet tremble when I think of the horrible thoughts that struggled for the mastery in my bewildered mind, in that moment of intense rage and surprise, and I gazed upon the guilty wretch—yet my daughter. How was the sacred atmosphere of that desolate, bereaved home, polluted by her presence?—by her, whom ten nights before, I had heard blaspheming in the streets, a sickening source of abhorrence to every virtuous passer-by? I could have cursed her, but words failed my utterance and I felt a choking sensation in my throat. I could have spurned her into the street whence she came; but my feet seemed rooted to the spot—so great was the revulsion of feeling for all the cruel wrongs she had heaped on me and mine. Sharp as a dagger's stab, the thought rankled in my heart, that my Ellen—my adored, departed wife, lay dead in the next room, and slain, as it were, by the cruelly bad conduct of the young, heartless, abandoned being before me.

"Reverend sir,—these terrible—these wicked and inhuman thoughts, rushed with the speed of a hurricane through my distempered brain;—but, blessed be God, they did not linger long there. This maniac, unchristian train of thought did not tarry long—not the tenth part of the time it takes to tell you now. It was a sore temptation; but the Almighty's grace came swiftly to my aid, and to hers also. My look of recognition, so blasting to the poor thing's trembling hopes, appalled her. She sank grovelling upon the floor—a moan, more like the howl of a wounded beast, than the voice from a human being, smote my ear, and wrenched asunder the tough fibres of revenge that were strangling my heart. She crawled to me upon her hands and knees, until she was within a yard of where I stood rigidly fixed in stony astonishment—her head bowed down—gasping—sobbing—and tears raining on the boards, and leaving their wet track behind her as she progressed in her path of humiliation. Was it one of repentance? The thought chilled me—perplexed me—almost maddened me. Would such a leprous thing as the crawling reptile before me repent? God forgive me?—I denied the truth of the proposition as instantly as it was started. A ringing—most horrible curse, was again swelling from my lacerated heart, and, but for my still paralyzing astonishment, would have poured hissing from my lips. Still she crept nearer. Inch by inch she now crawled and moaned; but her head was still bowed down—her tears still watered the floor. Briny—scalding—plentiful as they were, they affected me not in the remotest degree. I spoke not a word. I retreated by strawbreadths until my back touched the wall. Still the dread apparition of the matricide pursued me—crawling, weeping, and moaning. I could have screamed,—so great was my soul's agony—my abhorrence; but my tongue clove to my jaws.

"The spell was dissolved, and in an instant, by the single word of 'Father.' That word, which I never expected to hear again from *her*, at once melted and subdued my heart. I stooped down—raised her up—a mist overspread my vision—I felt her fall into my open arms, although I could not for some minutes discern her, nor rightly comprehend what had taken place.

"At length a sweet and holy pulsation glided through my frame—I kissed again and again the drooping brow of my child—and it was then I perceived she had swooned. Without relaxing my close embrace of the child of the dead mother within, I sprinkled her corpse-like face with cold water until she revived.

"'My father—my father!' she faintly, mournfully uttered.

"'My child—my Agnes,' I replied; 'do you repent? will you return again to your God?'

"'I will!—I will, father, if He spares me—if He gives me grace to do so.'

"'Agnes, I forgive you!' was my enraptured answer. 'Come again to my bosom; let the past be forgotten.'

"She remained weeping a long time within my sheltering arms. All my long-cherished resentments vanished into the thin air. The thought of Christ's mercy and forgiveness to Mary Magdalen completed the triumph of forgiveness over resentment, in my now softened heart. Why should I spurn this poor weeping repentant creature—my child—my repentant one—and now most infinitely dear to me? I declare to you, reverend sir, and that most solemnly, I felt for her more tenderness and affection than I had ever done before, even in the days of her innocence. My heart yearned to her, as did that of the good father mentioned by the Redeemer, in his beautiful parable of the Prodigal Son.

"'Look up, my child, and see whether your poor father does not now most heartily forgive you.'

"She raised her head a little—let it fall irresolutely upon my breast—raised it again, and looked me timidly, tearfully in the face. Oh! merciful God! what a change there was in that poor wasted face! No hideous paint, but a deadly pallor—no meretricious brightness flashing in her eye—it was dim and sunken with the tears she shed for her manifold transgressions. No words of guilty meaning then issued from her pale lips—they were closed—sealed with the true impress of humble repentance for the past. Scarce one vestige of her former beauty remained—so thin—so haggard—so woe-begone and miserable was her look, that my tears flowed fast as her own. And yet they were tears of heavenly joy mingled with much grief. I had recovered my child who was lost, and who was found—who was dead in sin, but who, I devoutly hoped, by the magnificent aids of our holy faith—by God's infinite and all-atoning mercy—would soon be restored to spiritual life.

"And, sir, see the immediate reward for this denial of my passion—this crushing of my resentment—this, through the all powerful grace of God, forgiveness of my erring daughter. My wife's death—my past griefs—my past and present poverty—my future probable destitution—were entirely forgotten, as I folded again and again in my arms my now repentant child, and whispered to her sweet hopes of her own forgiveness and reconciliation to her offended yet all-merciful God.

"She laid her cheek close to mine, and, in a gentle whisper, asked—'Where is mother?'

"I felt stung as if by an adder. Alas! I was again plunged in misery by that brief question. I writhed, groaned, threw from me the wasted, helpless form of my daughter as the devil rose within me, and felt as if I could have trampled her out of existence. But God's grace again came most immediate to my aid: I remembered those words of the Psalmist, 'I will have mercy and not sacrifice,' and—thanks be to God—I sacrificed my resentment, and for ever.

"I again raised my convulsed and agitated child—I soothed her—calmed her—prepared her—Heaven knows how, for I know not—but words were given me in that dread moment to prepare her for the knowledge of the death; and the sight of her dead mother.

"After a long fit of weeping, which, with its true sorrow, turned her heart, I trust, more and more to God, I led her into the chamber of death.

"I cannot reveal to you now, reverend sir, what passed within, between my child and myself, as we knelt and prayed, and wept beside the bed of death. Hours may have passed away in that most sad, yet purifying communion—the prayer for the dear and saintly departed—the prayer for the forgiveness of our own short-comings in affliction, in duty to her whose spirit had fled, and whose cold and mute effigy lay now stretched before us in its garniture of the grave. God assuredly heard the prayers of my child—I trust He did mine. We arose from our knees. 'Father'—said the poor child—'Father, may I kiss my own darling mother?'

"'Do so, my child,' I answered.

"'And at the instant of my concurrence she threw herself upon the corpse, and with pitiable, heart-rending terms of self-abasement, of self-accusation, she embraced the lifeless form of her departed mother, and bewailed her own black ingratitude to her, her own fall from innocence, and her neglect of the virtuous example held out by her, whose dead and cold arms she encircled with her own.

"I withdrew her gently, yet with difficulty from the corpse. She, poor thing, perhaps, would have willingly died in that embrace—the living with the dead—like me, in the first moments of my bereavement—but she had got her peace to make with Heaven. She arose and followed me into the next room.

"We sat down. I drew my chair close to hers—put my arm around her trembling form—and in that sheltering embrace begged her to tell me all: I was her father—no matter what she had done—I had forgiven her all, and that most heartily and sincerely.

"'Father,' said she, 'I will tell you all—I will conceal nothing that led to my fall, or its miserable consequences—for I feel that my days, ay, even my hours are numbered, and that I shall not long survive my angelic mother.

"'Father, you remember the fatal night I left you: I was almost determined to tell you all then—to have thrown myself upon your mercy and forgiveness. Oh! if I had—how much after-guilt and misery should I have spared! Father—three months before then I was ruined—ruined, body and soul. My seducer is now dead—it does not become such an abandoned wretch as myself to heap curses upon his memory, and as I hope to be forgiven myself, so do I now forgive him. Father, believe me my fall was not premeditated. He was a young gentleman of a good family in the neighborhood—he promised me marriage—I believed in his oaths and protestations, and in a moment of weakness and infatuation I was undone. Father, I never dared to look you in the face after that occured. But my crimes did not end here. I went to confession; but an overpowering sense of fear and shame prevented me from confessing my great sin. I shudder now to think of what I then felt when my venerable director pronounced the words of absolution, and I knowing I was perpetrating a sacrilege. From that day, and for months after, I endured a mental agony that no tongue can describe. My soul seemed saturated with sin—my heart corroded with remorse. He who had wronged me had gone to London. He wrote to me repeatedly begging me to come to him, and he would make me his wife. I believed him, Oh that I had confided in you! The night I left you, my mother's kiss seemed to blister my forehead—I felt so unworthy of her kindness and affection. I had then wickedly made up my mind to go to him at whatever risk. A friend of his was waiting for me with a gig about two miles out of town, in a by-lane. He brought a cloak and a few articles of dress which completely disguised me. He drove me across the country about ten miles, when he put me into the mail which was then passing. I arrived in town; was welcomed by my betrayer—was introduced by him to his landlady as his wife, and, by his cruel sophistry, he prevailed upon me to live with him as such until he could obtain his uncle's consent to marry me. Fool, wretched fool, that I was, to believe him; but I brought my punishment on my own head, and by my own act and deed.

"'Father, he soon tired of me, turned me over to one of his profligate friends, for he appeared to have none but such. For a while I lived in guilty splendor, but all the while the most exquisite mental torture was lacerating my heart. I could not subdue the terrible voice of conscience which was day and night upbraiding me. I endeavored to drown it in wine; but when the excitement was over, my despair and remorse was blacker and more unendurable than before. Father, I then became a drunkard, and fell, by swift degrees, from one stage of guilt and crime to another, each more dreadful than the last, until I became the abandoned wretch you saw in the Strand ten nights ago. Dear father, you would perhaps pity me, if you knew all that I have suffered, though I merited my sufferings most justly. The evil spirits of hell are surely not worse than those wretches with whom I was compelled to associate, nor their cruelty and malice superior to what I have endured. Oh, if every virtuous girl knew what it is to become a street-walker, she would never, never fall from her innocence; she would never pride herself on her beauty or her dress. Father, when you saw me in the Strand—when your terrible cry of 'Agnes!' reached my ear, intoxicated as I was, I knew you at once, though you were sadly changed. I believe the whole of that night I was raving mad. They tell me I tried several times to destroy myself. Father, the next night I did attempt it again. I felt that I was destined for hell fire, and the sooner I was in it the better. I thought I could not, even there, suffer more than I then endured. My external calmness deceived the Jewish hag that kept the brothel. She allowed me to go out. I rushed to Waterloo bridge—sprang upon the battlement—and threw myself headlong into the Thames. In the instant of falling I would have given worlds not to have done the deed. But it was then too late. I lost all consciousness before I reached the water. When I came to myself, I found myself in bed at a small public-house on the river side. A good waterman had put off in his wherry the moment he heard a woman had leaped the bridge. It was a moonlight night and he saw me floating about a hundred yards in advance, and by great exertion he happily saved me. Oh, father, where would my soul be now if I had then died?

"'The next morning I was taken before a magistrate. I promised faithfully never to repeat any rash act, and on expressing a great wish to leave my abandoned life, the good magistrate gave me half a sovereign to support myself until I could look out for some work to do. But my sole endeavor was to find you, my father. I searched for you everywhere, but to no avail, until, this evening, I met one of the men who helped you into the chemist's shop and accompanied you home. He gave me your direction. I flew here as fast as my fainting limbs would bear me. But when I got to the door, I sat down and cried bitterly—they were the first tears I had shed for many and many a day. They seemed to do me good and to relieve my over-pressed heart. The street door was fortunately open; at length I prayed to God for strength and courage to face you and poor mother—that too was the first prayer I had said since I left you, and it seemed to me that something, I knew not what, compelled me to go up stairs and seek your room. Father, you know the rest—and father,' continued my poor child, and throwing herself again on her knees, 'say again that forgive me.'

"I again assured her of my entire and hearty forgiveness, and that I would never reproach her for what had happened. Not one word of reproach did I utter for I then remembered the beautiful words of holy writ, 'the bruised reed thou shalt not break, the smoking flax thou shalt not extinguish.'

"The next day, sir, I buried my wife. Poor Agnes attended the funeral, leading little Mary weeping by the hand. Agnes did not survive her mother very long. But she died, I think, a model of true penitence. God's merciful grace was wonderfully bestowed on her in her last moments, and I do hope that my child's soul is now in peace. And I, sir, have struggled on since then with infirm health, which daily grew worse—so poor, that I have lived for some time on parish relief. As long as I could drag myself to the chapel, I fortified myself for my approaching end by the consoling ordinances of religion, and prayed within its walls for the holy repose of the soul of my daughter Agnes. You have now, sir, heard my tale of sorrow, but have I not reason to bless my God for all His infinite goodness to me and mine?"

The good man died the next day, I was with him when he died the glorious death of a true and faithful servant of God.

The good widow took charge of little Mary. She was, however, soon released of her charge. An uncle who had emigrated to America many years previous, and well to do, came to London on business. By one of the strange accidents in the chapter of life, he found out his orphan niece. He rewarded old Kitty Maloney most richly for her charity and motherly care of the child, and little Mary is now with her uncle on a flourishing farm in the finest and healthiest part of Upper Canada.

Death-Beds of the Poor

IT IS an April night in the present year of grace, 1849. It has been a day of not mere April sunshine and fitful showery inconstancy, the smile and the tear blended together, with an occasional, but rapidly retreating frown of this long-month's proverbially changing weather—it has been a day of unmitigated and stern conflict of the elements. Winter has again arisen in his chill garniture of snow. Hail and sleet, and drifting snow, howling wind and slanting deluges of ice-chilled rain, have held their riotous contest during the daylight hours; and now, in the dark hours of night, the elementary strife waxeth in intensity. Hurtling tiles and chimney pots from on high, fall with a loud crash upon the resounding pavement; and the few and miserable-looking passengers in the streets bend lowly as they stagger along in their vain endeavor to avoid the fury of the sweeping blast.

The small merchants who ply their busy trade in Clare market have long since, one by one, disappeared. The trumpet-tongued dealer in "live mackerel, oh!" has also moved off with his stock of doubtful freshness. The baked potato man has closed accounts with the squally night; the heavy rain has ruthlessly put out the fire of his portable steam-engine; and with a grunt and a volley of expletives—more congenial to that classic neighborhood than to propriety—he has evinced his unmitigated disgust at the sudden extinguishment of his calculated profits of the night. The stout, masculine-looking women, with their numerous stalls of vegetables—onions, radishes, salads, turnip-tops, water-cresses, celery, and parsnips—of very questionable quality and remote acquaintance with their mother earth,—have retreated, either to the dram shop to spend their scanty gains and imbibe a temporary supply of caloric, or home to their wretched hovels in Clement's Lane, and the yard-wide courts in its mucky vicinity. The threescore public-houses in the immediate neighborhood of this ancient market are crowded with noisy, riotous and drunken visitors. The stormy night is a god-send to the burly, sallow-faced landlords. In nearly every one of these emporiums of debauchery there is a nightly concert. Ogre-featured scarecrow lads, with lamp-blacked visages, African guitars, ear-splitting bones and noisy tambourines, play off the pitiful joke of black melodies and Ethiopian serenades. Sambo crossed in love, and the woes of the disconsolate Juno, and the hapless fate of the runaway Jupiter, affect to maudlin tears the sympathies of the cadgers, and the fancy men, and the costermongers of the chaste locality. And then, the copious libations of "cold without," give rise to pleasant and frequent displays of pugilistic acquirements. The half-drunken assemblage alternately fight and shake hands, as empty glasses are removed and a fresh supply of vitriolized gin and water is placed on the stained and filthy tables. Bull dogs and wiry terriers of every variety of breed and color, crouch glaring and sullenly at each other under their masters' chairs, and bare their white fangs and growl fiercely when the fray waxes warm, and are only restrained from a general onslaught on the combatants by sundry well-delivered kicks that send them flying across the sanded floor. Then the song and the roughly shouted chorus peal down from the hermetically sealed windows of those dens of iniquity, and make choral merriment with the yelling blast of the storm outside; and as each drenched and streaming incomer enters, and shakes the melting sleet from his battered hat and thrusts his numbed fingers and toes towards the blazing fire, an additional excitement is given to prolong the festive scene, to renew the bacchanalian orgies, in spite of starving wives and sickly and famished children at home.

As I noticed in passing to-night these scenes of sad and morbid festivity, I could not help breathing a prayer to heaven in behalf of the many children of want, who are now roaming destitute the streets of this great metropolis. God's pity and merciful help be to the homeless wanderer this wretched and killing night. Penniless, hopeless, desponding, and faint, chilled, too, and hungered, how must they wander about, vainly seeking a shelter and a warm fire to dry them, and a good meal's victuals to restore the exhausted energies of flagging nature! How must their maddened glance, attracted by the gas-light glare of these gin-palace windows, be pained; how must their sinking heart be cast down by the commingled chant of ribald bacchanalians which this night came swelling on my ear:

> "We won't go home till morning,
> Till daylight doth appear."

Home!—what a word to the homeless! What a mine of undiscovered depth to the pensive reflections of the barefooted wretch, through whose sieve-like rags the pelting storm pours most pertinaciously—whose only friend is God—whose stern foe is grim and pinching hunger and starvation! What a sight for him, poor wretch, as he stands, on and off by the hour together, by the corner cook-shop, and flattens his poor cold nose against the steaming pans of that splendid inner collection of roast legs of pork and juicy hams, goodly rounds of beef, most magnificent legs of mutton and well-stuffed fillets of veal! He resists vigorously, despite his almost fainting weakness and inanition, the assaults on his bare toes by sturdy urchins, who crowd around him to examine carefully the best cuts of those tempting elongated currant puddings—and who spy heedfully on which side the best and most plentifully sprinkled curuant slice may be had for the coin that now burns in their rejoicing pocket. He, poor wretch, has no gladsome penny to spend. He has been fasting all day; and his only rabid comfort now, is to gaze on the outspread dainties, to speculate on which savory joint he would like to revel, and to sniff up, by way of a most miserable succedaneum, the dense steam of commingled roast and boiled that issues from the cookery in the kitchen.

I saw one of these pariahs of society to-night thus occupied, and with his hands clutched convulsively behind his back. The temptation was irresistible. I slyly put a shilling within his cold fingers. He turned round hastily, but I had disappeared. He examined the coin eagerly with every withered feature puckered up to the most ludicrous state of excitement; tried it between his teeth; found it was good, and, with outstretched arms, he rushed into the goodly emporium of most savory food for hungry men. I had made one famished fellow-creature happy for the night.

But to those who meet with no relief, and who are thus pinched and maddened with hunger, who are sore-footed with many a day's weary flagging march, who have not a friend in the world to apply to for help,—how must every wholesome thought be driven clean out of their minds on such a night as this, as they stagger onwards in the vain and bootless quest of food and shelter, and rest for their aching limbs? If they sink down on a decent door step, and under its scanty porch shelter a little from the piercing blast their wearied frame, the authoritative voice of the policeman soon sends them adrift in their hopeless pilgrimage. If, by dint of repeated inquiry, they find the way to the nearest Union—often a long and weary walk to faint and hungered folk—they are met by the stern Cerberus at the gate with the harsh repulse: "It's no use in applying here—we are choke full and have no room for vagrants like you," The iron-barred wicket is banged in the face of the wanderer, and the indignant porter retires to his pipe and fire, to meditate upon the assurance of those "rascally Hirish," who give him no rest by day or night. And then the baffled applicant, who seeks only the bare means to prolong his wretched life, turns from the modern lazar-house of want—the indifferent representative of the old Catholic monastery, where poor and rich were fed alike in the days of England's unity in the faith with ungrudging and most cheerful hospitality—to seek kinder and warmer hearts to save him from famishing. He stops, with a pitiful cry of entreaty, a well-dressed gentleman who has, peradventure, just left a pleasant evening party, where music and rosy wine and creature comforts were abundant, and where, in fact, he enjoyed himself to the top of his bent. It is in vain that the moving appeal, "I am starving—for God Almighty's sake relieve me," reaches that charmed yet apathetic ear, which is yet rehearsing featly the entrancing strains of Rossini and Donizetti. A jerk of his elbow, and an impatient shrug of his well-cloaked shoulder, proclaims his disgust at this impertinent interruption to his reminiscences of the past evening's festivities. "Do, sir, for God's sake help me, I am starving!" again rings on his irritated ear. He would get rid of the suppliant and the annoyance together by a small donation, but his kid-gloved hands are too snugly ensconced beneath his cloak to risk a wetting by reaching out a penny to the dirty, miserable vagrant who pursues him. So he mends his vigorous steps and hastens onwards to his own warm and comfortable and cosy fireside, and his supplementary glass of grog, and consoles his half-troubled conscience with the trite reflection, that the poor-rates are amply sufficient to supply the wants of all such vagrants as these. At his second tumbler which he imbibes while putting on his carefully aired night-cap he gives vent to a virtuous fit of indignation, which makes him rail, in no measured terms, against the folly and ingratitude of the poor, who will starve rather than go into these respectable and well-ordered asylums. Alas! the good man little knows how many apply and are rejected because there is no room.

And when thus repulsed by him with whom God has dealt so bountifully, the wearied, maddened wretch staggers on again, half-blinded by the drifting sleet, almost indifferent to life; and but for the thought that still lingers faintly in his desolate heart, that it is God's holy will, and that it is better to suffer in this life than in the next,—he would be sorely tempted to end his life and his misery in the darkly flowing waters of the neighboring

Thames. God help and pity the houseless, homeless wanderer on such a night as this!

And I, too, have mingled for many weary hours in its turbulence and unseasonable severity. I, too, have breasted the storm in a long round of sick calls, and among the poorest of the poor, among the dying and the dead. I have witnessed both mental and physical suffering in its most appalling phases. My own petty griefs have flown to the winds in contemplating those of others, who had drank to the dregs of the chalice of affliction. My own discomforts, wet, tired and harrassed, were forgotten when I read again the familiar page of the acute and patiently borne sufferings of the poor.

I am now at home resting in dreamy thought in my old armchair, and by my own fireside, with my own silent but long-tried friends—my books—around me. I can listen abstractedly to the pelting storm without, and at times utter a grateful aspiration to Heaven for the many and daily mercies I receive from His all-bountiful hand. True, I am much wearied with the past exhausting labors of the day,—the more than usually lengthened round of sick calls, that have trenched far into the hours of this stormy night. What matter? I have been doing my heavenly Master's work. I have only, and perhaps barely and imperfectly, done my duty. I look not for my rest on earth. God grant that I may attain it in heaven. I have not had, like my brethren of old, the almost certain prospect of martyrdom before me; the previous torturing upon the rack, the hanging, the ripping open of the bowels while yet alive, the after quartering and beheading, for daring to administer the last sacraments to any of Christ's dying children of my flock. I have merely risked fever in the tainted atmosphere of the sick rooms of the dying poor; I have merely traversed, through a long protracted storm, many a slushy court, in which the Irish poor do congregate, and where I met with universally the kindest, warmest, and most affectionate welcome. God bless the poor Irish. Their hearts warm to their clergy; there is a rough sublimity in their attachment to their faith, in their deep reverence for its ordinances, in their almost impassioned welcome of its ministers, that throws a halo of religious beauty over their too often met with squalid poverty. I feel at home with them at once. I feel at the instant their father and their friend.

Though Judy Flannagan may be nothing more than a poor Covent-garden basket-woman, yet when the asthma is bad—brought on from her tramping sturdily, and in all weathers, under a load of vegetables that would make the strongest porter pause ere he encountered its enormous weight—still Judy Flannagan is one of nature's gentlewomen, frank, blithesome, and merry; patient, resigned, and most devout, vulgar-looking, certainly, to some fastidious tastes, in her half-male, half-female attire, her crushed and faded old bonnet, and her short dudeen ever pendant from her large and eloquently-formed mouth. Judy smokes; small blame to her. She works like a horse, and in all weathers. It is her only luxury, save a strong cup of tea. She has taken the pledge, and kept it faithfully. Judy is a childless widow; her boys and girls have all died; but she has reared an orphan child, whom she picked up one night half-dead with the cold and hunger, and has given it all a mother's warm and affectionate tending. Judy has also a little pusheen, whom she rescued, when a kitten, from some wicked urchins, who were worrying it to death with a costermonger's spiteful terrier. Pussy is now a fine, handsome, well-behaved cat, and Judy is not a little proud of her favorite; and nothing pleases the old lady better during her evenings of rest, after her day's gallop under her heavily-freighted basket, than to sit sipping her tea with pussy in her lap, and the little orphan child at her knee, reciting with sweet and serious earnestness his page of catechism for the ensuing day. She sends little Tim to our large and well-conducted school; and she bids him pray, morning, noon, and night, for the good ladies and gentlemen who subscribe to such an excellent charity.

Judy is now eight-and-fifty years old, but is hale and hearty, barring an occasional touch of asthma, and an impression on her heart, which comes on periodically upon the anniversary of her deceased husband's death. She then invariably stays at home, sports a bit of well-preserved crape about her cap, and says her beads all day, and most devoutly, for the repose of his soul. On that night she gives a solemn lecture to the light-hearted, laughing little Tim, as he cuddles up to his "granny's" knee, and whose curly-pated little brow she kisses, with many a tear, with many a fond Irish phrase of endearment. Her fondness for that child is wonderful. She knew his history. He was a child of shame. He was the offspring of a farmer's daughter of her own town-land in Ireland, who was betrayed and ruined by a villain, who had promised her marriage, but who never fulfilled his pledge. The poor girl fled from her home, followed her seducer to London, but all to no avail. She lay-in at a poor lodging house for Irish tramps, was neglected, and died broken hearted. The child was shifted about from one neighbor to the other; was alternately starved and petted, until it crawled forth, in the absence of its rough and temporary guardian, to a neighboring court, where old Judy found it; and who, on learning its history, deposited the chubby infant in that well-worn repository, the empty basket on her head, and trudged stoutly home with her precious freight to her little snug parlor in Bedfordbury. I have a faint recollection that upon this eventful finding of the grandson of her gossip, she rapt out a very suspicious oath, that as long as she had a bit and a sup to share, little Tim should be no ways beholden to any one for his support. Right faithfully has she kept her word. As regular as clock-work Judy comes to my confessional every Saturday night, and receives each Sunday morning, the Holy Sacrament. She has long made a beautiful preparation for heaven: God grant that she may get there, and pray for her director, if he should survive her.

Judy has had this last week a bad attack of asthma, is confined to her bed, and consequently out of work. A few shillings this afternoon made the old creature's heart and lips most eloquent with grateful thanks.

But my ministrations were not confined to her. My list of sick calls was long, and extended to many a remote and squalid locality. In many of these visits my inner mind was fed with many a thankful thought, with many a prayer of gratitude to God, on beholding the bright evidences of piety in the sick and virtuous poor—in those who forgot not God in the days of their youth, who persevered through the hard-working days of manhood;

and who, in the gray-haired, decrepit day of old age, sick and patient, resigned and dying, have so joyfully received the Church's last solemn and comforting administrations. God's peace and benison be with them. They, and such as they, are my greatest comfort; the holy souls whose last peaceful moments I feel the greatest reverence, the greatest hope, in witnessing. In them I feel most the wondrous power of my sacred ministry. In their upturned dying gaze of reverential love—in their sorrowful, and earnest tone of contrition for the past, and entire resignation to God—committing, with childlike, most innocent confidence the departing souls to the God that made them, saved them, preserved them, and sustained them to that terrible hour of nature's dread and last conflict with ever impending death—in their last yearning, pitiful look of love to their weeping children—in their tender and most Christian-like exhortation to them to lead good lives, to love their holy faith—in their peculiar and most touching piety in receiving the last sacraments of the Church,— in all this I have great joy, and wonderful compensation for the fatigues, annoyances, and risks I run in attending the sick beds of the poor.

And even when the dying Catholic has led anything but a Christian life, but has been favored by God's mercy with a long and protracted illness—when the mind has had time to enter into itself—when the great truths of eternity have had time and opportunity to penetrate into that hitherto closed heart, and sow in that hitherto sterile soil the seeds of true repentance— and when those blessed seeds of repentance have been watered daily, and hourly, and nightly, by tears of true contrition and bewailment—when the deep and darkened well of ignorance and despair has been sounded and enlightened by the bright and searching rays of God's ineffable faith and grace, and that cold and stony heart been warmed and softened with the merciful influences of the omnipresent, all-merciful Redeemer—the change is as great and glorious and consolatory as that upon which the two chosen sisters of Israel gazed—the resurrection of Lazarus from his four day's detention in the grave.

Such a sight as this I gazed upon this very afternoon. A poor old man, in a squalid and filthy court, and whom I have been constantly attending for the last three weeks. He is dying of asthma, and in a few days will be no more.

When I first went to him, he was perhaps of all men the most ignorant in what concerned his soul's salvation. He could not read. He had never been taught a single prayer. He had been an orphan from his childhood. He was at that tender age cast adrift, to roam the streets, to pick up his living where and how he could. He had no kind relative to take the little creature in, and breed him up in the knowledge of his duties to his God, to his neighbor, and himself; no kind, pitying friend, like the compassionate Judy Flannagan, to train him, and indoctrinate him in the maxims of honesty and morality. No one had compassion on the poor orphan child. He was dragged up the steep and rugged hill of fatal necessity, of rude and continually felt hardship; and that amidst the companionship of the dregs and the refuse of society, the waifs and strays of vice, the fragmentary shreds of corruption that prowl about our civilized towns and cities. He was left to roam where he listed, to herd with the devil's own cattle, to be penned within the hurdles of shameless, boasting vice and debauchery.

What did this poor creature then know of religion, of purity, of honesty, of meekness, of faith, of hope and charity? His training was to steal, to cheat, to lie, to swear and blaspheme; to wallow in obscenity amongst the wretched little shoeless drabs whom he herded in doorways, under dry arches, under thorny hedges, in lone and unfrequented commons—his precious efforts in crime gruffly applauded by veterans in guilt, and whose patronizing approval was the acme of his ambition.

To this little urchin, so circumstanced, so forsaken by all that was good, so contaminated by all that was vile and sensual and profligate, what wonder, under all these provocatives, under all these terrible bereavements, that the germs of baptismal grace, and God's inspirations to good, were crushed and annihilated? And so from childhood to boyhood; and so from youth to manhood; and so from maturity to the sear and withered leaf of old age. The blank, unsullied page of innocent childhood had been most terribly and foully stained. Damning and repeated characters had been therein inscribed. He became, in his old age, hopeless, despairing, and most miserably afflicted; conscience an incipient hell; the past a stormy career of shipwrecked years; the future a sea of heavy molten lead, crushing and scalding out every feeling of hope and happiness in the anticipation of the future.

Not a prayer could he say: he had never been taught a single word of supplication to God. Not one atom of the knowledge of God or of holy things had this poor and miserable dying sinner. He had, indeed, a glimmering knowledge of hell—he had often sworn by it, and believed that he must go there. He had again and again, and most repeatedly blasphemed by the Holy Name; but he knew not one iota of its sacred attributes. The name of Christ had often issued hissing from his lips with the foulest maledictions; but he was utterly unconscious of the saving influence of His redeeming blood. He was drifting among the engulfing breakers of death, like a helmless, sailless, deserted ship, the wreck of once fond hopes and magnificent baptismal endowments.

Such as he was I found him alone in his misery and despair. I was the first minister of religion that from his baptismal hour he had ever set eyes on or conversed with. I, too, was almost in despair. So much to be done, so little time to do it in: such an unkindly soil in which to work the blessed fruits of reformation. But I did not despond long, though my first advances were received gruffly enough. The sacred confidence of confession forbids me here to mention what passed in that memorable hour of that poor man's waning life. But I made the beginning of repentance; I dislodged the first stone of hardened indifference, and through which orifice I worked upon his better and hitherto dormant feelings. I aroused his fears. I convinced him of God's judgment upon sinners. I quickened him to the then feeble glimmerings of hope in his Redeemer, and of sorrow for his sins. I taught him the Lord's Prayer, and made him recite it after me to his Father and his God. I told him about Mary, the Mother of Jesus, the refuge of the penitent sinner, and how many sinners like him had been saved from their iniquity by her all-powerful intercession to her Divine Son. I then recited very slowly the Apostles' Creed, pausing at each important point, explaining and adapting its truths to his infirm state and limited capacity, in the simplest, yet most earnest language I could use. How that poor rugged, well-nigh heart-broken bosom heaved—how many a sob and choking exclamation of grief was uttered—how many a fervent expression of amendment was made before I left! I was amply rewarded. But, before I departed, I promised to send him two of the good Sisters of Mercy from the convent attached to my chapel, who, by their kind and angelic ministrations, would still further complete the good work of repentance and reformation—who, by their winning words of true Christian and most eloquent piety, by their fervent and continued endeavors, would prepare this poor sinner to make his peace with God, and receive, for the first time, the Sacraments of Penance and the Holy Communion.

In these good sisters I had most valuable pains-taking, and successful auxiliaries. They spared no effort. They prayed for the poor man with all the fervor of their innocent hearts. They taught him again and again, with all the sweet unruffled patience of a mother teaching her little one, all that was necessary for him to know. They read to him the beautiful prayers of the Church for repenting sinners, for preparing the first communicant; and by their unceasing efforts, continued day after day, he was at length fully prepared. I, too, visited him frequently; and at each visit he gradually disburdened his soul of its heavily accumulated load of guilt.

This afternoon I reconciled him to his God. This afternoon I made him again a child of God, by the second baptism of penance. His folded hands were meekly crossed and pressed upon his heart, when I gave him the solemn absolution and remission of his sins. A torrent of tears gushed down his pale and sunken face, as I assured him, in the consolatory words of Holy Writ, that if the sinner repented, confessed, and was absolved, "though his sins were as red as scarlet, they should be made whiter than snow." He had already penetrated, by a most devout faith, within the veil of the sanctuary. He believed, and most firmly, that Christ, his God, his Redeemer, was present in the most holy sacrament. He trembled at his own unworthiness, but Christian hope and confidence from on high sustained his humbling self-abasement. He received. He partook of the bread of angels. He banqueted upon the glorified body and blood of Him who died for his transgressions upon the cross, and who then visited, most mercifully, lovingly, and encouragingly, his humble bed, to prepare him for death and his appointed place in Paradise. O God! how wonderful are Thy works in the hearts of the contrite poor! how ineffable Thy mercies to those who seek Thee without guile, and in spirit, and in truth! Such, indeed, was the loving-kindness of my Divine Master to that poor, repentant, and aged sinner. It was evidenced in every tone, and look, and gesture. Though the storm beat heavily, and darkling, and coldly without, the peace, and light, and warmth, and purity of heaven itself seemed to shine and dwell within that poor and squalid chamber; and ministering angels were doubtless there,—unseen, though present,—praising and thanking the Most High, that another soul was snatched from the foul and damning influence of sin.

And then I anointed him. Precious anointing of the Church's holy Sacrament! Thanks be to God, I am a Catholic;—and still greater thanks be rendered to Him, that I have power to render to others that consoling, strengthening mercy of the last anointing of the sick. I, too, have been anointed. I too, myself, have experienced its soothing, sustaining, and healing powers. I, too, have known what it is to grapple with death—stricken down with fever and hopeless of recovery; the soul tossed about like a stormy sea at the sudden wrenching of the fastenings of life, the abrupt farewell to life, to friends, and all that the poor sinking, quaking heart holds most dear; the terrible future—unknown, untrod, and full of dark, mysterious, and shadowy forms to the brooding, restless imaginings of incipient delirium. From the depths of this troublous anxiety, this unutterable anguish, I was at once relieved by the holy anointing; so do I give it with a most profound faith to others in then like extremity; and so also do I frequently witness the like blessed results. It is good sometimes to be afflicted—you can then better feel for the calamities of others.

And I gave him the last blessing of the Church, and I read to him those consoling prayers which moved and turned his heart rapturously, confidingly to God. The poor dear man had no scriptural knowledge, or he might then have joyfully exclaimed: "Oh death, where is thy sting; oh grave, where is thy victory?" But his gratitude to God was too profound for many words. His looks proclaimed that he was very happy, quite resigned, and fully prepared to meet his God.

And after this blessed ministration of my sacerdotal duties, I went to other sick calls. Some were miserably discouraging, others appalling. Some had called me in the last hour of life, with the death-rattle in their throats, gasping for breath, wildly clutching the bedclothes—a most terrible despair in their filmy rolling eyes, the foam upon their dying lips, and their only shrieking cry of entreating to me, was to save them from the wrath to come. What could I do? This very night their souls will be before the judgment-seat. Their professions of sorrow; how were they to be depended upon? Poor wretches! I did what I could for them, though with a heavy and despondent heart. An evil life is a sad preparation for a sudden and unexpected summons by death. No preparation; and then the judgment—so stern, so relentless, so inscrutable.

And then I went to others whose friends had sent for me. Alas! the worst stage of all—despair or apathy. An utter rejection of God's grace, of God's infinite mercy in their last terrible moments of life. Hearts seared with a red-hot iron of hell's despairing influence; hearts deadened by the cold chill of indifference and torpidity from the long continued and deliberate neglect of their Christian duties; from living on in sin, on and on to the last moment, with a sometimes dreamy anticipation of dying the death of the just. What a jubilee for Satan is the death-bed of these unfortunates! What a triumph for him that he has at length lured the besotted fool to certain eternal misery, his companion victim in eternal torments; that he has added another soul to the hecatombs whom he crushed out of life and hope.

And then I went to take a last farewell of a little child, a young girl, who had been long delicate and fragile, with a fair sweet face to which early and long-continued suffering had given a grave and most spiritual expression. She was in the last stage of decline. The silver cord of life was now about to be loosened; the golden bowl of her most blameless existence to be broken at the fountain of eternity. She was this very evening dying in her innocence and her purity; her guardian angel only awaiting the kind summons of death to convey, with ineffable love, that spotless soul to the bosom of its God. Happy child, to die so young, so innocent, so pure! Thy little days of well-performed duties and of most fervent piety are now numbered. Against thee, since thy baptismal lustration, there has existed no terrible hand-writing upon the wall. Thou hast ever been the well-beloved child of the Virgin Queen of heaven: her praises, from the dawn of intellect, have been thy best and chiefest delight: her virtues the earnestly set model of thy fervent and continued imitation. And now thy acute and most patiently borne sufferings are about to cease. And now thy incessant cough will be soon stilled; thy little restless, painfully tossed limbs soon composed under the mighty hand of death; thy little form, parched, fevered, and moaning, yet still the cynosure of a fond mother's hopes and cares, mute and pale as Parian sculpture. But over thee will soon be tenderly uttered the Church's hymns of rejoicing, in the funeral obsequies of her departed saintly children: *Laudate pueri Dominum—laudate nomen Domini.* And yet in the intervals of thy hectic cough, thou pronouncest most tenderly, most lovingly, the holy names of Jesus and Mary. Thou lovest them both—the Mother and the Son. Thou believest, hopest in Him. Thou, with thy child's dying aspiration, supplicatest her to pray for thee in this the hour of thy death. And she will pray for thee, dear child; and she does pray for thee now, in the slight effort made by inexorable death, to take thee to thy God; and she will welcome thee there in blessed Paradise, her own, her dear, her darling child.

And now, when that moment of happiness has arrived for thee, though thy own poor desolate sorrowful mother feels assured thou art gone to heaven, yet she throws herself, weeping bitterly, on thy sinless corpse—kisses those cold mute lips of thine with that passionate vehemence a bereaved mother only knows. But she is ineffably consoled; the now angel child prays for its mother, and God's own tender mercy removes the burden and the bitterness of sorrow from her heart. She lives now but to rejoin her child. *

---

* The affection and devotedness displayed by this good woman for her dying child was singularly edifying. Before all was over, for thirty hours she scarcely for a moment quitted the bedside of her poor little Ellen. She continued kneeling by the sufferer, praying for her, often speaking to her about God and His holy angels, and begging her to pray for her poor mother when she got to heaven. And when the child got gradually weaker and weaker, when the last sigh was given, when the last filial look of undying affection was given to that poor widowed and now childless woman, when the last quiver of sentient mortality had ceased, and that most pure and innocent spirit was with God, she arose from her knees, closed with wonderful calmness the half-opened eyes, bound up most reverently the little saintly head to support the falling jaw, and folded carefully the little arms over the breast that yesterday had been the tabernacle of the most holy Sacrament. The child was only seven years old; but God gave her full consciousness of what she was receiving. I had fully prepared her. This good Christian mother then gave free vent, but for a little while, to the irrepressible gush of nature's sorrow. She threw herself upon the corpse of her dead child, her only one, and kissed long and passionately the lips of her little Ellen. She then knelt in quiet prayer by the bedside for the space of half an hour; and then arose, entirely resigned to God's holy and blessed will.

The Magdalen

CHAPTER I

ONE cold winter's afternoon—it is a long time since—I had a sick call to one of the most infamous localities in London. It was to a house situated in one of the many street of crime that infest the neighborhood our large theatres; and this particular street, or rather lane, was the worst of its class. Every house was consecrated to the demon of impurity, and the atmosphere seemed tainted with the pollution of hell. Yet to this den of iniquity I was summoned, and my duties compelled me to visit it.

A slatternly young woman brought the sick call. I summoned her to my room, and questioned her as to the urgency of the case, who the sick person was, and what was the matter with her. The girl evaded my questions for some time with great dexterity, as she seemed to imagine that I was ignorant of the wretched locality and its infamous reputation. But I gave her pretty concisely to understand that I was perfectly aware of its character, and insisted on knowing more about the sick person before I went.

"It is a young lady who lodges with missus," was the pert rejoinder.

"Who sent you?" I asked.

The girl colored; her mouth quivered, and a tear—perhaps an unwonted visitant in that begrimed visage—stole down her cheek.

"No one, sir," she stammered out, with a hesitating tone. "She didn't tell me to come but she is so bad, sir."

"Are you a Catholic?"

"God forgive me, I am, sir," was the sad reply.

"How then, my poor girl, can you live in such a wicked place?"

"Starvation, sir, compelled me to it. I had been out of place three months. I had pawned all my clothes but those I stood upright in. I hadn't tasted food for two days, and was going to drown myself, or go on the streets, when an old fellow-servant told me of this place; and rather than do worse, I took it."

I had not the heart to scold this poor girl much for What she had done; but advised her to leave it as soon as possible, and then inquired again about the sick person.

"Is she an unfortunate girl?" I asked.

"She is, sir; but one of the best of her class. I would go through fire and water to serve her and I am sure she was driven to it from great trouble. She does nothing but cry when she is alone."

"How long has she been ill?"

"About a month, sir. She took ill with a bad cold from walking all night in a heavy rain, and the misses wouldn't let her change her things when she came in, but abused and beat her for not bringing home any money, and locked her in an empty garret till morning. She was never herself after that, and this last week she has been very bad indeed."

"Has she had a doctor?"

"Oh dear no, sir. Missis never has a doctor for any of the girls. When they get very bad she packs them off to the hospital. She says she can't afford to spend money on doctor's stuff. But Miss Margaret was trying to pray this afternoon, and I asked her if she would not like to see the priest. She said she was sure no clergyman would come to such a lost wretch as she was, or to such a place of iniquity. But I told her I was sure you would; and oh, sir," she passionately added, falling down upon her knees, "for God Almighty's sake, do come—pray do, sir."

I soon relieved her anxiety by promising to go immediately.

I had that morning attended the death-bed of a saintly child, who died pure and innocent as an angel. What a contrast to the sick bed I was hastening to! It was only a few minutes after the girl when I arrived. I found her in a violent dispute with a fat, blear-eyed, hooked-nose, old Jewess, the vile mistress of the establishment. She was taking to task her ill-paid drudge for having been absent without leave.

"Don't tell me, you good-for-nothing huzzy; don't tell me: I won't have any popish priest come into my house. I hate them! They robbed me of three of my best girls, by making them go to confession, and sending them to an asylum. He shan't come here, I tell you."

At this stage of the affray I entered. It is needless to state how I subdued the ferocity of this she-wolf, or how I obtained admittance to the sick girl who was expecting my spiritual attendance. Suffice it to say, that, after a long, and to me most painful parley, I was ushered up stairs by the housemaid who came to me with the sick call.

The house was large and old. It had in other times been the residence of fashion and gentility; but there is no telling to what strange uses the mansions of the great may come. In a miserable garret, with no fire-place, almost denuded of furniture, and its every accessory of the meanest and most squalid character, I found the object of my visit. She lay on a wretched truckle-bed, in a small recess near the iron-barred casement. Having told the servant to wait outside the door till I wanted her, I approached the bedside.

The poor miserable girl's face was turned eagerly towards me; yet her eyes were downcast, as if from shame, and an intense feeling of degradation, and she trembled violently. She then covered her closed eyes with her hands, and sobbed long and piteously.

I drew a chair near her bedside, and seating myself, I told her who I was, and for what purpose I had come. I spoke as kindly and as soothingly as I could; told her not to despair but to hope in the infinite mercy of her Redeemer, who rejected not the tears and repentance of Mary Magdalen, who had been a sinner like her. I pointed out to her briefly, but earnestly, the miserable consequences of her present unhappy life, its damning guilt, and the swift and sure justice of God upon those who live and die in the foul embrace of sin. The souls of her lost and suffering sisters in crime, now expiating in eternal torments their sad career upon earth—oh what would they now give if they had her opportunity of making her peace with a God of infinite mercy, who still opened to her his arms of forgiveness, "who came not to call the just, but sinners to repentance." I told her that I had attended many in her unfortunate situation; that her crimes, grievous as they were, were no strangers to me as a Catholic priest; and that many, like her, had repented, confessed, and had enjoyed the unspeakable blessing of a renewed peace with God in the forgiveness of their sins, and a hearty and entire amendment of life.

Still no answer, but renewed and violent sobbing. I could not see her face; her small delicate hands covered the greater part of it, and through her slender fingers the big tears forced their way in a quick and ceaseless shower. A profusion of rich auburn hair, which was unbound, fell streaming in wavy brightness over her neck, and the bed-clothes heaved with her quickly-drawn and hysterical breathing.

"My dear child," said I, "let your sorrow lead you with humble hope to the foot of the Cross—to a true repentance, and a good confession of your past sins. Come, begin now; I will help you; it is never too late to return to God - as long as there is life there is hope for the repentant sinner."

And a change, sudden and unexpected, came over that poor, unfortunate girl. She started up in bed, looked at me long and anxiously, gave a low and agonized, and moaning cry, and sank back fainting upon her pillow. She recognized me, and I, alas! recognized her.

In that terrible recognition I saw before me the daughter of an old and valued friend! once the cherished, almost idolized, inmate of a happy Christian home, once beautiful, innocent and good; with all the charities of life budding forth in her young and sinless heart; but now the diseased, and blighted, and wretched inmate of a brothel!

It was too much for me. I too sank back in my chair, nearly overpowered with surprise and grief. The child whom I had so tenderly loved; who had lisped her infant prayers at my knee; whose whole heart had expanded in innocence and purity to my oft-repeated instructions: who had received her first communion from my own hands, and whose eternal interests I had so long watched over with an almost parental solicitude, whom I once thought, from the exceeding purity and piety of her life, would have made, God willing, the happy inmate of a convent; that she should now lie cowering before me in that hellish abode, lost, polluted, and undone! The thought almost turned my brain, and some time elapsed ere I had strength or self-possession enough to summon the servant outside to her assistance.

Alas! how sadly altered she looked as she lay like a pale and inanimate corpse before me on the bed. Some five years had elapsed since I had seen her last. She was then sixteen, bright, blooming, and beautiful,--joyous as the little lark that wings his way up to the soft and delicate clouds, and carolling in irrepressible glee his thrilling strain of melody. Then happy hearts were around her, and she was the source of all loving, and home-felt, and home-imparted charities, Then she loved her God, and served Him faithfully. Her days were passed in the perfect discharge of duties light and easy of fulfilment. A mother's smile of heartfelt approbation—the frequent caress of parental love rewarded her every action, and at night she slept the sweet sleep of innocence and peace. But now, how changed, and miserable, and wretched her lot! What had she done? What had she suffered? How had she sinned? This at present I could not learn, as all my endeavors were centred upon restoring her from her state of insensibility. Her fainting fit lasted long. With my help and the maid's assistance she at length recovered her consciousness, and once more opened the heavy and closed lids of her deep blue eyes that still retained much of their former beautiful expression. I held a glass of water to her trembling lips; she drank it eagerly;

it revived her and gave her the power of speech. We were again alone.

"Father, father," she faintly murmured, "curse me not. I have sinned, sinned, I fear, beyond redemption, and would have died rather than you should have beheld me thus. I thought, long since, to have buried my shame and life together in the cold waters of the Thames. Thank God I was not a suicide. I should have been lost—lost—lost. But I am lost! Am I not, sir? What hope can there be for a wretch like me? I have tried to pray for mercy, sir, for grace and opportunity to change my wretched state of life; but the words stuck in my throat; they choked me; live coals seemed to consume my heart to a cinder as often as I tried to pray; it seemed as if the devils of that miserable abyss into which I fear I shall be shortly plunged, were laying on this wretched heart of mine before its appointed time the eternal fire to which I am doomed. Oh, sir, that I had died before you were sent for." She wept bitterly, and wrung her hands in the extremity of her grief, and shame, and despair.

Grief I could manage, had been accustomed to, and could generally assuage, or mitigate it by the consolatory voice of religion; shame too I had generally overcome; but despair it was indeed difficult to cope with. The foundations of hope seemed severed beneath the feet of the hapless sufferer.

"My dear Miss Challoner," I said, "remember that I was once your friend—a dear friend: I am that friend still: nay more than ever. However unfortunate your present position may be, remember that you have one near you who pities your misfortunes, and would rescue you from them if possible."

"Oh, sir, do not speak to me so kindly—I cannot bear it—I am so unused to it—I have not deserved it. Alas! where is the fruit of your patient kindness, your good instructions, now? I am lost, sir, beyond redemption."

"Your mother, my dear child, still loves you—still prays for you; your sister Anastasia still mourns for her poor sister Margaret. Think not that you are entirely abandoned."

Twice she started as I pronounced these words of more than talismanic force. The voice of religion had sunk cold and unheeded upon her ear; her heart was well-nigh petrified by her grief and remorse; but there was one fibre of that wasted heart that yet quivered at the still venerated names of mother and of sister.

"Oh, sir, tell me—for God's sake tell me—do they yet live? Are their hearts yet unbroken by my profligacy—by my shameful fall, and life of infamy?"

"They are alive, and well," I replied. "I cannot say they are happy; but you, my dear child, would restore them to happiness, by again embracing a path of virtue."

"Too late, sir—too late. As I have lived so must I die. It is vain for me to confess; my repentance would be a mockery. I feel that I have not long to live: and how can the few fleeting moments of my abandoned life make reparation for the grievous sins and scandals that I have committed? Oh, sir, leave me to die! Tell not my poor mother or my sister of my sad fate. God grant they may be ignorant of it:—I have carefully concealed it from them;— it has been my daily and nightly fear, lest I should meet them. Thank God, I did not; I should have died that instant, or gone raving mad. I feel almost mad now sir; and forgive me when I say your presence makes me worse. I could have borne a stranger's visit better."

I will not here relate how I mitigated this feeling of intense shame and terrible despair. Suffice it to say, that after much communing, and many soothing and hopeful words, I gradually tranquillized her excited state of mind. I cheered her with the hope of rescuing her very soon from her degraded course of life and she promised me earnestly, that, when she was out of that accursed house, she would endeavor to make her peace with God by a good confession. She was too weak, too exhausted, to attempt it then; and, though she seemed very ill, yet I apprehended no immediate danger, and so deferred this important duty. For some weeks I bitterly regretted it.

Never shall I forget the look of gratitude she gave me when I parted from her. Her old and childlike confidence and affection for me seemed revived. Though the mere wreck of what she was once, yet she still possessed the beauty and grace of a fallen angel:—its heavenly characters blurred and blotted: but still the faded outline was there, sufficient, and more than enough, to make my heart ache bitterly, at the rapid change for the worse in my once dear little favorite Margaret Challoner.

I lost no time in having recourse to my good friend the physician, whose kind offices I had so often employed in behalf of the poor. I went to him; explained, in confidence, briefly the nature of the case, and begged him to go immediately to the unfortunate girl. In a trice the worthy doctor's hat was on his head, and he was on his road. Before departing, I requested him to let me know that night how his patient was, and whether immediate danger was to be apprehended.

He came to me about two hours after, and expressed his fears for the worse. She was delirious, brain fever had set in; and, in her enfeebled state, and the wretched attendance in the house, fatal consequences were almost sure to ensue.

I asked him if she could not be removed.

"Certainly," he said; "no danger in that tonight, but to-morrow it may be too late."

I thanked him cordially for his kind attention; ordered a cab, and drove at full speed to the house of Mrs. Challoner.

Chapter II

I will, ere I resume my narrative, give the reader some insight into the early history of the unfortunate subject of this sick call. She was the daughter of a brave and meritorious officer in the army, who died when she was about nine years old, leaving a widow and two young daughters to deplore bitterly his loss. Margaret was the younger, and her father's favorite. Happy it was he died in her days of innocence. Mrs. Challoner removed with her family to a quiet and secluded village in —shire, where, with her small independent fortune, she lived retired and happily with her children. She had no governess for them, for she was highly accomplished, and took great pains in cultivating the voice of little Margaret, which was a magnificent contralto. It was at their beautiful cottage that I became first acquainted with them. A few days after their arrival, I was told they were Catholics: and I rode over to welcome them to my parish, and to offer my humble services as far as they found them needful. They were gladly accepted; and we soon became intimate friends.

Anastasia, the other daughter, was a meek-eyed, gentle little girl; shy at first, but very loving and trusting when you gained her confidence. I soon found out they were musical; and my violin, and the harp and piano, worked out some famous trios. After the fag of the day, I rarely spent more pleasant evenings than with Mrs. Challoner and her charming children. They were intellectual in the highest sense of the word; and as time ripened our acquaintance, or rather friendship, I looked upon the house as a second home.

Years sped on; my two young favorites had become accomplished and graceful young women, and blessed with every virtue that a kind and loving Providence could bestow. Their happiness seemed complete. Their mother lived with them as an elder sister; they had perfect confidence in each other; and. the slightest word of dissension was a stranger to their happy home. Religion, in its purest form, sanctified the innocent tenor of their daily life; a devout and regular attendance at the distant chapel, frequent communion, family prayer, and the morning's meditation made without fail showed they were in earnest in their duty to God; and nothing could be more edifying than their constant and well-timed charities to their poor neighbors in the village.

Little Margaret was often the chosen messenger of benevolence. She was a hardy child; and, with a small basket on her arm, nicely covered with a napkin, she would trudge a mile or two, regardless of frost or snow, to carry a bottle of wine, some tempting delicacy of the table, or a little tea and sugar, to a sick widow, or some famishing patient of a good doctor of the union. And the little girl's heart would glow within her, when she trotted home at a brisk pace, accompanied by Carlo, a fine Newfoundland dog, who invariably carried back between his glistening teeth the empty basket, and was too proud of his burden to take his customary roll in the snow, or, if the weather was mild, his usual headlong rush into the pool on the common; but sedately wagging his huge tail, and eyeing his little mistress with a look of dignified protection, he seemed a fitting guardian for that innocent and happy child. And then, when she returned home from her visit to widow Brown, glowing with exercise, and humbly conscious of having done her duty to the poor, she would throw herself into her dear mother's arms, twine her little arms around her parent's neck: and then the family concert in the evening would proceed with more spirit and precision than usual, and the trios would be played or sung with more than usual melody and expression. And why? Because their hearts were filled with peace and happiness, and no blighting reproof of conscience marred the calm flow of their innocent enjoyments. They were days of happiness indeed; soon sped and never to return.

When Margaret was about sixteen, I left the mission in which I had spent so many quiet years. I corresponded with my old friends occasionally, and especially with Margaret. The first few letters showed the same undisguised confidence; then they grew more reserved : and finally ceased altogether. I suspected something wrong, but felt a delicacy in making any inquiry.

About a year before my narrative opens, Mrs. Challoner came to reside in town. She had given up her country establishment, and took a small house in the neighborhood of Russell square. I was agreeably surprised one Sunday after vespers, to receive a visit from my old and valued friend. We shook hands cordially: but I observed there was a restraint in her manner, a care-worn expression in her look, that showed she was ill at ease. I inquired after her daughters. The muscles of her mouth slightly quivered.

"Anastasia is well," she at length said, after a hesitating pause.

"And how is my old favorite, Margaret?" I added, etermined to know the worst.

"She burst into tears. Then poured forth the mother's pent-up griefs in a long and heartrending detail.

About three years since, a gentleman came on a visit to a neighboring family of distinction. Margaret was staying at the Grange for a week, for she was on intimate terms with the family. Her acquaintance, from her amiable disposition and musical attainments, was highly prized. This gentleman—or fashionable villain, for he was nothing else—paid Margaret great attention, and was enthusiastic in his praise of her singing. Margaret's vanity was touched; she began to admire this polished, well-dressed stranger; her eyes often used to meet his—invariably when she arose from the piano; and he soon learned the secret of her attachment. Then followed moonlight walks in the beautiful shrubbery and mazelike plantations: he poured his insidious tale of passion into her credulous ear; and, without knowing one atom of his heart, or mind, or moral principles, she surrendered her affections into his unholy keeping. This was to be kept a profound secret; for the villain well knew the character he bore for successful intrigue, the many hearts he had betrayed, wrung, and broken with anguish; but he was tolerated in society for his agreeable manners, and his stores of anecdote and repartee. Margaret went home an altered being. Her flow of spirits and cheerfulness were gone; her color faded, her eye grew drooping, and her gait was listless. If she played or sang at her mother's request, it was done mechanically. The morning and nightly kiss was given coldly and reluctantly. It was in vain her mother questioned her; she remained silent and abstracted, or answered vaguely that nothing was the matter. Then her religious duties were neglected: she went seldom to confession and communion, and at length stayed away altogether, but all this time she was receiving letters from the man who had won her affections, through the agency of an unprincipled person in the village, to whom they were sent under cover.

Things went on in this unsatisfactory way until the next summer. When one evening, (which had passed over with the same listless apathy on the part of Margaret,) taking up her chamber-candlestick to retire, she stood some moments as if lost in thought; then laid it down on the sideboard, knelt at her mother's feet, and begged her blessing. Her mother raised her, clasped her fervently to her heart, and murmured, amid tears and kisses, the fondest blessings over her much-loved child. She thought that the gloomy cloud was departing from her daughter's mind and heart, and that she would soon be herself again. Never was she more miserably deceived.

The following morning, Mrs. Challoner and Anastasia assembled in the breakfast-room, with the servants, to read morning prayers; but no Margaret appeared. Her maid, too, was absent. Anastasia went to her sister's room; but her sister was fled. A note lay on her dressing-table; it was hastily opened, and the unhappy reader screamed, and fell heavily on the floor in a state of insensibility.

Mrs. Challoner rushed up stairs upon hearing her daughter scream. She foreboded misfortune, but not the tithe of what had happened. The note informed her that Margaret had left her home for ever; that she was going to be married, but stated not to whom; implored her mother's forgiveness for the rash step she had taken, but stated that circumstances compelled her to act thus secretly.

And then there was wailing, and lamentation, and distress, and anguish, in that hitherto happy and united family. It was in vain that her mother set every engine at work to discover the retreat of her misguided daughter, or to learn what had become of her. From that moment to the present, she had lost all traces of Margaret, save that she and her maid went by rail to London, and then disappeared.

And day after day, night after night, that bereaved mother poured forth her cry of agony to God, that He would restore to her, her child:—guilty or innocent, she would clasp that trembling prodigal to her aged heart, and weep over her the fond tears of reconciliation and forgiveness. Her prayers were at length heard; and now about to be granted.

I had a painful duty before me, and which I trembled at performing. How was I to break to a mother's startled ear the lost and abandoned condition of her child, her present state, and polluted residence! Alas! I knew not: and, ere had framed the remotest idea of what I should say, I was at the door of Mrs. Challoner's residence.

I cannot remember now how I broke this mournful intelligence. She bore it with wonderful firmness. True, she turned for a few minutes to an ashy paleness, and gasped strugglingly for breath with hysterical emotion; but she neither cried nor fainted. Grief and surprise seemed to have dried up the fountain of her tears, and she acted promptly and heroically.

She was alone when I broke to her Margaret's state and retreat. She rang the bell. The housekeeper obeyed the summons. This good old creature had been many years in the family and loved them all with a passionate devotion.

"Mrs. Williams," said her mistress, "I have an important favor to beg of you."

The housekeeper gave a look of assent, mingled with much inquiry.

"I have heard of my child who has been missing so long—"

"Oh, thank God, dear ma'am! How glad I am! Where is she? when will she come home?"

"To-night, dear Williams; and you must fetch her."

The poor lady then sank upon a chair, covered her face with her handkerchief, and nature was relieved with a copious flood of tears.

I then spared her the horrible necessity of explaining where her daughter was, by briefly informing the housekeeper of every necessary particular. She, too, after her first astonishment and dismay had subsided, was wonderfully collected. A hackney-coach was sent for; a blanket, and a large cloak, for the sufferer, were provided; and good Mrs. Williams, with a purse amply stored to meet any demands from the vile Jewess, departed upon her errand of mercy.

I then prepared Anastasia for her sister's arrival. Oh, what happiness was in her look when I told her I had found her sister! At every word I uttered she advanced nearer, her lips parted but voiceless, her eyes fixed on me with a steady gaze of intense inquiry; and when she heard the whole—for I concealed nothing from her,—she looked like the holy Martha awaiting the return of the repentant Magdalen from the supper-hall of the Pharisee.

It was midnight before I returned home; and ere I laid my head upon my pillow, I offered up another and a renewed prayer of thanksgiving to God for His mercies of the past day.

Chapter III

It was not till the third day that Margaret awoke from a deep stupor; and her sister's anxious and unremitting care was rewarded by the assurance of her medical attendant, that, unless any sudden shock brought on a relapse, her reason was safe; her life might be spared, but of that he was very doubtful. It was thought better that she should not, as yet, see her mother, as, in the present feeble state of her faculties, the sight of that parent's grief might bring on a fatal relapse.

Her sister alone was with her when she awoke from her death-like trance. Margaret looked at her with an air of troubled consciousness. Her poor thin arms were stretched out imploringly; her eyes were then downcast, as if shame held down their trembling lids; and the tears of awakened consciousness and sorrow flowed rapidly down her cheeks. Her sister threw herself weeping upon her bosom; and that sisterly embrace lasted long and silently. Her first words showed that nature's strong instinct was still uppermost in her distracted mind.

"My mother! where is she? where is my mother?" said she, in a low and broken voice.

"Your mother is safe and well, dearest Margaret; do not be anxious about her, but try and sleep again."

The poor girl sank back upon her pillow,—a smile of ineffable happiness lit up her every feature.

"Thank God! thank God!" she feebly murmured, and then fell once more into a deep and death-like sleep.

Towards evening Margaret awoke again. Consciousness had fully returned. She raised herself up in bed, and looked around her with an expression of bewildered astonishment; she held her hand up to her head, as if to clear her troubled perceptions,—she started, for all her beautiful tresses had been cut off. "It was necessary, dearest," said her sister, "that you should lose your hair; you have been very ill, but now, thank God, you are so much better, and will soon be quite well."

"Where am I, Anastasia? where have I been? I have had such horrid dreams." And then she lay down and pondered awhile;

and, one by one, the broken links of memory's chain were gathered up again and reunited, until the dark career of her latter days was made fully manifest to her restored recollection,—a crimson flush spread over her pale and attenuated countenance; she trembled much and violently, turned her face to the wall, and wept long and heart-breakingly.

"Anastasia," she wildly cried, starting up and grasping her sister's arm "does my mother forgive me? Does she know that I am here?"

"She does, Margaret; she indeed forgives you, and will see you when you are strong enough to bear her presence."

"Oh, no, I can never see her!" she exclaimed shudderingly; "the sight of her would kill me, after all I have done to blast her peace of mind. Oh, my mother, would that I had died while an innocent child in thine arms! thy grief would then have been nothing to what I have caused thee since. Soul and body lost! lost—condemned to perdition!"

It was in vain that her sister tried to soothe her agony of remorse with words of hope and tenderness: she would not be comforted. She felt, perhaps for the first time, in all its intensity—in all its appalling clearness—that, by her own desperate act and deed, she had incurred woman's most dreadful punishment,—shame and dishonor; that she was an outcast from the companionship of the virtuous, a by-word, a reproach, and a mark for the finger of scorn to point at, the butt of ridicule and taunt for those who forget their Saviour's sublime injunction: "Let him who is without sin cast the first stone at her."

Anastasia felt there could be no present comfort for grief like this, and she waited in silence till the first burst of agony was over, praying fervently the while for the unhappy sufferer. And long she had to wait, for many days elapsed before Margaret could listen to any words of consolation. She lay silent, motionless, tearless, shrinking even from meeting her sister's eye, the touch of her hand, or the sound of her voice, as if they made her feel her shame and degradation the more acutely.

But at night, when the poor child of sin and sorrow slept the heavy sleep produced by opiates, her mother would steal gently into her room, and hang with speechless agony over her erring daughter. Perhaps her child was never so dear to that widowed and broken heart as she was then, lying on the verge of the grave,—the blighted flower that she had so long cherished in her bosom: and then tears would flow from that still loving and forgiving mother's eyes as she gazed on her sleeping child, and the oft' repeated prayer would be tremulously uttered, "My God, my God, Oh! spare my child!" And then, on leaving, her maternal kiss would be gently imprinted on that pale and still beautiful brow, and the tears would fall unheeded on the sunken cheek of the sleeping Margaret, who lay unconscious of these mute caresses, and who, in her waking moments, shuddered at the thought of her mother's presence.

The mother's love for her child is a well of affection deep and inexhaustible; no sin or ingratitude can dry it up. Why does the mother's love ever descend upon a child with such a full and gushing flood of affection? Why does the child's love return to its parent's heart in such a slender and oft-interrupted current?

At length Margaret consented to see me, I found her very much altered. She was so thin and pale; her skin was of an alabaster whiteness and transparency, you could see the blue vein beneath; and her fatal malady was too surely indicated by a red and hectic spot on each cheek-bone; her eyes were preternaturally large and bright, they shone with that luminous appearance so often seen in young persons who are dying of consumption; her breathing was quick and labored, and a hollow cough at times impeded her utterance.

Divine grace had by this time operated most blessedly and beneficially on her heart. The storm of turbulent grief had passed away; and though it left her shattered and dying, a calm sunset of peace shone mildly and beautifully over her departing moments. Remorse, too, had fled from her; it was succeeded by the true penitence of the heart,—that repentance which, while it led the poor sinner to detest most profoundly her sins, brought her to the foot of the cross of her dying Saviour: there hoping, there praying, there embracing those wounded feet of His, she seemed to hear, with Mary Magdalen: "Many sins are forgiven her because she has loved much." And all her ancient love of God seemed to have returned, and more. There was infinite gratitude mingled with that love: God had spared her; had not cut her off in the midst of her sins; but had brought her out of the mire of iniquity, even to her mother's house, to die in peace. These wonderful graces, which she received, and felt, and most touchingly acknowledged, came chiefly after her confession. Never had I administered the sacramental rite of absolution with more blessed results. She remained silent long after the absolution was imparted, devoutly communing with God; and a glow of happiness lit up every look of her erstwhile desolate features. She pressed my hand fervently when I departed; and the light of Heaven shone in her grateful eyes.

She remained alone at her own desire, for a few hours,—hours so precious to the newly, reconciled penitent—hours passed with God alone in the very centre of that now purified heart. What happiness for her, poor child, to reflect, in grateful thanksgiving, that her sins were indeed forgiven, and that the gates of Heaven's mercy were thrown wide open to her, and for ever! Eternity, to which she was so rapidly hastening, now lost all its previous terrors. The infinite tenderness of an all-merciful Redeemer was then shown, doubtlessly, in her loving and rapturous communing with Him; and though many tears were shed, they were tears of peaceful joy and hope. Her sins forgiven! Mountains of terrible and crushing woe seemed liberated from her heart; and that heart was now steadfastly, earnestly consecrated to God, and for ever.

Towards evening she sent for her sister. Anastasia came, rejoicing to congratulate the now reconciled child of God. With passionate fervor she now strained her to her heart, and kissed again and again that now unclouded brow.

"Oh Anastasia," said she, "I feel so happy; I can see my mother now: would that I had strength to throw myself at her feet, and, in the words of the prodigal son, say: Mother, I have sinned against heaven, and before thee and am not worthy to be thy child. Will she come? and will she tell me that she indeed forgives me?"

The assent was given in looks and gestures, for her sister's heart was too full to allow her to speak.

The mother came to her child: her knees trembling, and her heart throbbing and melting within her. The mother came to her child, but she came alone. The scene was too solemn—too sacred to bear a witness save God and His holy angels. Hour after hour passed rapidly and unheeded by. The mother's arms were around her child; the mother's loving and sheltering bosom sustained that dying head; the mother's tears fell fast and soothingly on that wasted countenance, that now blushed and beamed brightly with excess of joy. The mother's sacred kiss of reconciliation, of entire forgiveness, was given again and again, and angels in heaven might rejoice exceedingly over that blessed scene.

Then was entire confidence restored—never again to be broken. Then was a full and free detail given by Margaret to that loving mother of all she had done, of all she had suffered, of all that she had sinned. Happy confidence! How much had they both been spared if the sacred bond of affection had never been broken!

Mrs. Challoner afterwards made me acquainted with the outlines of her story, and gave me permission to make use of it for the good of others.

The villain who had lured her from her home had sworn solemnly and repeatedly that he would marry her immediately after she came to London. He was a skilful profligate, and had ample resources to carry out his nefarious plans. A forged license and a needy scoundrel dressed like a clergyman did the business. This atrocious mockery of a religious rite was perpetrated in the drawing-room of the house whither his accomplice conveyed the unfortunate Margaret on her arrival in town. Her maid and her betrayer's valet were the only witnesses.

For three months Margaret had no suspicion of this diabolical deception; and then the horrible truth was at once made known to her. The seducer left England for the Continent, sending by the post a cold and insolent letter; gloried in having deceived her, and left her, as a handsome recompense, the furniture of the house she was in.

She read the letter with distended eyeballs; she read it through, and fell stunned on the floor as if she had been shot.

"I was never right in my head, mother, after that. I remember rushing out of that house in which I had received such cruel wrong. I remember wandering distracted about the streets all night until my aching limbs could bear me no farther. I remember sitting faint and sobbing on a door-step, when a woman came up to me and kindly inquired what made me cry so. I believe I told her all; my heart was too full—it would have burst if I had not told some one, and I seemed to cling to the first human being who showed pity to me. I know not what persuasion she used, or what means she employed; but I soon found myself in the wretched house from which you, my mother, rescued me.

"At first they were kind to me, but I was not suffered to go out. And oh! my mother, they could not prevail upon me then to join their horrible trade; they beat me so, especially the old Jewess; but I said I would rather die than do it. And then, mother—they drugged the glass of wine I took at supper, and, in a state of insensibility, my ruin was again effected. It was then that I became reckless, frantic, and despairing. I flew to drink to drown my misery, to escape the reflections that worked my brain to madness. I then plunged deeper and deeper into guilt. I thought there could not be a worse hell for me than that which I then endured.

"And, mother, dearest mother, when on the cold winter's nights I have walked the streets till two, three, and four o'clock the next morning, famishing with hunger, my limbs aching with the cold, wet through and through with the driving rain and sleet, abused and insulted by drunken men, who were careless of what I felt at the inhuman curse, the brutal gibe, or the ruffianly blow:—Oh! how bitterly I thought on my late innocent home, and how I thought of you! Often and often have I gone down a dark entry to hide the tears that would flow in spite of all my endeavors to prevent them, How bitterly did I contrast your tenderness, your devoted love, with the brutality to which your poor child, the street-walker, was subjected; your happy home with that fiend-like place of debauchery I lived in. And, mother, I was in a constant tremble when I was out, for fear I should meet you.

I sometimes wished that when my last hour might come—and I then cared not how soon—that you might then be with me, and forgive me ere I died. It was for that chance, the distant forlorn hope of dying at your feet, and, receiving your forgiveness, that I so long resisted committing suicide. Oh! I was terribly, terribly tempted. For hours together in the dead of night have I paced the bridge, leaned through the balustrades, and gazed upon the dark and silent water beneath. One plunge, and my sorrows and my shame, as far as this life was concerned, would be at an end. But the thought of dying without your forgiveness preserved me; or rather, it was the unsought pitying mercy of God that restrained my maddened longing for the suicide's dishonored grave I could not then pray. My parched tongue clove to the roof of my mouth; the words choked me when I attempted to utter a prayer to Heaven for mercy and forgiveness.

"And you forgive me, my own dear, darling mother; and though the world may heap coals of fire upon my memory, you will think kindly of me when I am gone?"

The poor mother was powerfully affected at this sad and simple narrative of much cruel wrong and grievous suffering. Blinded with tears, she could only clasp her daughter to her heart, and in broken whispers assure her that never did a mother love a child as she did her own dear Margaret then. Their tears, their sighs, their sobs were mingled together, their mutual prayers ascended to Heaven for each other.

Sweet is the hour of reconciliation. It lingers long like a precious perfume in the memory.

The next day I gave her the Holy Communion in the form of viaticum. With deep humility, she would have knelt, supported in her bed, to receive the most blessed Sacrament; but her weakness was too great, and I would not allow her. As I repeated thrice those holy words—"*Domine non sum dignus ut intres sub tectum meum,*"—she also, repeated, in a tone of thrilling earnestness, "Lord, I am not worthy that thou shouldst enter under my roof: say but the word, and my soul shall be healed."

Her communion was to her a heavenly banquet, full of renewed peace and consolation; the seal of divine love stamped in undying characters upon her heart. It prepared her wonderfully for that heaven, to which she was now rapidly hastening.

After a few days' quiet recollection with God, I anointed her. This holy unction being received in a state of grace, and with a most devote preparation, produced its inevitable salutary effects. It removed entirely those terrible temptations to despair, with which the enemy torments the last moments of those who have sinned much and often. Margaret's faith, and hope, and charity, and contrition were strengthened and sustained by this holy anointing. The charity of God had cast out all fear from her now truly repentant heart and she awaited, in calmness and peace, her last hour.

But God still deferred her last hour, for wise and merciful purposes. He gave his beloved child, time for still greater purification—time to make atonement, by the angelic patience and resignation with which she bore her sufferings. She desired meekly even to suffer more; she said, she deserved infinitely more; and that the Almighty was too good to her. Her life hung by the slenderest of threads, that daily became more and more attenuated; still it snapped not in twain, and she survived to the spring.

*****

It was the beautiful spring-time of the year,—a time of renovated hopes, of joyous pulsations. The mother watched beside her dying child; and how differently was that season of happy sensation measured by her, who watched hoping against hope, the last feeble flickerings of that life which was the light of her existence. With all a mother's infinite tenderness, Mrs. Challoner watched beside her dying child. She counted not the hours like happy mothers. She reckoned them by each pulsation of that fading frame, by each change of that feeble countenance, by each failing intonation of her daughter's voice. Her world lay within the narrow precincts of that sick room: her hopes, within the last remnants of her daughter's strength, that hourly sank more rapidly and visibly. She watched beside her night and day; and gazed, hour after hour, in silent sorrow upon her child's altered features, where death was already imprinting his mysterious characters. In the solemn hour of midnight, or when the gray dawn was stealing over a sleeping metropolis, that mother watched and prayed beside the bedside of her dying child, sustained her feeble head in the paroxysms of coughing, and soothed her gently to sleep in her arms. And as she lay thus, cradled again in those sheltering arms, she looked sinless as an infant sleeping. Her features wore, then, the calm and placid expression of her infant years; and the mother's breathing was almost repressed lest she should wake her child.

And the hour came—the solemn mysterious hour of death, that sets free the immortal spirit from its frail and worn-out tenement of clay. She awoke from a long slumber. It was a lovely morning in May. The bright sun was up, scattering his golden rays upon a smiling and renovated earth. Fresh scents of beautiful flowers wafted their odors through the opened windows of that sick room; and the dying Margaret awoke cheerful and happy.

"Oh, mother," she said, in a low, sweet tone. "I have had such happy dreams. I have heard such strains of heavenly music in my sleep, and I saw, though not distinctly, such beautiful forms welcoming me to a place that seemed full of heavenly contentment."

And then she lay silent awhile with closed eyes, and her lips moving softly, as if in quiet prayer. And then the gray shadows of approaching death stole gently, but surely, over that angelic countenance, depriving it of its hectic bloom; and her lips became colorless. And then I read the consoling prayers for a departing soul; her mother and her sister, and the good Mrs. Williams, kneeling by the bedside of that dying saint. And when those prayers were over, that have winged so many to heaven, she once more open her eyes—gave each of us a look of fond and grateful affection—and then the dear child slept with God.

The Famished Needle Woman

HAPTER I

ONE Sunday afternoon last winter, 1848, I had just finished Vespers, and was disrobing in the sacristy. My mind was full of vague, fleeting, yet happy thoughts—the tones of the beautiful psalms, and snatches of holy melody, were yet lingering in ear—those beautiful, consolatory words of the Psalmist, "Nos qui vivimus, benedicimus Domino"—"We who are alive, do bless the Lord," came again and again to my recollection, and I felt renewed gratitude and thankfulness that the late cruel pestilence had not committed greater ravages among my flock, and that I had again the happiness of imparting to them the benediction of Him, their Redeemer, their all-merciful Saviour, in His last legacy of love and most holy sacrament. I laid aside my cope, stole, etc., and was preparing to leave the sacristy, when my meditations were disturbed by the entrance of a young girl apparently about sixteen or seventeen years of age. She was very meanly dressed, and had a hungry, care-worn expression of countenance. She was in tears, and for some seconds could not speak from her hysterical sobbing. At length, in broken accents, she informed me that her sister was very ill, was dying, she feared of starvation, and that her two little children were in the same miserable state. I asked if she was married.

"Her husband, father, died of the cholera just three months ago, and since then I lost sight of her, for she moved to another lodging, and where it was I could not find out till this afternoon, though I often inquired; and if I had known how poor Jane was so badly off, I would have pawned the shoes off my feet, the gown off my back, rather than have found her as I did this afternoon. Oh, father, for God's sake come to her, for I fear she is dying, and no one in the house will do any thing for her."

I promised I would see her sister immediately. Hastening to my room I summoned my housekeeper, and told her to get ready for me some sandwiches, and wrap them up in paper as quickly as possible. I then poured some port wine into a pocket flask, which had often done duty on like occasions, and having got ready every thing requisite for a sick call, I hurried off to my destination. It was Charles street Drury-lane: a place of ill-famed notoriety; a street, which, for more than a century, has been thronged, rather than inhabited, by the lowest, the vilest of human beings. Abandoned women of the lowest grade, thieves and burglars, costermongers and ballad-singers, dog-stealers and medicants, formed the bulk of its population; the rest was eked out by the poorest of the poor artisans, who take in slop-work from the clothes salesmen in the neighborhood, and the other waifs and strays of distressed humanity. I had forgot to mention that the poor girl who brought the sick call, could not return to her sister, as she was obliged to go back to her place; her monthly two hours' liberty having expired.

I was no stranger to this wretched locality, Charles-street. I never enter it unless compelled from duty; though now, thank God, it is not nearly so perilous as it was a few months ago. Then a mission was opened in Charles-street, in the very centre of pollution, by Father Hodgson, for the express purpose of reclaiming those poor unfortunate young women, who literally swarm in the street. It was continued for several weeks, and with the most happy effect. Many of them, who came to curse, and jeer, and blaspheme, remained to weep, and pray, and confess their sins; many a repentant Magdalen has been rescued from that den of vice and debauchery, and is now doing holy penance in a Catholic asylum. Oh! would to Heaven we had the means—for if the requisite funds could have been obtained, a whole shipload of those unfortunates, (repentant, reconciled to God,) might have been sent off with advantage to Australia, and have been put out of the way of temptation for the future. But, it could not be done. A few only of the most promising could be provided for; and for the rest, there is much and serious misgiving. Who will employ them? Who will receive into their homes the poor reclaimed girl of the town, who has wept scalding tears of repentance for her sins, and who sincerely promises she would rather die than return to her former hated course of life? *

If there be one charity more acceptable to God than another, methinks it is to stretch forth the helping hand to the lame and halt in virtue—not to be discouraged by their past career—not to be disgusted overmuch with the leprous state in which they have lived—but to encourage them to persevere by kind and prompt assistance in their first feeble steps to a thorough amendment of life. Such a charity as this the angels in heaven rejoice at, and God Himself most warmly approves.

Within a quarter of an hour after receiving the sick call, I was in Charles-street. It is a long, narrow street, formerly known by the appellation of Leukner's-lane, and runs from Drury-lane parallel

---

* This is no exaggeration. The writer of these "Sick Calls" has been the instrument of reclaiming very many of those unfortunates, and who have happily persevered in a virtuous life—many of them weekly communicants, and some, now departed, had most saintly deaths. They all assured him of the dreadful loathing they had for their horrid life—so full of misery and physical and mental suffering. They had lived in it from an apparently fatal necessity. There seemed then no outlet of escape. No one would trust them with employment: without a character no one would give them service. The fount of hope was frozen in their desolate hearts, till God's hand was stretched out so wonderfully to deliver them.

with the back of Great Queen-street. I entered it I may say, with disgust and a strong feeling of abhorrence, as I always do when compelled from duty to visit that pestilent locality. At nearly every door were a group of girls, whose looks and attire betrayed their infamous calling. Not a word was uttered as I passed along, and the eyes of many were cast with shame to the ground. They knew I was a priest, and many, I fear, were Catholics; driven, perhaps, by cruel want or sore temptation, to the streets. Some of the poor wretches curtsied, and a tear—it might be one of repentance—stood, and trembled on their eyelids. God help them! I pitied them, and prayed for them as I passed. I had no difficulty in finding the house—it was too well known to me—I had been there before, to attend a dying man who was mortally wounded in a drunken brawl. I had forgotten to ask the girl who summoned me what room in the house her sister inhabited. This annoyed me; for I was compelled to knock at the parlor door, and inquired of the landlady, a wretched gin-drinking termagant, with whom I had had a feud for some years in consequence of her keeping such a disorderly house. This time, however, and for a wonder, she was sober and tolerably civil. Deferring any remonstrances to another time, I asked her in what room in the house Jane Larkins lived?

"In the back garret, your reverence; and she has been there too long. She owes me three weeks' rent, and four days to the back of that; and if it wasn't for fear she'd die in the streets, I'd have turned her out long ago."

"Do you know she is dying of hunger."

"No, your reverence, not I—and it's nothing to me if she is. I have my own children to provide for, and taxes and rent to pay, and I can't take the bread out of my own babies' mouths to give to the likes of her."

She would have gone on much longer in her inhuman torrent of volubility, had I not checked her by abruptly passing her door, and mounting the first flight of the steep and slippery stairs. It was dusk when I arrived, and within it was pitchy dark.

"Stay, sir," said the relenting virago, "I will light a candle; for our staircase is rather dark, and the stairs want mending, and the banisters maybe are not so good as they ought to be—bad luck to them that stole them for firewood—and it mayn't be safe for you to go alone by some of the room doors, for I have two dog-fanciers in the two-pair, and their bull-dogs are apt to worry a stranger. Now, sir, follow me, and take care where you tread.

I followed the burly landlady, and with difficulty climbed to the top staircase of the house. Every room that I passed, and there were three on each floor, contained one or more families. From some of these wretched, squalid rooms issued the hoarse tones of a fierce brawl, the shout of blasphemy, and the dull, heavy sounds of blows—the shriek, the wail, the choking sob of woman beaten and reviled by her drunken helpmate, and her pitiful appeal for mercy—the agonizing cry of children; "Oh, father, don't kill poor mother!"—and many other sounds indicative of brutal and drunken violence, of maudlin rage, of reckless profligacy—assailed my unwilling ear as I crept heedfully up the dangerous stairs.

My conductress at length stopped panting at the door of one of the back attics. She gave a single loud knock with her bony knuckles, and a low voice from within bade her enter. This, however, she refused, and placing the candle in my hand, she hastily retreated. I lifted the latch and entered.

It was then that I saw one of those sights of misery that are seldom witnessed but by the parish doctor or a Catholic priest. The garret had no ceiling but the tiles and rafters of the roof. The light was feebly admitted through a small window, a leaden lattice which held green and knotted panes of coarse glass—some of them were broken, and mended with paper. Through this window was dimly seen, by the misty light of the now rising moon, a vast mass of roofs of houses, thickly covered with the discolored snow of central London. In a small grate lingered the embers of a nearly extinct fire of coke, which diffused a stifling odor through-out the room. An old deal table, with two worn-out rush-bottomed chairs, and a diminutive chest of drawers, apparently the refuse of Brokers-alley, formed the principal furniture. Against one of the rafters hung an old Leghorn bonnet, and beside the wall by the fireplace was a letter-holder, full of those vouchers of poverty, pawnbrokers' duplicates. And beside that miserable fire crouched a little girl about three years old, with the remnant of a blanket around her skeleton frame. Famine was stamped on her thin, pale countenance. She seemed to try in vain to keep herself warm. The child was weeping. There was no mistaking that faint and moaning cry. It was the wailing cry of famine, a cry most agonizing to the ear, and which haunts the recollections of those who have once heard it, to their dying hour. On the bed near the door—if bed it might be called, for it was nothing but a heap of straw and shavings, covered with a tattered rug—sat the young mother of the famishing child. She was rocking herself to and fro, and vainly endeavoring to give nourishment to an infant, whose little wan features bore the ghastly hue of approaching death. Still the little creature paddled with its blue fingers about the milkless breast; and the hot scalding tears of the mother fell on its gray shadowy face, as it feebly moaned for the want of food. And she, O God! how pitifully wasted and miserable she looked as her eye met mine and she recognized in me her spiritual director. But she thought not of herself, her only anxiety was for her infant.

"Oh! sir—my baby's dying—dying of starvation—and I have no milk to give it!" And then she clutched with frantic eagerness the poor nestling to her thin, wasted bosom, and rocked herself to and fro, and moaned exceedingly pitiful to hear.

The first glance told me that the innocent babe was fast hastening to paradise, to be a little angel rejoicing in the kingdom of its eternal Father. No human aid, no human medicament could prolong its life. I gave the mother and the little girl, who was cowering over the now extinct embers in the grate, sparingly to eat, a little now, a little more then, and a sup of the generous wine in my pocket flask. The child ate most ravenously; the mother seemed choked almost in the effort to swallow—grief surged at her heart; and again and again would she pause in the act of deglutition, peer earnestly in the face of her babe, and offer it the breast again and again. But the innocent sucked in vain, the fount of life was dried up by cruel, relentless famine. And then, when it had lain for some minutes profoundly still, and gave utterance to no feeble cry of pain, the anxious mother gazed long and earnestly in its apparently sleeping face—and then a horrid suspicion seemed to dart like lightening through the brain: she seized hold of her child—hugged it convulsively to her breast, and called it by its name, and with the most passionate terms of endearment she glued her own still hungry lips to his little pale and wasted cheeks, felt his limbs—they were stiff and of marble-like coldness—placed her hand upon his heart—listened with distended eyeballs for a few seconds' space—and shrieked out, "My God! my God! my child is dead!".

Chapter II

The young mother swooned over the dead body of her child as she pronounced those terrible words, "My child is dead!" An old crone, who gained a precarious living by vending lucifers, and who dwelt in the adjoining attic, came opportunely to my relief in restoring this poor afflicted creature to a state of consciousness. Alas! what a resuscitation for her! Her eyes opened with a shuddering, tremulous movement—closed again—then opened with a wild and mournful stare, so full of desolation that my heart fairly ached within me; and used as I was to scenes of terrible affliction, I was on the point of bursting into tears, but by a powerful effort I restrained my deep emotion.

"My child, my child! where is my baby?" She had not yet recollected her loss, and was looking earnestly around the room for the innocent, whose last sigh had, a brief section of an hour before, been exhaled upon her bosom. It had been laid out with as much reverence and decency as possible upon the deal table, and covered with a cloth. Her eye assumed a frenzied aspect as its gaze fell, and rested upon the mysterious burden on the table. With one bound she arose from her recumbent position, and withdrew, with quivering haste and trembling hands, the covering that still hid from her departed infant. She looked for a long time silently upon the face of the dead. There could be no mistake about that aspect. The half-opened mouth; the half-closed eyes; the rigid features; the marble fixedness of the sunken cheeks; the stiffened pointedness of the bony fingers of that little attenuated hand; the elongation of the limbs; the drear and awful silence—all revealed with frightful distinctness, the reality of death.

And then she bowed herself to the ground, moaning and crying most bitterly in her agony of bereavement. Her little girl, who had hitherto remained unnoticed by the now fireless grate, now crept shivering to her mother's side, entwined her arms round her mother's neck, and nestled her face in her bosom. The action, simple as it was, turned the heart-broken woman's attention from the dead to the living—suspended for a while her deep distress—and reopened the closed fountain of maternal solicitude. She felt that she was not yet childless, and that though one was gone to God, another had yet claims upon her maternal exertions. Sad, yet resigned, was the look she cast upon me, as I endeavored to console and comfort her in those glorious promises of Holy Writ which are so bountifully spread throughout the sacred volume. That most comforting one, "Suffer little children to come unto me," I applied to her special case, and with signal advantage. I told her how blessed the change her departed child had met with, in leaving a world of sin and sorrow before its innocence had been tainted, to enjoy the clear sight and possession of God, and that for evermore. It would no longer hunger or thirst; it would no longer be cold, and afflicted with cruel pain; but it would be among the pure, angelic spirits of God, and be comforted for evermore. She was now sure of its eternal salvation, and it would pray for her—for her, its own suffering mother, that she might rejoin it in heaven.

But the stern reality of her loss at times made her refuse all comfort, all consolation. At times she wildly apostrophized death as a cruel foe, who had taken from her her darling Willy, and prayed earnestly that the same inexorable enemy might take her also. She expressed a frantic eagerness to die. When I combated this painful outbreak she turned to me and said, "Oh, sir, you know not what it is to be a parent and lose a child. The greatest blessing you can hold out to me is, that I may soon die." And when I told her that we must not wish for death independently of the will of God; that the gift of life is one that may not slightly be thrown away; that God had given her this cross to bear, and would give her grace to bear it with a Christian spirit of resignation if she humbly prayed for it—she impatiently murmured, "I have borne my troubles long enough—I can bear them no longer. The grave is the only resting-place for the poor and wretched such as I. That is one comfort which the poor have in their misery, they need not fear death if they are only prepared to die; they have nothing to lose in losing life, but every thing to gain. Father—can you wish me to live? What have I to live for? Poor, friendless, helpless, to me life is one continual scene of starvation and misery."

I will not weary my readers with the detail of what further arguments I used, to mitigate the grief of this afflicted and suffering young creature, for she was barely twenty years of age. She had married foolishly and thoughtlessly at the age of sixteen, contrary to her mother's wish, and had reaped bitter fruits of misery in consequence of her disobedience. She plunged at once, a mere foolish, giddy girl without experience, without a parent's blessing into the cares and trials and difficulties of the marriage state. Her husband was a young and thoughtless fellow, equally inexperienced with herself. Hence the usual result naturally followed,—a young family, and scanty means to maintain them. He was a tailor by trade, but an indifferent workman; fond of his pleasure, his pipe, and his pot, and his idle Monday to play at skittles in the back-yard of some low public-house; and that with drinking, and smoking, and shirking his work, he, in the second year of his marriage state, lost his employment, and was reduced to the occasional and ill-paid drudgery of slop work.

It was at this time, when want and hunger often stared them in the face, that they both attended a missionary retreat, given by the late saintly priest, Father Dominic. Their poorly-paid work was slack, and they had much time to spare in attending his moving exhortations. They produced a powerful effect on the minds and hearts of the poor young tailor and his wife. They both went to confession to him, who was an angel of mercy and compassionate tenderness to them in their sin and sorrow. He encouraged them to the utmost to bear with patience and resignation their appointed trials and gave them sage and paternal advice for the better management of their domestic economy. His advice was needful, and was strictly followed.

Poor Larkins soon after lost his health, and became dreadfully rheumatic. His fingers swelled so, and became so painful, that he could only, at rare intervals, employ his needle. The whole support of his family fell upon his young, and still girlish wife. And right nobly did she then redeem her promise given, perhaps lightly, on her espousal day, "for better, for worse, for richer, for poorer, in sickness, and in health, till death do us part." She literally wore her fingers to the bone to procure him, and her children, bread to eat. And literally, they had little else, and but a small modicum of that at times. When work was slack, and that not unfrequent, a penny worth of bread, and a little weak tea, formed the whole daily sustenance of Larkins, his wife, and their infant daughter. And what was that work? And how was it paid? Shirts at from five farthings to fivepence half-penny each. The latter nobly-remunerated garment, took a day and a quarter to make, from the fine work and elaborate stitching required by the merciless contractor. Trowsers also were hemmed, and basted, and stitched, and button-holed, from fourpence to eightpence per pair; and three-pence half-penny a day, of sixteen or eighteen hours' drudgery, was all the profit the poor seamstress received after deducting the, to her, heavy expense of thread, and needles, and pins, and candlelight. The rent *must* be paid; and it would never have been paid, had not the indefatigable Jane got an occasional job of better paid needlework from a tradesman's family in the neighborhood.

And then poor Jane lay in of her second child, the infant now departed—and sad, and sore was the struggle with adversity endured by this much tried couple. They would have perished, had not her husband applied to the tradesman's wife who supplied them with an occasional job of work. She kept Jane alive by her well-timed charity. She sent her food, and paid the midwife's bill.

A still heavier calamity awaited the unfortunate seamstress, which indeed bowed her to the earth, and tried sorely her newly awakened faith and trust in God.

Chapter III

AND then the cholera came in 1848, and Frederick, her husband, was among the first of its victims. He died resigned and fully prepared to meet his God. Happy for him that the day of adversity had been for him a chastening, purifying ordeal; and that he had applied himself earnestly, and with perseverance, to his religious duties and a hearty amendment of life, before the death summons came. He prayed trustfully to his God before he died, that He would protect the poor wife and children, and be to them a father and a friend.

Jane moved off then to her present poor abode. Her late one was saddened to her by too many mournful recollections. And she still struggled on, weak and ailing as she was, to give bread to herself and children by the same painful and never-ceasing toil of needlework; and that, too, slackened. So many women were starving, that with frantic eagerness they besieged the doors of the slop-sellers, and underbid each other to the lowest minimum of payment, in the wild hope of getting work to do. For days together, and that frequently, poor Jane's and her little daughter's sole sustenance, was a halfpenny worth of bread and cold water, and sometimes none at all. She had had no work for a week previous to my visit, had been two days without food, giving the sole remaining crust of mouldy bread to the little Emily. No wonder that she was famishing—half dead—her milk dried up—and her baby *in articulo mortis,* when I was called in to see her, and to supply her wants in this her cruel and deadly necessity.

And, thanks be to God, I did supply her wants as far as in me lay. By the charity of a revered friend, I had a few pounds placed at my disposal for cases like this. I paid off her arrears of rent to the she—Cerberus of a landlady. I removed her to the clean homely, motherly lodging of a good old Irishwoman, who kept a fruit stall in Drury-lane, and who devoted many a day, and many a sleepless night, to soothing the sorrows, and nursing the precarious health of Jane and her child. I had the dear infant buried, and paid the undertaker's bill. Jane's gratitude was boundless, that I had spared her the humiliation of accepting parish relief in the funeral rites of her departed child. With the kind, motherly nursing of good old Kitty McCarthy, and good and plentiful nourishment, Jane and her little Emily thrived wonderfully; and in a few weeks no one would have taken them for the starved, skeleton-like objects they had been before, and that so lately.

Kitty McCarthy was a character. She was hot-tempered, but of a generous, unsuspicious, confiding heart. She was all heart, and sometimes had too much of that curious commodity! She would often strip herself to the last farthing, and consign her whole disposable stock of valuables to the kind keeping of the pawnbroker, to relieve a distressed countrywoman, especially if she was a "Grecian."*

"The craythurs," she would exclaim, with many an Irish shrug, and twist of her large and eloquently formed mouth,—"sure they are unused entirely to the ways of this big blackguard of a town, that's filled with Turks and Haythens more than Christian people. Sure I'll never be the worse for lending them a helping hand; and when old Kitty's gone—glory be her bed!—sure, won't they pray for the old woman that tuck them in when they were quite starved and dissolute, and wandering about the cold streets, and the 'peelers' too often ready and willing to take them off to jail!"

Thus, her little room was often tenanted by a poor wandering family of Irish immigrants; and Kitty minded her stall all day, and did a little washing at night for a neighbor, and slaved like a horse, that she might feed, and scold, and joke with, and give the "bit and the sup" to the poor starving creatures around her. And they blessed her in their inmost souls; and their blessings and their prayers old Kitty valued more than a king's ransom.

One slight failing old Kitty had—she dearly loved a glass of *"potheen;"* but it was in moderation. She said it did her good, and

---

* Natives of Erin recently imported into England, are invariably so called.

cheered the cockles of her heart. And may be it did; and maybe I was wrong to blame her, and press the old lady to be a tee-totaller.

"I'm not intemperate, yer riverence,—I never gets drunk, nor makes a baste of meeself—no one, glory to Heaven! ever saw old Kitty disguised in liquor, nor the least ways intosticated, barring once at a wake, when the tobacco smoke overcame me entirely—and sure it wasn't the fault of the liquor; and then maybe I didn't get sarved out for it—for in the scrimmage wasn't my best silk bonnet and cap smashed to smithreens, and my two eyes blackened and knocked out of my head; and me, a dacent, vartuous woman, flung like a rope of inions clane over the corpse! Catch Kitty Carthy getting a drop too much to the fore again! It was a warning to me, and as good as a fairy blast to me, and will be, as long as I can tell a ripston pippin from a China orange. And sure your riverence wouldn't begrudge me one glass of the cratur, now and again, when I'm perished with cold, sitting all day on my little basket, minding my little stall of fruit, in the cold, wet street, when the rain and the sleet has chilled me to the bone, and the rheumatiz crippling my limbs—sure thin, father dear, you wouldn't penance me with cowld water, and make me take the pledge, and I as sober a woman as any in the parish?" Nor did I.

Most of my readers must have often admired the patient fortitude with which the poor apple women of London bear their hard lot of life. In summer, their "lines" run tolerably smooth but in winter, their sufferings at times are dreadful. Often aged, infirm, rheumatic, they bear in the open air, without shelter, and that the livelong day, and often far into the night, the severity of our changeful seasons without a murmur or a word of complaint; and that, too, often for the slender profit of fourpenee or sixpence a day on their scanty stock of fruit. Hours may pass away—hundreds of passengers may go heedlessly by, without regarding the old Irish woman and her basket of apples; but how are those weary hours of suspense and disappointed hopes spent? Not in murmuring, or repining, or envying those who are better off, and well fed and well clothed—but in prayer and devout meditation. If you examine that aged woman's lips narrowly, and without her perceiving it, you will generally see them moving gently and quietly, in her supplicatory prayers to Heaven. She may be said to say her beads the livelong day. The constant burden of her prayer is, "Holy Mary, Mother of God, pray for us sinners, now and at the hour of our death. Amen." That good old soul has fortified herself for her daily struggle with life and its attendant ills, by a devout attendance at early Mass. She receives the most Holy Sacrament weekly; and her love of God, her veneration for the sufferings of her Redeemer, are singularly deep-seated and fervent. No wonder such extraordinary graces are given her, to bear with such beautiful patience the many trials to which she is exposed. No wonder that when her last hour comes, it finds her so gloriously prepared to meet her God. Her end is most devout, edifying, saintly. Every London priest that I have ever spoken to on the subject, has mentioned in like manner the good old Catholic applewomen of their flock. God's holy peace and blessing be unto them! and God bless dear old Kitty McCarthy; for she is not the worst of her venerable sisterhood, as we shall shortly see in the freshly turning trials of the young widow, Jane Larkins, and her child.

Chapter IV

By the month of February, time, care, and the goodness of God brought Jane Larkins nearly round to a tolerable state of health and resigned frame of mind. She still lived with old Kitty McCarthy, who declared she would not part with her for a crock full of gold. "Maybe, it isn't she, the purty darling, who makes my little place snug and comfortable for me when I come in out of the cold—the bright cozy fire—the kettle laughing and singing on the hob—the bit of warm toast—and my pipe of baccy well filled for me to have a good comfortable smoke!" for Kitty did smoke when she had taken her cup of tea, she said it did her good, and kept the asthma from choking her, and I believed it did. Jane was now much better off as to worldly circumstances; her grinding, pinching toil of slop-work, at fourpence a day, was over: I got her constant employment from an army clothier in the neighborhood, to whom I mentioned her case, and she could now earn, with moderate exertion, about ten shillings a week—a magnificent sum to her, and which enabled her to support herself and child, and pay Kitty something for the share of her bed, and the use of her room, They all lived right happily together.

But soon their happiness and contentment was clouded. Another sore trial, another sore trouble came. Little Emily had never entirely recovered the cruel hardships she endured at the time her infant brother died. She was a delicate, beautiful child, with blue large eyes and flaxen hair, and a most winning, affectionate disposition. She was idolized by Kitty, who said she was too good for this world; God would not let her remain long with them—and her prophecy was soon fulfilled. She sickened of the scarlatina, then rife in the neighborhood. For a month, the little innocent struggled against this dread malady, in general so fatal to children. She died, making the sign of the holy cross, and her last word of innocent, confiding prayer was, "Holy Mary, pray for me." She went on angel's wings to rejoin her infant brother in heaven.

Jane's grief was inconsolable. The nearest, dearest ties that had bound her to life were now snapt in twain. Death had fearfully despoiled her. Husband, infant, and child—all gone within a few brief months! Her constitution sunk under these repeated prostrations. Notwithstanding all the care and affectionate ministrations of old Kitty McCarthy, Jane dropped daily. She never fairly held up her head again after her return from the funeral of little Emily. The day too was cold, dreary, and depressing. A chilly mizzling rain saturated the atmosphere. The next week a febrile attack set in, and she was soon prostrate, delirious in her bed.

Then broke the fever out, and in all its virulence and strength. Then came that burning—ever burning heat, after the shivering which seemed like the coldness of the tomb. Then came starts, and visions, and fearful sounds close to the bewildered head, and whispering voices that tantalized the sufferer, and faces of those long since gone to their rest—and glimpses of loved ones, and feared ones—ever and ever the thirst—that fiend of the sick bed—proclaimed that fever—wasting fever, had set in and held its way.

A week or more of fierce delirium ensued; and those who tended the sufferer, knew not, in the shrieks and frenzied violence, the gentle crushed spirit of that hapless being. And oh! what suffering—what untold suffering marks the ravages of typhus! The hopeless craving for rest; the throbbing burning head, and aching limbs, and the terrible visions of the night, commencing with sunset, and continuing in drear, shadowy, agonizing intensity to the mid-hours of night! Events of by-gone days long-forgotten, now shape themselves in phantasmagorical procession through the scared and troubled brain: ghost stories heard, or read in childhood and since discarded, unthought of, now throng on the pathway of the bewildered mind. Now, the sufferer is engaged in the horrors of a shipwreck—all have perished save herself—a black and misty sky is overhead—the artillery of heaven is crashing and pealing in her throbbing ears—the forked lightings flash on her closed, but aching eyeballs. Now she is whelmed in the surging wave—now sinking in the fathomless abyss, and vainly striving to maintain her breath amid the suction of the waves.

And then, from the brown and incrusted lips of the sufferer, would issue cries the most appalling, and screams of entreaty to save her from perishing.

Anon, she is struggling with the swathing clothes, the shroud, and the coffin—a living, yet buried captive in the grave! and she throws the bed-clothes wildly about, and wrestles with her clenched hands, and has to be restrained in her bed by the utmost force of her good old nurse.

Anon, she is whirled through the pathless fields of air, impelled by some unknown power. She traverses millions of miles through the regions of space. She views with eager eye the distant resplendent orbs of the universe; she flies towards them, wingless, yet most agile, to behold and contemplate those mysterious shining planets—but as she flies towards them, they still recede from her, until the faintest yet luminous speck is barely visible—and then,—down—down she is plunged into the lowermost depths of the earth. She is there scorched in the womb of the huge volcano that vomits forth its showery spray of liquid fire—and then she is drifting along the cold and shivering confines of an iceberg—wandering along for years amid the frozen fields of the Polar Ocean.

Drink! drink! drink! Poor helpless sufferer—take thy prolonged and grateful draught of cooling fluid, of juice of orange and lemon, and other luxuries for the thirst—lave thy hot brow with ether and let the cool breath of heaven play on thy burning head, and tost and restless frame:—thou needest all the alleviations that science and humanity can devise, procure, and administer.

This crisis came. One fearful night, nature sank beneath the struggle. The fluttering pulse could no longer be counted in its quick, faint, tremulous and intermittent movement. The limbs were cold—the features sharp, clammy, and sunken—the lips at times rigid, and the convulsively twitching—the hitherto restless arms were still—and there lay the young and worn-out sufferer;—she slept not—she was conscious.

I had been seated by her bedside for more than an hour. Mrs. McCarthy had sent for me, as she perceived a change. She opened her poor, dying, blue eyes—they rested on me with a grateful, loving look, and in a very low yet distinct whisper, she said:

"Oh, sir, I have had such a happy dream! I have seen my mother—I have seen her, sir, with that smile of affection which, long remembered, has sustained me since her death in many an hour's bitter and trying sorrow; and now, sir, pray for me and with me. Things that I thought once innocent, now press heavily upon me. The nearness of death is very awful. It is, indeed, hard to one so young—but God's holy will be done."

I knelt down and read one of Gother's beautiful and consoling prayers for the sick who are near their end; it greatly comforted her. She had, up to the time of her fever, gone most devoutly every week, to the sacraments;—she had, therefore, little difficulty in preparing herself for her last confession, and the reception of the holy viaticum.

Most thankfully, reverently, sorrowfully, yet most hopefully, did she receive the last sacramental absolution of her sins. Most devoutly, and with profound adoration and love, did she receive the adorable body and blood of her Saviour in his thrice holy sacrament. He was her all, her Helper, her Comforter, her Sustainer, in this, the hour of her trial—the soul's transition from the visible to the invisible world. She lent on Him for support, embraced in spirit, with tears of love and gratitude, His adorable feet, and again offered every sin of her past life to be washed away in His precious blood. Thrice holy sacrament—the viaticum for the dying! How wondrous are thy consoling gifts, thy sustaining strength, to the departing Christian, who receives thee, full of faith, contrition, and love! High privilege it is for thy servant, O God, to stand and administer thy adorable body to thy departing children—to give thy Almighty strength to thy sinking child—to wield thy powers, to put to flight the concentrated efforts of the evil one—to pour thy mercy, thy forgiveness, thy charity into that soul which is so soon to stand before thy judgment-seat! High privilege it is, indeed, to stand beside the bedside of thy dying child—to act there as thy representative—invested with thy powers—to loosen the bonds of sin—to sanctify, and to save, by the reverent administration of the sacraments of thy holy Church!

Yes, it is there, O Lord—in the bosom of thy one holy Church, that thou art found, and that thou art the true Comforter, and that most especially in the hour of death. Cold and profitless are all other creeds compared to thine. They act the part of a most cruel step-dame to the children in life—they most cruelly abandon them in the hour of death, when they stand so much in need of thy sacramental aids. Broken cisterns—waterless—tainted with the foul dregs of heresy, are then given to their parched souls to drink from, as their last strengthening in the final conflict with the dread enemy of man's salvation. Unannealed—unabsolved—uncommunicated with thy Almighty viaticum—with the intercessory prayer of her, the Mother of God, and thy blessed saints and angels rejected as a blasphemy—with faith so dubious—with hope so feeble or so presumptuous—with charity so imperfect—with contrition so vague and aimless—how fares it with the children of error in their last awful moments of expiring mortality? Let the teachers of Protestantism expound this saddening problem. They have knowledge—they have opportunities—they cannot plead invincible ignorance—they have their ritual, which commands them to absolve the sick and dying Christian if he heartily desires it and confesses his sins, however doubtful they be of their own power to impart that absolution—they have their own Bible, which commands the sick man to be anointed and the prayer of faith to be said over him, although their shadow of a Church forbids them to do so—they have the solemn words of Christ ringing in their ears, "This is my body, this is my blood," when they read their unauthorized consecration over the sacramental elements, and when they give this dubious Anglican rite to the dying one; and when he craves the body and blood of Christ as his viaticum to strengthen him for his last perilous journey through the valley of the shadow of death, he is told that it is only bread and wine he receiveth; told to feed on Him by faith. Oh then! do they not act the part of a rending wolf that devours and scatters, rather than that of a true shepherd to their flocks? And then, to show the earthly nature of their creed—when all is over—when the cold clay testifies that the unassisted, unassoiled spirit is fled—not far—but to the judgment-seat of God, there to account—not one single prayer to Heaven for mercy to that poor betrayed soul escapes the cold stern lips of the minister of error.

How it fared with the poor dying Catholic, Jane Larkins, we have seen—her last remaining moments are now to be chronicled.

How differently had she been provided for in these her last moments by her tender and solicitous mother the Holy Catholic Church! Poor as she was—lowly as was her bed—the same magnificent aids were afforded to her as to a dying princess—no difference, not an iota; if any, with an advantage. If a priest is a priest indeed, and acts as Christ wishes him to act, his fervor will expand to an unlimited extent, when he stands beside the dying bed of the virtuous poor. Are they not the Church's jewels? Are they not the brightest gems of her coronal of grace and sanctity?

Are they not the peculiar people of Heaven? Are not their cruel sufferings—their long-tried patience—their deep humility—their unbounded faith—their matchless adherence to that faith, through weal, through woe, in a land of heresy and temptation, to be rewarded then and there?

Ay, reader, it is; and that in a manner that "Scripture readers," and "city missionaries," and Puritan declaimers little dream of, when they assail so bitterly the faith of the poor distressed Catholic, and endeavor, with Judas-like bribes, to turn him into the damning sin of apostasy. Poor Jane Larkin's dying heart was wonderfully comforted when she received the last sacramental absolution of her sins. She knew that I had power to absolve, and that the words I pronounced were not the mockery of an absolution. She knew that when I held in my hand the Adorable Sacrament, and pronounced those sacred words, *"Ecce Agnus Dei, ecce qui tollit peccata mundi,"*—Behold the Lamb of God, behold him who taketh away the sins of the world,—she knew, and that without the shadow of a doubt, that it was verily and indeed the Body of her Lord—no misgiving about feeding upon Him by faith; and if the faith was weak there would be no contact of her heart with the glorified body of her Lord. But her preparation for death was Catholic—with all the bountiful aids of the Catholic Church—and that made the difference between her last moments, and the death hour and last preparation, and last ministerial sustainment of the dying Protestant.

And then after a few minutes spent in rapt adoration and thanksgiving, succeeding her holy communion, I anointed her; then good old Mrs. McCarthy weeping all the while. The sight had left the eyes of the dying Jane; but she smiled sweetly, and whispered as I bent over her with outstretched hand to give her the last solemn blessing of the Church—"Father, I feel so happy,—God is so good to me—I am sure, my sweet mother in heaven, the holy Virgin Mary, is praying for me now. God bless you, father, for all that you have done for me—and God bless you, dear, dear Mrs. McCarthy, for you have been more than a mother to me—kiss me before I go—"

The fine-hearted old woman whose eyes were blinded with tears, but who was wonderfully self-possessed, threw herself upon her knees beside the dying girl, placed her feeble head upon her motherly bosom and kissed her with all a mother's passionate tenderness for a dying child. A seraphic look of love lit up every feature of the departing one, and with one gentle sigh, she slept in God.

The End

Appendix*

How to Help the Dying

☦ Do not flatter the sick person with hopes of life when there are little or no grounds for hope; rather encourage him to make the best use of the time that remains to him, by receiving the Holy Sacraments with fervent dispositions, and accepting his sickness from the Hand of God with perfect resignation to the Divine Will, in union with the sufferings of his dying Saviour and in satisfaction for his sins. Many, through a mistaken affection, are cruel to the dying, and keep from them what it is all important for them to know,—or at least fear to speak to them of those things which would prepare them to meet their God. Do not imitate these. Affection at the deathbed must be unselfish—*the first thought of all should be the soul that is soon to appear before God.* How beautiful is the charity of those who help their loved ones to die well, instead of adding to their difficulties and distress by their own unrestrained sorrow!

☦ Take out of the room such things as profane pictures and anything likely to disturb or tempt the dying person. Place near him, where he may easily see them, a crucifix or picture of Jesus crucified and of His Blessed Mother, that he may be reminded to commend himself frequently to Jesus and Mary. Holy water should also be near, so that he may easily reach it.

☦ Visitors who might disturb or distract the dying person should not be allowed in the room. Keep away therefore all bad, idle, and talkative people, any who have been the occasion of sin to him, any who have done him a great injury, any who would

---

* The Publisher, 2022, has gathered this appendix material from various traditional Catholic sources that have Ecclesiastical Approval.

talk to him of vain and worldly things, or disturb him by their grief, or make him grieve too much.

☨ Bad people should not be left to take care of the dying, above all should not be left alone with them. There are instances of bad persons who, being left alone with the dying, ruined the soul instead of saving it. If a woman is dying, and someone has to sit up with her, it should be a woman.

☨ Whilst helping the dying, do not forget to say your own prayers. Some people forget their prayers, and so lose the blessing of God on what they do for the dying.

☨ The devil is very busy in the room of the dying. He tries to ruin them by fearful temptations, and often makes them see terrible things which frighten them very much. Often, therefore, suggest to them acts of contrition, confidence, patience and the love of God. As temptations to despair are among the most frequent with which the dying are assailed, it is seldom advisable to speak to them of the Divine Justice, of the pains of hell, or of the grievousness of their sins. Encourage them rather to put all their trust in the mercy of God, in the Passion of Christ, and in the prayers of the Blessed Virgin and the Saints. Remind them also that a remedy against all temptations is to make often the sign of the Cross, and to invoke the holy names of Jesus and Mary. The dying should be sprinkled with holy water, especially during their agony, and when they show signs of fear and trouble.

The Last Sacraments

It is an immense blessing to receive the Last Sacraments. They are given to us by God in His goodness to comfort and strengthen us in our Last Agony, and they help us wonderfully to die a happy death. Try therefore to rouse in the dying person a great desire to receive them, and to prepare carefully for them.

I.—Confession.

This Sacrament will remit all his sins, restore to him the friendship of God, and open heaven to him again.

II.—Extreme Unction, a.k.a. The Anointing of the Sick.

"Is anyone among you sick? He should summon the presbyters of the church, and they should pray over him and anoint him with oil in the name of the Lord, and the prayer of faith will save the sick person, and the Lord will raise him up. If he has committed any sins, he will be forgiven." *James 5:14-15.*

III.—The Holy Viaticum.

When Holy Communion is given to the sick in danger of death, it is called the Holy Viaticum, or food for a journey. A dying person has a long and dangerous journey to take. He has to go from this world to the next, and to pass through many enemies. Our Blessed Lord knows how weak he is, and comes Himself to strengthen him, to protect him from all dangers, and take him safely to heaven.

Help him to thank so loving and faithful a Friend, who, when all go away, will not leave him, but remain with him faithful to the end.

The Last Blessing

The Church grants to her priests the power of giving the Apostolic Blessing with a Plenary Indulgence to her children who are near their end. Though a considerable time may elapse between the granting of this Indulgence and the moment of death, it will produce its effect at this last moment, if the dying person is in a state of grace.

To receive the benefit of this Blessing and Plenary Indulgence, he should renew his sorrow for the sins of his whole life, and his resolution never more to offend God by sin; make an act of faith in all that the Church believes and teaches; unite himself to God by fervent acts of hope and charity; and resign himself entirely to His Most Holy Will.

Praying

Let him pray as well as he is able. Remind him often of the suffering of his dying Saviour, which will sustain his patience, and comfort him in all his pains. Let no long time pass without suggesting to him some short aspiration; though apparently unconscious, he is likely to hear. He will unite with you, and your words will strengthen and encourage him. O how his Guardian Angel will bless you for helping him with that good thought, with that little prayer, at a moment when of himself he could not have made the effort to direct his thoughts to God.

Place the crucifix in his hands, and now and then give it him to kiss, with some short, tender words of love:

- ◊ Jesus, sweet Jesus, dear Jesus!
- ◊ My Jesus, mercy!
- ◊ Jesus, I am Yours; save me.
- ◊ Jesus, I trust in You!
- ◊ Dear Jesus, I kiss Your Feet; hide me in Your Wounds.
- ◊ Jesus, for You I live; Jesus, for You I die; Jesus, I am Yours in life and in death.
- ◊ Jesus, Jesus, Jesus.
- ◊ Holy Mary, pray for me.
- ◊ St. Joseph, pray for me.
- ◊ Mary, my mother, help me.
- ◊ St. Michael, pray for me.
- ◊ My good Angel, pray for me.
- ◊ My dear Patrons (*name them*) pray for me.
- ◊ St. Joseph, in union with thy divine spouse, the Blessed Virgin, open for me the bosom of divine Mercy.
- ◊ Jesus, Mary, and Joseph, I give you my heart and my soul.
- ◊ Jesus, Mary, and Joseph, assist me in my last agony.
- ◊ Jesus, Mary, and Joseph, may I breathe forth my soul in peace with you.
- ◊ My sweetest Jesus, be not my Judge but my Savior.
- ◊ Into Your hands, O Lord, I commend my spirit.
- ◊ O Lord Jesus Christ, receive my spirit.
- ◊ Holy Mary, mother of grace, mother of Mercy, defend me from the enemy, and receive me at the hour of death.
- ◊ I die in the Holy Roman Catholic Faith!
- ◊ I believe all the Holy Church believes!
- ◊ O my God, I believe in You!
- ◊ O my God, I hope in You!

- ◊ O my God, I love You above all Things!
- ◊ O God, make haste to help me!
- ◊ My God, my hope, my all!
- ◊ O Jesus, be my Saviour and my deliverer!
- ◊ Jesus, I wish to die, that I may expiate my sins.
- ◊ Jesus, I wish to die, because You have died for me.
- ◊ Jesus, I wish to die, that I may see You and love You eternally.
- ◊ O Lord Jesus, in You have I trusted; let me never be confounded.
- ◊ O Mary, show yourself a mother to me!
- ◊ O Mary, pray for me now in the hour of my death!
- ◊ O clement, O pious, O sweet Virgin Mary!
- ◊ Jesus, be always in my heart.
- ◊ Jesus, be always in my thoughts.
- ◊ Jesus, be always on my tongue.
- ◊ Jesus, my last thought, my last sigh.
- ◊ Jesus, I believe in You.
- ◊ Jesus, I hope in You.
- ◊ Jesus, I love You above all things!
- ◊ Jesus, be merciful to me a poor sinner!

Guide his hand to make the Sign of the Cross, and often repeat the holy names of Jesus and Mary.

When the agony begins, kneel down reverently, and recite with those present the Recommendation for a Departing Soul,* the Divine Mercy Chaplet,* the Rosary, the Litany of the Blessed Virgin, or any suitable prayers,—such as:

- ◊ We beseech Thee, help Thy servant, whom Thou hast redeemed with Thy Precious Blood.
- ◊ Mary, Mother of Grace, Mother of Mercy, defend us from the enemy, and receive us at the hour of our death.
- ◊ Refuge of sinners, pray for him.
- ◊ Holy Mary, Mother of God, pray for us sinners now, and at the hour of our death.
- ◊ Jesus, mercy! Mary, help!

---

* See next sections of this Appendix.

During the agony, often sprinkle the bed and the dying person with holy water, especially when he shows signs of fear and trouble. The acts suggested now should be chiefly love and contrition, the simpler the better,—and they should be short. When he is near his last moment, repeat them without pausing:—

◊ My God, I love You, I love You.
◊ I am sorry for all my sins.
◊ Lord Jesus, receive my soul.
◊ My Jesus, mercy!
◊ Holy Mary, pray for me.
◊ St. Joseph, pray for me.
◊ Jesus, Jesus, Jesus.

After the Passing of the Soul

The soul has gone into eternity, but prayers can reach it and help it still. A very few souls go straight to heaven; most souls must spend some "years" in Purgatory. How then can those who loved it in life forsake it now in its extreme need, and leave it to suffer unpitied in the fearful fires of Purgatory! Do not forget it because its voice can no longer reach your bodily ears. Go in spirit to the gates of Purgatory and hear its cry: "Have pity on me, have pity on me, at least you my friends—you who watched by me, and cared for me to the last, and promised never to forget me—do not forsake me now." Can you turn a deaf ear to this piteous prayer? Now is the time to prove your love, not by feasting in the house of death; not by squandering money in costly flowers and outward show of grief when the body is committed to the grave; but by thinking of the poor soul, which, unless you come to its help, must suffer so long and so terribly. Send it help continually; you can do it so easily.

Your prayers for the departed soul will find their way to Purgatory, and show the soul you love that you have not forgotten it. They will comfort it, they will ease it in its pains, and hasten the time when it will be freed from them, and go to enjoy God for ever. There, before His Throne, it will remember you, its benefactor, for the Blessed are most grateful. It will pray for you and help you amid the dangers and trials of this life, and will come to your assistance when you too shall have passed the gates of death, and stand in need of the charity you have shown to others. Blessed are the merciful, says our Divine Lord, for they shall obtain mercy. Mt 5:7.

Remember that to have a Mass said for those you love is the greatest proof of affection you can give them. One Mass will help them more than all you could do for them by prayer and good works. A dying child said to her sorrowing parents:—"When I am gone give me no flowers, but Masses, Masses." A traditional option is to request Gregorian Masses (30). You can send the appropriate offering (which, as of 2022, is typically $10 per Mass, so $300) to an organization that does these Masses.*

Let your charity be persevering. Many souls have to remain long in pain and weary waiting, because those they loved grew tired of praying, and after a few days or weeks forgot them.

And whilst you pray for the soul that is gone, think also of those who have the same journey to make before very long— Today for me, tomorrow for thee, is the lesson every death-bed should teach us. Listen to our Lord's solemn words—Watch— Be ready. Mk 13:33. He does not say Be getting ready, but Be ready. And ask yourself—Am I ready? Shall I be ready? What must I do to be always ready?

---

* One such organization is Alliance for International Monasticism, 345 East Ninth Street, Erie, PA 16503. The Mass stipends are sent to monasteries in developing countries, so you will be helping not only the departed soul, but monks and nuns, and the poor.

The Divine Mercy Chaplet

Jesus said to St. Faustina in 1938, "When anyone prays this Chaplet in the presence of the dying, I will stand between my Father and the dying person, not as the just Judge but as the Merciful Savior." *Divine Mercy in My Soul, Diary of St. Faustina.*

May be prayed on a regular Rosary.

Make the Sign of the Cross

Pray the opening prayers:

You expired, Jesus, but the source of life gushed forth for souls, and the ocean of mercy opened up for the whole world. O Fount of Life, unfathomable Divine Mercy, envelop the whole world and empty Yourself out upon us.

Blood and Water, which gushed forth from the Heart of Jesus as a fount of mercy for us, I trust in You! (Repeat three times.)

Pray the Our Father

Pray the Hail Mary

Recite the Apostles' Creed

On each Our Father bead, say the Eternal Father prayer:

Eternal Father, I offer You the Body and Blood, Soul and Divinity of Your dearly beloved Son, Our Lord Jesus Christ, in atonement for our sins and those of the whole world. Amen.

On each Hail Mary bead, say the prayer:

For the sake of His sorrowful Passion, have mercy on us and on the whole world.

Repeat the above two prayers for the next four decades

The Divine Mercy Chaplet

PRAY THE CONCLUDING DOXOLOGY THREE TIMES:

*Holy God, Holy Mighty One, Holy Immortal One,
have mercy on us and on the whole world.*

PRAY THE CLOSING PRAYER

Eternal God, in Whom mercy is endless, and the treasury of compassion inexhaustible, look kindly upon us, and increase Your mercy in us, that in difficult moments, we might not despair, nor become despondent, but with great confidence, submit ourselves to Your holy will, which is Love and Mercy Itself. Amen.

END WITH THE SIGN OF THE CROSS

Recommendation for a Departing Soul

The leader [preferably a priest] sprinkles the sick, his bed and the bystanders with holy water, saying:

Aspérges me, Dómine, hyssópo, et mundábor: lavábis me, et super nivem dealbábor.

Sprinkle me, O Lord, with a hyssop, and I shall be purified; wash me, and I shall be whiter than snow.

The leader then presents an image of our crucified Savior to the sick, that he may kiss it. Having lighted a candle, all kneel, and together devoutly recite the following short litany:

Kýrie, eléison.	Lord, have mercy on us.
Christe, eléison.	Christ, have mercy on us.
Kyrie, eléison.	Lord, have mercy on us.
Sancta Maria, *ora pro eo (ea).*	Holy Mary, *pray for him (her).*
Omnes sancti Angeli et Archángeli,	All you holy Angels and Archangels,
Sancte Abel,	Holy Abel,
Omnis chorus Iustórum,	All you choirs of the Just,
Sancte Abraham,	Holy Abraham,
Sancte Ioánnes Baptista,	St. John the Baptist,
Sancte Ioseph,	St. Joseph,
Omnes sancti Patriárchæ et Prophetæ,	All you holy Patriarchs and Prophets,
Sancte Petre,	St. Peter,
Sancte Paule,	St. Paul,
Sancte Andréa,	St. Andrew,
Sancte Ioánnes,	St. John,
Omnes sancti Apóstoli et Evangelístæ,	All you holy Apostles and Evangelists,
Omnes sancti Discípuli Dómini,	All you holy Disciples of the Lord,
Omnes sancti Innocéntes,	All you holy Innocents,
Sancte Stéphane,	St. Stephen,
Sancte Lauménti,	St. Lawrence,
Omnes sancti Mártyres,	All you holy Martyrs,

Sancte Silvéster,	St. Sylvester,
Sancte Gregóri,	St. Gregory,
Sancte Augustíne,	St. Augustine,
Omnes sancti Pontífices et Confessóres,	All you holy Bishops and Confessors,
Sancte Pater Benedícte,	St. Benedict,
Sancte Francísce,	St. Francis,
Sancte Camílle,	St. Camillus,
Sancte Ioánnes de Deo,	St. John of God,
Sancte Pius de Pietrelcina,	St. Padre Pio of Pietrelcina
Omnes sancti Mónachi et Eremítæ,	All you holy Monks and Hermits,
Sancta María Magdaléna,	St. Mary Magdalen,
Sancta Lúcia,	St. Lucy,
Sancta Teresia a Jesu Infante,	St. Therese of Lisieux,
Omnes sanctæ Vírgines et Víduæ,	All you holy Virgins and Widows,
Omnes Sancti et Sanctæ Dei, intercédite pro eo (ea).	All you holy Saints of God, intercede for him (her).
Propítius esto, parce ei, Dómine.	Be merciful, spare him (her), O Lord!
Propítius esto, líbera eum (eam), Dómine.	Be merciful, deliver him (her), O Lord!
Propítius esto,	Be merciful, deliver him (her), O Lord!
Ab ira tua,	From Thy anger,
A perículo mortis,	From death's dangers,
A mala morte,	From an unholy death,
A pænis inférni,	From the punishments of hell,
Ab omni malo,	From every evil,
A potestáte diáboli,	From the power of the devil,
Per nativitátem tuam,	Through Thy birth,
Per crucem et passiónem tuam,	Through Thy cross and passion,
Per mortem et sepultúram tuam,	Through Thy death and burial,
Per gloriosam resurrectiónem tuam,	Through Thy glorious resurrection,

Per admirabilem ascensiónem tuam,	Through Thy wonderful ascension,
Per grátiam spíritus sancti Parácliti,	Through the grace of the Holy Spirit, the Consoler,
In die iudícii,	In the day of judgment,
Peccatóres, te rogamus, audi nos.	We who are sinners, we implore Thee, hear us.
Ut ei parcas, te rogámus, audi nos.	That Thou wouldst spare him (her), we implore Thee, hear us.
Kýrie, eléison.	Lord, have mercy on us.
Christe, eléison.	Christ, have mercy on us.
Kýrie, eléison.	Lord, have mercy on us.

When the soul has entered upon its last agony, the following prayers are said:

Oratio. Orémus. — Collect. Let us pray.

Profiscíscere, ánima christiána, de hoc mundo, in nómine Dei Patris omnipoténtis, qui te creávit: in nómine Iesu Christi, Fílii Dei vivi, qui pro te passus est: in nómine Spíritus Sancti, qui in te effúsus est: in nómine gloriósæ et sanctæ Dei Genetrícis Vírginis Maríæ: in nómine beáti Ioseph, íncliti eiúsdem Vírginis sponsi: in nómine Angelórum et Archangelórum: in nómine Thronórum et Dominatiónum: in nómine Principatuum et Potestátum: in nómine Virtútum, Chérubim et séraphim: in nómine Patriarchárum et Prophetárum: in nómine sanctórum Apostolórum et Evangelistárum: in nómine sanctórum Mártyrum

Go forth from this world, O Christian soul, in the name of God the Father almighty, Who created you; in the name of Jesus Christ, the Son of the living God, Who suffered for you; in the name of the Holy Spirit, Who has been poured forth upon you; in the name of the glorious and holy Mother of God, the Virgin Mary; in the name of St. Joseph, her illustrious Spouse; in the name of the angels and archangels; in the name of the thrones and the dominations; in the name of the principalities and the powers; in the name of the virtues, the cherubim, and the seraphim; in the name of the patriarchs and prophets; in the name of the holy apostles and

et Confessórum: in nómine sanctórum Monachórum et Eremitárum: in nómine sanctárum Vírginum et ómnium sanctórum et sanctárum Dei: hódie sit in pace locus tuus, et habitátio tua in sancta sion. Per eúndem Christum Dóminum nostrum.
℟. Amen.

evangelists; in the name of the holy martyrs and confessors; in the name of the holy monks and hermits; in the name of the holy virgins and of all the saints of God. May peace be your dwelling today, and may your home be in holy Sion. Through Christ our Lord.
℟. Amen.

Oratio

Collect

Deus miséricors, Deus clemens, Deus, qui secúndum multitúdinem miseratiónum tuárum peccáta pæniténtium deles, et præteritórum crí¬minum culpas vénia remissiónis evácuas : réspice propítius super hunc fámulum tuum N. (hanc fámulam tuam N.) et remissiónem ómnium peccatórum suórum tota cordis confessióne poscéntem deprecátus exáudi. Rénova in eo (ea), piíssime Pater, quidquid terréna fragilitáte corrúptum, vel quidquid diabólica fraude violátum est; et unitáti córporis Ecclésiæ membrum redemptiónis annécte. Miserére, Dómine, gemítuum, miserére lacrimárum eius; et, non habéntem fidúciam, nisi in tua misericórdia, ad tuæ sacraméntum reconciliatiónis admítte. Per christum Dóminum nostrum.
℟. Amen.

O God of compassion and kindness, Who in Thy boundless mercy dost erase the sins of the penitent and remove the guilt of past wrongdoing by the grace of forgiveness, look with kindness on this Thy servant N., and listen to his (her) prayer as he (she) asks with his (her) whole heart for the remission of all his (her) sins. Make new in him (her), O most loving Father, whatever has been damaged by earthly weakness and profaned by the deceit of the devil; and incorporate into the Body of the Church this member who has been redeemed. Listen with mercy to his (her) sighs, O Lord, look with mercy on his (her) tears; and as his (her) trust is only in Thy mercy, admit him (her) to the mystery of reconciliation with Thee. Through Christ our Lord.
℟. Amen.

Comméndo te omnipoténti Deo, caríssime frater (caríssima soror), et ei, cuius es creatúra, commítto; ut, cum humanitátis débitum morte interveniénte persólveris, ad auctórem tuum, qui te de limo terræ formáverat, revertáris.

Egrediénti ítaque ánimæ tuæ de córpore spléndidus Angelórum cœtus occúrrat: iudex Apostolórum tibi senátus advéniat: candidatórum tibi Mártyrum triumphátor exércitus óbviet: liliáta rutilántium te confessórum turma circúmdet: iubilántium te Vírginum chorus excipiat: et beátæ quiétis in sinu Patriarchárum te compléxus astringat sanctus Ioseph, moriéntium Patrónus dulcissimus, in magnam spem te érigat: sancta Dei Génetrix Virgo María suos benígna óculos ad te convértat: mitis atque festívus Christi Iesu tibi aspéctus appáreat, qui te inter assisténtes sibi iúgiter interésse decérnat. Ignóres omne, quod horret in ténebris, quod stridet in flammis, quod crúciat in torméntis. Cedat tibi tetérrimus sátanas cum satellítibus suis: in advéntu tuo, te comitántibus Angelis, contremíscat, atque in

Dearest brother (sister), I commend you to almighty God, and I entrust you to Him Who created you, so that when by your dying you have paid the debt to which every man is subject, you may return to your Maker, to Him Who formed you from the clay of the earth.

And then, when your soul goes forth from your body, may the radiant company of angels come to meet you. May the assembly of the apostles, our judges, welcome you. May the victorious army of white-robed martyrs meet you on your way. May the glittering throng of confessors, bright as lilies, gather about you. May the glorious choir of virgins receive you. May the patriarchs enfold you in the embrace of blessed peace. May St. Joseph, beloved patron of the dying, raise you high in hope, and may the holy Mother of God, the Virgin Mary, lovingly turn her eyes toward you. And then, gentle and joyful, may Christ Jesus appear before you, to assign you a place forever among those who stand in His presence. May the most foul Tempter, with his mob, fall back before you. May he tremble at your coming with your escort of angels and flee into the dread chaos of eternal

ætérnæ noctis chaos immáne diffúgiat. Exsúrgat Deus, et dissipéntur inimíci eius, et fúgiant qui odérunt eum, a fácie eius. Sicut déficit fumus, defíciant: sicut fluit cera a fácie ignis, sic péreant peccatóres a fácie Dei. Et iusti epuléntur, et exsúltent in conspéctu Dei. Confundántur ígitur et erubéscant omnes tartáreæ legiónes, et minístri sátanæ iter tuum impedíre non áudeant. Líberet te a cruciátu Christus, qui pro te crucifíxus est. Líberet te ab ætérna morte christus, qui pro te mori dignátus est. Constítuat te Christus, Fílius Dei vivi, intra paradísi sui semper amœna viréntia, et inter oves suas te verus ille Pastor agnóscat. Ille ab ómnibus peccátis tuis te absólvat, atque ad déxteram suam in electórum suórum te sorte constítuat. Redemptórem tuum fácie ad fáciem vídeas, et, præsens semper assístens, manifestíssimam beátis óculis aspícias veritátem.

Constitútus (a) ígitur inter ágmina Beatórum, contemplatiónis divínæ dulcédine potiáris in sæcula sæculórum.
℟. Amen.

Oratio

Súscipe, Dómine, servum tuum

night. May God arise and His enemies be scattered; and may those who hate Him flee before His face. As smoke vanishes, so let them vainsh; as wax melts before fire, so may sinners perish before God. But let good men feast, and rejoice in the sight of God. May shame and confusion strike the cohorts of hell; and may the slaves of the Tempter not dare to bar your way.

May Christ, Who was crucified for your sake, free you from excruciating pain. May Christ, Who died for you, free you from the death that never ends. May Christ, the Son of the living God, set you in the ever green loveliness of His paradise, and may He, the true Shepherd, recognize you as one of His own. May He free you from all your sins and assign you a place at His right hand in the company of His elect. May you see your Redeemer face to face and, standing in His presence forever, may you see with joyful eyes Truth revealed in all its fullness.

And so, having taken your place in the ranks of the Blessed, may you enjoy the happiness of divine contemplation for ever and ever.
℟. Amen.

Collect

O Lord, in Thy mercy, receive

(ancíllam tuam) in locum sperándæ sibi salvatiónis a misericórdia tua.

℟. Amen.

Libera, Dómine, animam servi tui (ancíllæ tuæ) ex ómnibus perículis inférni, et de láqueis pænárum, et ex ómnibus tribulatiónibus.

℟. Amen.

Libera, Dómine, ánimam servi tui (ancíllæ tuæ), sicut liberásti Henoch et Eliam de commúni morte mundi.

℟. Amen.

Líbera, Dómine, ánimam servi tui (ancíllæ tuæ), sicut liberásti Noë de dilúvio.

℟. Amen.

Líbera, Dómine, ánimam servi tui (ancíllæ tuæ), sicut liberásti Abraham de Ur Chaldæórum.

℟. Amen.

Líbera, Dómine, ánimam servi tui (ancíllæ tuæ), sicut liberásti Iob de passiónibus suis.

℟. Amen.

Líbera, Dómine, ánimam servi tui (ancíllæ tuæ), sicut liberásti Isaac de hóstia, et de manu patris sui Abrahæ.

℟. Amen.

Líbera, Dómine, ánimam servi tui (ancíllæ tuæ), sicut liberásti Lot de sódomis, et de flamma ignis.

Thy servant into the place of salvation which he (she) is hoping to receive from Thy mercy.

℟. Amen.

Deliver, O Lord, Thy servant from all the dangers of hell, from constraining punishments and from all distress.

℟. Amen.

Deliver, O Lord, the soul of Thy servant, as Thou didst deliver Enoch and Elias from the death that all in this world must die.

℟. Amen.

Deliver, O Lord, the soul of Thy servant, as Thou didst deliver Noah from the flood.

℟. Amen.

Deliver, O Lord, the soul of Thy servant, as Thou didst deliver Abraham from Ur of the Chaldees.

℟. Amen.

Deliver, O Lord, the soul of Thy servant, as Thou didst deliver Job from his sufferings.

℟. Amen.

Deliver, O Lord, the soul of Thy servant, as Thou didst deliver Isaac from becoming a sacrifice at the hand of his father, Abraham.

℟. Amen.

Deliver, O Lord, the soul of Thy servant, as Thou didst deliver Lot from Sodom and its flames.

℟. Amen.
Líbera, Dómine, ánimam servi tui (ancíllæ tuæ), sicut liberásti Móysen de manu Pharaóins regis Ægyptiórum.
℟. Amen.
Líbera, Dómine, ánimam servi tui (ancíllæ tuæ), sicut liberásti Daniélem de lacu leónum.
℟. Amen.
Líbera, Dómine, ánimam servi tui (ancíllæ tuæ), sicut liberásti tres púeros de camíno ignis ardéntis, et de manu regis iníqui.
℟. Amen.
Líbera, Dómine, ánimam servi tui (ancíllæ tuæ), sicut liberásti Susánnam de falso crímine.
℟. Amen.
Líbera, Dómine, ánimam servi tui (ancíllæ tuæ), sicut liberásti David de manu regis Saul, et de manu Golíæ.
℟. Amen.
Líbera, Dómine, ánimam servi tui (ancíllæ tuæ), sicut liberásti Petrum et Paulum de carcéribus.
℟. Amen.
Et sicut beatíssimam Theclam Vírginem et Mártyrem tuam de tribus atrocíssimis torméntis liberásti, sic liberáre dignéris ánimam huius servi tui (ancíllæ

℟. Amen.
Deliver, O Lord, the soul of Thy servant, as Thou didst deliver Moses from the power of Pharaoh, King of Egypt.
℟. Amen.
Deliver, O Lord, the soul of Thy servant, as Thou didst deliver Daniel from the den of lions.
℟. Amen.
Deliver, O Lord, the soul of Thy servant, as Thou didst deliver the three young men from the fiery furnace and from the power of the unjust king.
℟. Amen.
Deliver, O Lord, the soul of Thy servant, as Thou didst deliver Susanna from an unjust condemnation.
℟. Amen.
Deliver, O Lord, the soul of Thy servant, as Thou didst deliver David from the power of King Saul and the might of Goliath.
℟. Amen.
Deliver, O Lord, the soul of Thy servant, as Thou didst deliver Peter and Paul from prison.
℟. Amen.
And as Thou didst deliver blessed Thecla, Thy virgin and martyr, from three cruel torments, so deliver the soul of this Thy servant, and cause him

tuæ), et tecum fácias in bonis congaudére cæléstibus.
℟. Amen.

Oratio

Commendámus tibi, Dómine, ánimam fámuli tui N. (fámulæ tuæ N.), precamúrque te, Dómine Iesu Christe, salvátor mundi, ut, propter quam ad terram misericórditer descendísti, Patriarchárum tuórum sínibus insinuáre non rénuas.

Agnósce, Dómine, creatúram tuam, non a diis aliénis creátam, sed a te, solo Deo vivo et vero; quia non est álius Deus præter te, et non est secúndum ópera tua.

Lætifica, Dómine, ánimam eius in conspéctu tuo; et ne memíneris iniquitátum eius antiquárum et ebrietátum, quas suscitávit furor sive fervor mali desidérii. Licet enim peccáverit, tamen Patrem, et Filium, et spíritum sanctum non negávit, sed crédidit; et zelum Dei in se hábuit, et Deum, qui fecit ómnia, fidéliter adorávit.
℟. Amen.

Oratio

Delicta iuventútis et ignorántias eius, quæsumus, ne memíneris, Dómine; sed

(her) to rejoice with Thee in the good things of heaven.
℟. Amen.

Collect

We commend to Thee, O Lord, the soul of Thy servant N., and we beg of Thee, O Lord Jesus Christ, Saviour of the world, that Thou wouldst not refuse the welcoming embrace of the Patriarchs to this soul for whose sake Thou didst, in Thy mercy, come down upon earth.

Recognize him (her), O Lord, as Thy creature, made not by strange gods but by Thee, the only true and living God, for there is no God other than Thee, and no works like Thine.

Give joy, O Lord, to his (her) soul by the sight of Thee. Remember not the sins and intemperance he (she) has committed, urged on by the madness and fever of evil desire. Indeed he (she) sinned; yet never did he (she) deny the Father, the son, and the Holy spirit but believed in Them, had zeal for God's cause, and faithfully adored Him Who made all things.
R Amen.

Collect

We pray Thee, O Lord, do not remember the faults of his (her) youth and his (her) ig-

secúndum magnam misericórdiam tuam memor esto illíus in glória claritátis tuæ. Aperiántur ei cæli, collæténtur illi Angeli. In regnum tuum, Dómine, servum tuum (ancíllam tuam) súscipe. suscípiat eum (eam) sanctus Míchaël Archángelus Dei, qui milítiæ cæléstis méruit principátum. Véniant illi óbviam sancti Angeli Dei, et perdúcant eum (eam) in civitátem cæléstem Ierúsalem. suscípiat eum (eam) beátus Petrus Apóstolus, cui a Deo claves regni cæléstis tráditæ sunt. Adiuvet eum (eam) sanctus Paulus Apóstolus, qui dignus fuit esse vas electiónis. Intercédat pro eo (ea) sanctus Ioánnes, eléctus Dei Apóstolus, cui reveláta sunt secréta cæléstia. Orent pro eo (ea) omnes sancti Apóstoli, quibus a Dómino data est potéstas ligándi atque solvéndi. Intercédant pro eo (ea) omnes sancti et Elécti Dei, qui pro Christi nómine torménta in hoc sæculo sustinuérunt; ut, vínculis carnis exútus (a) pervenire mereátur ad glóriam regni cæléstis, præstánte Dómino nostro Iesu Christo: Qui cum Patre et spíritu

norance; but rather, through Thy great mercy, be mindful of him (her) in the splendor of Thy glory. May heaven open for him (her); may the angels rejoice with him (her). Receive Thy servant, O Lord, into Thy Kingdom. May he (she) be taken up by holy Michael, the Archangel of God, who leads the armies of heaven. May the holy angels of God come to meet him (her) and take him (her) into the heavenly city, Jerusalem. May he (she) be welcomed by blessed Peter, the Apostle to whom God gave the keys of the kingdom of heaven. May he (she) be aided by St. Paul, the Apostle who was worthy to be God's chosen instrument. May St. John, the favored Apostle of God to whom were revealed the secrets of heaven, intercede for him (her). May all the holy Apostles, on whom has been conferred the power of binding and loosing, pray for him (her). May all who have endured great sufferings in this world for Christ's name, the saints and the chosen of God, intercede for him (her), so that, freed from the bonds of the flesh, he (she) may attain to the glory of the kingdom of heaven. Through the help of our Lord Jesus Christ, Who with the Fa-

Sancto vivit et regnat in sæcula sæculórum.

℟. Amen.

Oratio

Clementíssima Virgo Dei Génetrix, María, mæréntium piíssima consolátrix, fámuli (fámulæ) N. spíritum Fílio suo comméndet: ut, hoc matérno intervéntu terróres mortis non tímeat; sed desiderátam cæléstis pátriæ mansiónem, ea cómite, lætus (a) ádeat.

℟. Amen.

Oratio

Ad te confúgio, sancte Ioseph, Patróne moriéntium, tibíque, in cuius beáto tránsitu vígiles astitérunt Iesus et María, per hoc utrúmque caríssimum pignus, ánimam huius fámuli (fámulæ) N., in extrémo agóne laborántem, eníxe comméndo, ut ab insídiis diáboli, et a morte perpétua, te protegénte, liberétur, et ad gáudia ætérna perveníre mereátur. Per eúndem Christum Dóminum nostrum.

℟. Amen.

ther and the Holy spirit lives and reigns world without end.

℟. Amen.

Collect

O Virgin most kind, Mary, Mother of God, most loving consoler of those in distress, commend to your son the soul of His servant N., so that, because of your motherly intervention, he (she) may be freed from the terrors of death, and may joyfully arrive, in your company, at his (her) longed-for home in heaven.

℟. Amen.

Collect

To you do I turn for refuge, St. Joseph, Patron of the dying, at whose happy death bed Jesus and Mary stood watch. Because of this two-fold pledge of hope, I earnestly commend to you the soul of this servant N., in his (her) last agony; so that he (she) may, with you as protector, be set free from the snares of the devil and from everlasting death, and may attain to everlasting joy. Through Christ our Lord.

℟. Amen.

AT THE MOMENT OF DEATH

When the moment of expiring is approaching, all the bystanders kneel down and earnestly pray. The dying person, if possible, should invoke the name of Jesus; if he or she can no longer do so, the priest or one

Recommendation for a Departing Soul

of the bystanders should pronounce for him or her in a clear tone of voice and repeatedly JESUS, JESUS, JESUS. Moreover, such words or phrases as the following should be repeated again and again in his or her ear:

◊ In manus tuas, Dómine, comméndo spíritum meum.

◊ Into Thy hands, O Lord, I commend my spirit!

◊ Dómine Iesu Christe, súscipe spíritum meum.

◊ Lord Jesus Christ, receive my spirit.

◊ Sancta María, ora pro me.

◊ Holy Mary, pray for me.

◊ María, mater grátiæ, mater misericórdiæ, tu me ab hoste prótege, et hora mortis súscipe.

◊ O Mary, Mother of grace, Mother of mercy, protect me from the enemy, and receive my soul at the hour of my death.

◊ Sancte Joseph, ora pro me.

◊ St. Joseph, pray for me.

◊ Sancte Joseph, cum beáta Vírgine sponsa tua, áperi mihi divínæ misericórdiæ sinum.

◊ O St. Joseph, with your spouse, the Blessed Virgin, open to me the heart of the divine mercy!

◊ Iesu, María, Ioseph, vobis cor et ánimam meam dono.

◊ Jesus, Mary, and Joseph, I give you my heart and my soul!

◊ Iesu, María, Ioseph, adstáte mihi in extrémo agóne.

◊ Jesus, Mary, and Joseph, assist me in my last agony!

◊ Iesu, María, Ioseph, in pace vobíscum dórmiam et requiéscam.

◊ Jesus, Mary, and Joseph, in your blessed company may I sleep and rest in peace.

When the soul has departed from the body, the following prayers are immediately said:

℟. Subveníte, Sancti Dei, occúrrite, Angeli Dómini, * Suscipiéntes ánimam eius, * Offeréntes eam in conspéctu Altíssimi. ℣. Suscípiat te Christus, qui vocávit te, et in sinum Abrahæ Angeli dedúcant te. Suscipiéntes ánimam eius, of

℟. Come to his (her) aid, O saints of God; Come forth to meet him (her), angels of the Lord: * Receiving his (her) soul, * Presenting it to the Most High. ℣. May Christ, Who has called you, now receive you, and may the angels bring you to Abraham's bosom. Receiving his

feréntes eam in conspéctu Altíssimi.

℣. Réquiem ætérnam dona ei, Dómine: et lux perpétua lúceat ei. * Offeréntes.

℣. Kýrie, eléison.
℟. Christe, eléison.
Kýrie, eléison.

℣. Pater noster, *secreto usque ad:*

℣. Et ne nos indúcas in tentatiónem. ℟. Sed líbera nos a malo.

℣. Réquiem ætérnam dona ei, Dómine. ℟. Et lux perpétua lúceat ei.

℣. A porta ínferi. ℟. Erue, Dómine, ánimam eius.

℣. Requiéscat in pace. ℟. Amen.

℣. Dómine, exáudi oratiónem meam. ℟. Et clamor meus ad te véniat.

℣. Dóminus vobíscum. ℟. Et cum spíritu tuo.

Oratio. Orémus.

Tibi, Dómine, commendámus ánimam fámuli tui N.,* (fámulæ tuæ N.), ut, defúnctus (a) sæculo, tibi vivat: et quæ per fragilitátem humánæ conversatiónis peccáta commísit, tu vénia misericordíssimæ pietátis abstérge. Per Christum Dóminum nostrum.
℟. Amen.

(her) soul, presenting it to the Most High.

℣. Eternal rest grant unto him (her), O Lord, and let perpetual light shine upon him (her). * Presenting.

℣. Lord, have mercy on us.
℟. Christ, have mercy on us.
Lord, have mercy on us.

℣. Our Father, *silently until:*

℣. And lead us not into temptation. ℟. But deliver us from evil.

℣. Eternal rest grant unto him (her), O Lord. ℟. And let perpetual light shine upon him (her).

℣. From the gates of hell. ℟. Save his (her) soul, O Lord.

℣. May he (she) rest in peace. ℟. Amen.

℣. O Lord, hear my prayer. ℟. And let my cry come unto Thee.

℣. The Lord be with you. ℟. And with your spirit.

Collect. Let us pray.

O Lord, we commend to Thee the soul of Thy servant N.* that when he (she) departs from this world, he (she) may live with Thee. By the grace of Thy merciful love wash away the sins that in human frailty he (she) has committed in the conduct of his (her) life. Through Christ our Lord.
℟. Amen.

In the meantime the bell is rung as a token of the decease, according to the custom of the place. The corpse is then brought into a decent place with light, and a small Crucifix is placed between the hands of the deceased. The corpse is sprinkled with holy water, and until it is taken away, those that are present pray for the defunct.

(*) If the deceased was a priest, the word Sacérdos *(priest) is added after the baptismal name.*

Bringing you spiritual riches
of the Holy Roman Catholic Tradition
at the most affordable prices possible.

CaritasPublishing.com